LIFE WITHOUT PLASTIC

The Practical Step-by-Step Guide to Avoiding Plastic to Keep Your Family and the Planet Healthy

Chantal Plamondon
and Jay Sinha

founders of Life Without Plastic

PAGE STREET
PUBLISHING CO.

DEDICATION

For Jyoti, who started us on this journey and illuminates the way every day.

PAGE STREET
PUBLISHING CO.

Copyright © 2017 Chantal Plamondon and Jay Sinha

First published in 2017 by
Page Street Publishing Co.
27 Congress Street, Suite 105
Salem, MA 01970
www.pagestreetpublishing.com

Distributed by Macmillan, sales in Canada by The Canadian Manda Group.

21   20   19   18   17   1   2   3   4   5

ISBN-13: 978-1-62414-425-7
ISBN-10: 1-62414-425-X

Library of Congress Control Number: 2017937731

Cover and book design by Page Street Publishing Co.
Illustrations by Robert Brandt / Photography by 123rf.com: page 97 (left and right of center); Abeego: page 97 (third down); Alamy: pages 6 and 19; Burstenhaus Redecker: pages 95 (bottom picture) and 119; Eco Nuts: page 95 (top image); Franziska Heinze: page 186; Getty Images: cover and page 3; Home Depot: page 135; iStock: pages 6, 85, 97 (far left), 101 (first from the bottom), 102, (bottom two), 113, 153 and 160; Life Without Plastic: pages 97 (far right), 101 (top two), 102 (top four), 138 (all in the center circle except for the Stainless Steel Laptop Tray, and all in the outer ring except for the Stainless Steel Snack Container, Stainless Steel Dip Container and the Thermal Stainless Steel Container), 116, 144 and 146; Lunchbots: pages 101 (second from the bottom and bottom) and 138 (Thermal Stainless Steel Container, Stainless Steel Snack Container and the Stainless Steel Dip Container); Planetbox: page 138 (Stainless Steel Laptop Tray); Re-Uz.co.uk: page 97 (center); Shutterstock: page 160.

Printed and bound in China

FSC
www.fsc.org
MIX
Paper from
responsible sources
FSC® C016973

1% FOR THE PLANET
MEMBER

trustees

CONTENTS

FOREWORD
by Beth Terry

Ten years ago, I read an article about ocean plastic pollution—a problem I'd never heard of—and saw the shocking image that changed my life. The photo revealed the decayed carcass of a baby albatross who'd starved with a belly full of plastic, plastic it had been fed by its mother who mistook lighters, toothbrushes and bottle caps floating in the ocean for food. My heart broke as I realized that my personal choices could be causing harm to creatures thousands of miles away, and that very day, I embarked on a mission to see if it would be possible to live without plastic. I created a blog to report on my progress eliminating everyday plastics: disposables like single-use bottles, bags, cups, straws, food wrappers, shampoo containers, lip balm and toothpaste tubes and, yes, toothbrushes, but also durable plastic items like food storage containers and ice trays that I no longer wanted in contact with what I was going to put in my mouth.

Finding a Tupperware replacement proved difficult. All of the stainless steel containers I had tried were fine for short-term use in the refrigerator, but they weren't airtight or leakproof, so I couldn't store food in the freezer long-term or use them to carry soup for lunch without worrying about making a mess in my backpack. A year later, I finally found Life Without Plastic, an online shop offering an ingenious series of airtight and watertight stainless steel containers that could solve my problem. I emailed the owners for a sample to review, and that's how I met Jay Sinha and Chantal Plamondon, authors of this book and dear friends.

Of course, all relationships have their ups and downs, and ours started out a little less than perfect. When I finally received my beautiful new Life Without Plastic container, I was dismayed to discover that the container itself came wrapped in a thin plastic bag inside the box. I thanked them for the container but mentioned that I wished it had come without plastic packaging. I honestly didn't expect my message to do much good, so I was delighted when they responded, agreeing that the plastic wrap wasn't great and that they would try to phase it out. And then, they actually went to work doing just that. Life Without Plastic is one of the few for-profit companies whose main purpose for existing is to combat the plastic pollution problem, and Jay and Chantal are some of the most ethical business people I have met during my plastic-free journey.

In 2012, I included profiles of plastic-free heroes Jay and Chantal in my book, *Plastic-Free*. And today, I am thrilled to introduce their book, *Life Without Plastic*, the newest addition to a growing body of literature on plastic pollution and actions individuals can take to reduce plastic in their own lives. Unlike other practical how-to books, Jay and Chantal discuss the topic from the point of view of business owners who have seen aspects of the supply chain that are hidden from most of us ordinary consumers. And they provide the most up to date information on the problem, as well as details on different types of plastics and related toxicity issues and the pros and cons of various alternatives. I hope you will read and enjoy this book, and most of all, put it to use. All of us can be part of the solution to plastic pollution!

Beth Terry is the creator of the website MyPlasticfreeLife.com and author of Plastic-Free: How I Kicked the Plastic Habit and How You Can Too.

INTRODUCTION

"I have an idea!" exclaimed Chantal.

For Jay, those words have always been a source of excitement and wonder, and sometimes trepidation. Chantal often has ideas that appear as flashes of creativity, fresh and raw and untamed by practicalities; ready to be molded into action through a plan developed together. Of course, the challenge is always picking and choosing which ideas to actually implement using our limited life energy and resources. Focusing where we can have the greatest impact while living our values. Sometimes we don't even think about all that. We just go for it.

This one was a keeper.

"What about an online store selling alternatives to plastic products?" said Chantal.

We were on a road trip from our 1930s-era third-story apartment in Ottawa to Chantal's father's suburban home in Sainte-Thérèse, Quebec, just north of Montreal, on our way to a family get-together. Our two-year-old son was fast asleep in his snug car seat. Road trips—like walks in the forest or on the beach—have always been fertile ground for our idea generation and development.

There was an electricity around this online store idea—we had been searching for a way to reduce our impact on the planet through a business that could support our lifestyle and values, and getting rid of plastics was a high priority. Our skill sets and interests fed into it nicely. Chantal had a passion for ethical business, and had always wanted to start her own. Jay had a scientific background spanning biochemistry and ecotoxicology. Combined with our shared love of the natural world and healthy living, the potential was vast. The idea quickly grew into a tangible entity.

Then came the really fun part . . .

"So, what should we call it?"

When we say the word "plastic," what is the first thing that comes to your mind?

Maybe a crinkly, cellophane-like grocery bag, or a white-capped, clear single-use water bottle. Maybe a toy. LEGO? A Tonka truck? A doll, perhaps?

Maybe you think of credit cards. It's so easy these days to pay with plastic. And even the actual physical currency is plastic in some countries. In Canada, for example, the paper bills are no longer paper; they are biaxially-oriented polypropylene plastic, and you can see through them.

Or, if you're already attuned to this plastics issue, maybe you see that bag caught in a tree, or that bottle or rubber ducky floating down your local river. Perhaps you've seen a massive patch of floating plastic somewhere out on the high seas of the North Pacific Ocean—which, by the way, just to bring your vision into ominous focus, is actually a ubiquitous soupy smog rather than a giant solid island. Or maybe you've seen an autopsy being done on a seabird to reveal a stomach full to bursting with colorful pieces of jagged, lethal plastic—plastic we use in our everyday lives, perhaps just for a few minutes, before trashing or recycling it.

Hold your image.

An all too common sight: a discarded single-use disposable water bottle floating in the ocean

Now consider this string of words: *Life without plastic*.

What comes to mind?

Probably the word "impossible," right?

So, is it possible to live without plastic?

No, you're absolutely right—currently it's *not* possible. Not on this precious planet. Unless perhaps you're part of an indigenous community living a pure subsistence existence in Amazonia, or homesteading it deep in the backwoods, growing and gathering all your own food . . . but even then, plastic will find you.

Plastic is pretty much everywhere in the world now, stemming from microscopic levels. It's in the air, it's in the soil, it's in the water. That is the reality, borne out of increasing amounts of scientific research documenting our global plastic footprint.

Beyond the miniscule plastic particles around us that we can't even see, it just isn't feasible for most of us to live *completely* without plastic in this day and age given the modern urban setting the majority of us inhabit. Plastic is very hard to avoid. The keyboards we are typing on as we write these words are plastic. Same with our phones and tablets. Cars sport a hefty percentage of molded plastics. Most homes are riddled with plastic throughout, from the walls to the floors to the light fixtures. And then there's the ubiquitous plastic packaging, which envelops practically every product imaginable, from apples to eggs, foam bath to lipstick, toy cars to printer cartridges.

We are surrounded by the toxic polluting conundrum that versatile convenient plastic has become. But . . . there are lots of ways to *avoid* plastics in everyday life— wherever you are, whatever you do. All it takes is a little awareness and initiative. Educated action, we like to call it.

Life without plastic is the goal. We'll never reach that absolute goal in our lifetimes—plastic lasts way too long for us to outlive it—and that's not the point. It's the effort that counts, and an all-out effort to avoid toxic, polluting plastic by as many humans as humanly possible is what our world desperately needs right now. Living without plastic is a goal worth working toward for the simple reasons that plastic can be toxic to the health of all living beings and it is rapidly polluting every nook and cranny of our planet.

CHAPTER 1

FRAMING THE ISSUE
Through Our Plastic-Free Journey

We recognize that many plastics have amazingly useful properties, such as being lightweight, flexible, moisture-temperature-chemical resistant, durable and relatively inexpensive. We also recognize the important roles durable plastics play in certain settings such as hospitals and for computers, phones, safety and industrial equipment. While we hope to eventually see a product design revolution that replaces plastic across the board with safer non-polluting materials, our focus here is on the plastics that cause the most harm and that can be easily avoided in everyday life.

Plastic-free living is a goal we have spent much of the past decade working on and helping folks around the world strive to achieve. We have a few things to say about it that we hope will help you on your plastic-free journey.

But first, we'll tell you a bit about our journey into plastic-free living . . . how that road trip led to those three words—Life Without Plastic—and how it changed everything for us.

We never planned to become plastic-free living experts and crusaders. It just happened as we sought a healthy, low-waste lifestyle. But there were some pretty powerful triggers that helped us along the way . . .

It all started back in 2002 when we became pregnant, Chantal in particular. She began doing lots of future mother research and reading and came across an article describing how chemicals leaching out of plastics have the potential to cause problems for living beings. The article explained how those most at risk of adverse health effects from exposure to such chemicals include children—especially babies and infants, whose wee systems are in early development—and their mothers, who have oodles of hormones coursing through their fertile, life-giving bodies. This shocked and scared us.

We were already eco-conscious from many angles—recycling, composting, eating organic, consuming lots of granola and hugging trees (the latter two more Jay's pursuits)—but we had not considered the inherent problems associated with plastics. We would wash and reuse single-use water bottles over and over, thinking we were being super eco-aware by preventing them from being recycled after a single use or heading straight into the trash and, ultimately, a landfill. We didn't realize each use and wash was breaking down the cheap, unstable plastic more and more, and increasing the potential for chemicals and microscopic bits of plastic to leach into our drinks. There's a reason why they are intended for single use!

During the year before our son was born, we started experiencing strange physical symptoms that seemed to come out of nowhere: runny noses, rashes, sore eyes, chronic fatigue, achy joints. Chantal was pregnant, so fatigue and strange new body sensations were to be expected for her, but something more was going on here. And we both were feeling it.

When Chantal was eight months pregnant, inspectors found black mold in our damp basement, and they were certain that spores released from the mold were coming up into our apartment through the ventilation system. The mold spores were the likely cause of our symptoms. They suggested we move out *that day*, especially for the safety of Chantal and the baby in her womb.

This mold experience made us even more sensitive—intellectually and physically—to the toxins that surround us in everyday life.

Fortunately, when our son came into this world very early one frigid January morning, he was a healthy seven-pound (3-kg) baby full of life, joy and magic, and seemingly unaware of the drama that preceded his birth.

His name is Jyoti, which means "radiance" or "ray of light" in Sanskrit and Bengali. And that he is. In so many ways it has been he who has illuminated our path toward plastic-free living. After he was born, Chantal breastfed him, but there were times when we needed to store her milk. We couldn't bear the thought of putting that antibody-rich, life-giving nectar in plastic bottles that would have to be boiled to be sterilized. We were by now very concerned about chemicals leaching out of plastic food and drink containers, especially when they were exposed to temperature extremes such as boiling. So Chantal began looking everywhere for glass baby bottles.

If we go back thirty or forty years, glass baby bottles were the norm. Not so in 2003. Baby bottles then seemed to be made only out of plastic. She eventually found one possibility. Evenflo, based in Ohio, was still making the glass ones. She contacted them to order some. No problem, they said, but the minimum order was 1,000! They only dealt in wholesale quantities. We were able to find some secondhand glass baby bottles for our immediate needs, but that experience stuck with us and planted a fertile new seed.

We also decided to get a non-plastic water bottle. Easier said than done in 2005. Some Internet research led us to what appeared to be a solid possibility from a California company called Klean Kanteen. Chantal ordered a couple. We tried them out and loved them. Another seed.

Chantal had always wanted to start her own business. This plastics issue seemed like the perfect pathway to fulfilling that dream. We spent a couple of years daydreaming about how to make a contribution to reducing the massive quantities of plastic that are consumed every second of every day around the world. We wanted to address the damage that toxin-leaching plastics can cause to human and animal health and the environmental disaster that the increase of plastic waste is causing. We soon realized—based on our own experiences of often searching in vain for everyday products made out of non-plastic materials—that to effectively help people reduce their plastic use and exposure we had to be able to point them toward non-plastic alternatives. We also knew from our own searching that there were still very few alternatives to plastic consumer products on the market, especially for food and drink containers. Then that pivotal road trip conversation took place.

In 2005, we were both working for the federal government and having difficulty finding good caregivers to be with Jyoti. This was just the catalyst we needed. Once again, that cute little kid was shining his light to lead us in the direction of living without plastic. Chantal took a leave from her job and set to work building the company while caring for Jyoti. Thus began Life Without Plastic, our online store with the all-encompassing tagline of offering safe, high quality, ethically-sourced and Earth-friendly alternatives to plastic products for everyday life.

It began with just a few products, and you can probably guess what some of those first ones were . . . Klean Kanteen stainless steel water bottles in various sizes, Evenflo glass baby bottles, as well as some stainless steel food containers Chantal found at a product trade show in Asia.

From the start, the idea was to offer people solid information about the harm plastics are causing to human health and the environment. With this information in mind, they could then choose to take action and reduce the use of plastic in their lives. If they were looking for alternatives to replace their plastic products, we had some to offer that we had tried out and used regularly in our own lives.

At that time, there was some scientific research out there on the adverse health effects of chemicals leaching out of certain plastics, but not a lot, and it was difficult to find conclusive studies—though there were some. The public view of plastics was rather benign and uninterested, apart from those like us who had a personal reason to do their own research. We knew there was something wrong with plastics and we preferred to take a precautionary approach and try to avoid them. Most, however, had no idea that using plastics could adversely affect their health. The minimal public interest in toxic chemicals leaching out of plastics began to change in 2007 when the media started talking about something called bisphenol A (BPA).

You've likely heard of BPA. It's a synthetic plastic chemical that is the building block of hard clear plastics known as polycarbonates and some epoxy resins. Polycarbonates are used to make things like drinking bottles, tableware, CDs and DVDs, and BPA-based epoxy resins are used as the lining for metal food cans and on cash register receipts. The problem with BPA is that it is an endocrine disruptor, meaning it disrupts normal hormonal processes in the body; in particular, it mimics the female sex hormone estrogen and has been linked to health problems ranging from obesity to cancer, potentially with even miniscule exposures.[1]

In 2007, the environmental group Environmental Defence Canada compiled rapidly growing scientific research and began spreading the word about health problems associated with BPA and calling for a ban on BPA in consumer products. Some Canadian retailers pulled polycarbonate water and baby bottles from their shelves. We were constantly getting calls to do media interviews about the issues related to BPA and plastics in general.

For us, this is when things really took off as the demand for non-plastic bottles exploded almost overnight. We realized that the issue was here to stay and we were going to play a key role in spreading the word while helping the world decrease its addiction to plastic. We were regularly in close contact with our fast-growing stainless steel bottle supplier in the United States, trying to increase quantities and speed up shipments of bottles. During one conversation, a Klean Kanteen employee reeling with the voluminous demand for their bottles from the Great White North asked, "What in the world is going on up there in Canada?!"

What was going on was that Canada was in the process of becoming the first country in the world to impose a ban on BPA. The federal government's 2008 ban was restricted only to baby bottles and the lining of containers of infant formula, but it paved the way for other similar bans around the world, including in the United States and Europe. And broader, more precautionary bans will likely come eventually—restricting the ban to baby bottles ignores the fact that BPA is in a multitude of other products that surround us and our food daily. The number of scientific studies documenting health issues related to BPA and other chemicals leaching out of plastics continues to grow and grow.

1   F.S. Vom Saal & C. Hughes (2005) "An Extensive New Literature Concerning Low-Dose Effects of Bisphenol A Shows the Need for a New Risk Assessment," *Environmental Health Perspectives* 113(8): 926–933; Breast Cancer Fund (2012) "The State of the Evidence on Bisphenol A (BPA)" (accessed 4 March 2017: http://www.breastcancerfund.org/clear-science/radiation-chemicals-and-breast-cancer/bisphenol-a.html).

In tandem with the revelation of all the health issues linked to plastics, we observed the staggering environmental impact of plastic pollution—it's especially vivid in the oceans—gaining increasing media and global attention. We spread word of the issues through our own channels: our website and social media, blog posts and media interviews. We raised awareness in our home community of Wakefield, Quebec by organizing a campaign to reduce plastic bag use, providing bulk stainless steel water dispensers for local festivals and events and organizing film screenings. All the while we were continuing to seek out new plastic-free alternatives to offer in our online store. We also got to know more of the passionate visionaries around the world working on the front lines of the plastic toxicity and pollution movement. Yes, it was becoming a global movement.

One of the galvanizing forces of this movement has been the California-based Plastic Pollution Coalition (PPC), which was founded in 2009 with the mission of stopping plastic pollution and its toxic impact on humans, animals and the environment. We have been active PPC members from the start and proudly offer their products in our store with proceeds going directly to supporting PPC's global mission.

So, what's the solution? There are many, many solutions—we are limited only by our imaginations and desire for change. We will touch on a wide variety of solutions throughout this book with the tips and alternatives we offer you. But we think the key big picture fundamental elements of the overall solution are that we need to:

- Stop plastic pollution and poisoning at the source by avoiding plastic and using alternatives. Plastic is too microscopically dispersed around the world to try and clean it all up at this point. The flow of new plastic into our lives has to decrease. If we use less plastic, our health is at less risk and there is less plastic pollution. Prevention and avoidance should be engraved in our minds.

- Change our perception of existing plastic as waste to be disposed of, and see it as a valuable—albeit potentially toxic—resource to be carefully recycled and reused in safe non-food, non-polluting applications.

- Move toward a circular economy system where plastics never become waste; rather, they all re-enter the economy through recycling and reuse.[2] Plastic products should be designed from the start never to become waste. The materials for making plastics should shift away from fossil fuels and synthetic chemicals to safe, renewable, chemical-free bio-based sources.

- Embrace individual action and local, community-based initiatives. While global solutions are needed, it is at the individual and community levels that change is implemented on the ground in day-to-day life. This is where the most tangible, accessible-to-anyone, plastic-free change happens. Realize that your individual decisions DO make a difference. The beauty of our now interconnected, social media–infused world is that as individuals we ALL are now global decision makers having world-wide reach with the press of a button.[2]

This is the upshot of what our plastic-free journey has taught us to date. And this is part of the message we bring to you now. The other part of our message is what is contained in the rest of this book: more in-depth info on plastics and the best alternatives, coupled with some easy and practical tips, tools and tricks to avoid plastic in your everyday life.

2   Ellen MacArthur Foundation (2016) "The New Plastics Economy: Rethinking the Future of Plastics," World Economic Forum (accessed 4 March 2017: https://www.ellenmacarthurfoundation.org/publications/the-new-plastics-economy-rethinking-the-future-of-plastics).

We have our radiant son to thank for helping us begin this journey into Life Without Plastic, and for holding our hand through the process. He continues to do so to this day, helping out by packing plastic-free toothbrush and floss orders and creating videos such as the stop-motion journey of a playdough creature escaping from a stainless steel container and the unboxing of a Japanese wooden alternative to traditional plastic LEGO. Yes, he is, and always will be, the passionate shining core of why we do what we do.

ABOUT THIS BOOK

Consider this book a plastic-free living primer to help you reduce plastic in all aspects of your life, but without feeling overwhelmed by the enormity of the issue and all that you could—or possibly feel you should—be doing. Guilt is not the goal. You've got to go with what works for your life, and we're great believers in small steps toward significant, meaningful goals. Through this step-by-step guide, we'll take your hand and gently walk you through ways to avoid plastic in all aspects of everyday life.

We are plastic-free living advocates, and we look up to the examples of others striving to live with less plastic, such as Beth Terry, founder of the blog My Plastic Free Life, and the folks running visionary organizations for positive plastic-free change, such as PPC, Algalita Marine Research and Education, the 5 Gyres Institute, the Plastic Soup Foundation and Plastic Oceans. We also learn from and connect with those in the fast-growing "zero waste" movement, such as bloggers Lauren Singer of Trash Is for Tossers and Bea Johnson of Zero Waste Home. They have taken their self-aware, elegant lifestyles to levels of beauty and creativity that provide powerful, inspiring examples of ways to avoid plastic in everyday life. Zero waste is a natural, all-encompassing sister perspective and approach to plastic-free living, but please note that this book is not focused specifically on zero waste living.

This book is not about deconstructing the plastic pollution argument. It is based on the strong premise that plastic pollution must stop because it is choking our oceans, blanketing our land masses and affecting our health right now and potentially for generations to come. Anyone can Google something that might say that disposable plastics are better for the environment than durable goods based on one narrow environmental perspective. We have no desire to go there and engage in that sort of back-and-forth discourse. We have chosen to battle plastic toxicity and pollution, and we are sticking to that mission.

The purpose of this book is not just to try and convince you to embrace the goal of living without plastic. Only you can change yourself. By changing yourself in this direction you become a powerful force for change as an example to others. When you take your reusable grocery bags with you when you go shopping, other people see you, including your neighbors and children, and what had to be justified to every cashier at the store soon becomes normal behavior for all.

We're primarily here to explain why living without plastic is a worthy goal for all of humanity to consider, and to help everyone get started with tangible tips and tools. Tackling the full goal head-on from the start can be daunting for many who are new to the idea of living with less plastic. For some, like Beth, Bea and Lauren, and maybe you too, embracing it fully in all aspects of your life can be approached as an exciting challenge, rather than a colossal task, but they are inspiring exceptions compared to many of us, who are doing our best in our own way. Wherever you are on your journey, our purpose is to help you start the process of being aware of the plastic around you, and to be open to taking action to reduce your plastic use by seeking out alternatives.

If you are just starting out on your plastic-free journey, you may wish to heed an initial piece of important advice: As excited as you may be to embark on this journey, be careful about fully embracing plastic-free living cold turkey, and trying to do it all at once. Once you start noticing the plastic around you, it could overwhelm and discourage you quickly. Start with one change. Incorporate it into your life and routine. Move on to another. That's why this is a step-by-step guide. Take it one step at a time. This is all about changing habits, and that takes time, effort and patience.

We want to help you make simple changes in your life to improve your and your family's health, and the health of our shared global environment. Health is a fundamental focus for us. We believe in a precautionary approach, especially when the scientific research keeps uncovering more and more confirmed and potential adverse health effects being linked to exposure to chemicals leaching out of plastics. We are firm followers of the Precautionary Principle, which holds that if there is a risk of harm to health or the environment from an activity or product, then preventive action should be taken—even if the scientific evidence is not complete or clear.

We'll share tips we've learned along the way through our own always ongoing research and the insightful feedback and suggestions we constantly receive from our loyal tribe of plastic-free, alternative-seeking clients and followers. So whether you are looking for your first reusable water bottle or are a seasoned plastic-free-living aficionado wondering about options for non-plastic yoga mats, there are lots of suggestions and ideas here for you.

As for how we've laid things out in the pages that follow, we start with some quick action to get you engaged right away, a few super easy and impactful plastic use reduction actions anyone can do right now, anywhere. We then walk you through the plastics landscape, explaining what plastic is and some key terminology. We highlight the different types of common plastics and how they can be dangerous to your health and the environment. Is recycling the solution? We'll show why it's not enough. How about bioplastics? Only in part. And we'll do a quick run through of a variety of alternative raw materials out there for replacing plastics in everyday life products.

We'll help you assess the current level of plastic in your personal space, and then through the home we go, offering up suggestions for plastic-free alternatives to help create a healthier living space. We'll be by your side wherever you may be headed outside your home: a restaurant, the gym, the office, school, university, a hike in the woods or traveling to the other side of the world.

Finally, we'll offer up suggestions for moving beyond your personal sphere of life to radiate a plastic-free lifestyle. If you're feeling like you need to spread the word about living without plastic farther and wider, we'll provide you with ideas and tools for plastic-free events and community initiatives, including highly impactful and even artistic individual actions with the potential for global reach.

Throughout this book we provide tips and techniques—the "how to's"—but we also offer up some suggestions for actual product brands in our resources section at the end of the book. Rather than sprinkling them throughout the book, we put them all together in one section at the end to make it easier to see them all at a glance and compare more easily. The order in which they are presented follows the flow of the book. You can find numerous alternatives to plastic products in our online store, but this book is not intended to be a catalog for our products. Whether we carry them or not, we point out products we have found that we feel comfortable suggesting based on our core health and environmental criteria for living plastic-free. We have not necessarily tried out every single thing we suggest, but based on our research and experience we trust the sources we offer up. We are just scratching the surface here. There are most certainly lots more plastic-free products out there that we have not highlighted. Always be on the lookout for new alternatives!

Keep in mind that even we, who have written this book and started a business called Life Without Plastic, do not live completely without plastic. We do live with less plastic than the norm—it helps to have easy access to some of the latest alternatives—but our home and lives are far from plastic-free and sometimes we still even purchase things packaged in plastic. We don't feel guilty about not being completely pure in our living with less plastic. We know we are making a difference. We do our best to refuse-reduce-reuse-repurpose-repair-reinvent-recycle, and, as Bea Johnson would say, "rot" (i.e., compost)!

Plastics really do surround us all regardless of where we happen to be on this magnificent planet—from polar ice caps to deep ocean realms to your bedroom, bathroom, kitchen and office. It is never too early or too late to start reducing your plastic exposure and footprint.

Our son, who sparked our journey toward living without plastic, is now fourteen. We want him to be able to grow up in a world where breathing-drinking-eating microplastic particles is not normal, and finding plastic bags and bottles on the beach is a travesty of the past. Our world is not there yet, but together we can get there. We hope you'll join us on this journey toward plastic-free living and better health for us all, including you, your loved ones and our magical, shared Mother Earth.

Onward!

CHAPTER 2

THE SUPER EASY "PARETO PLASTIC-FREE LIVING"
Quick Start Guide

If you just happened to pick this book up out of curiosity because you've heard about the plastics issue and the title piqued your interest, we're going to help you take action right now to improve your health and the health of the environment by reducing your plastic footprint and increasing your awareness about the plastics in your life. Yes, *right now* you can decide to do a few things in your everyday life that can have a huge impact. And yes, we did just say in the Introduction to take it one step at a time, but these things are so straightforward and complementary that it's fine to tackle them in tandem. They all flow in the same plastic-free, habit-forming direction.

Why do we call it the "Pareto" Plastic-Free Living Quick Start Guide? The Pareto principle—or 80/20 rule—states that roughly 80 percent of the effects come from 20 percent of the causes. So if you are just starting out on your exciting plastic-free journey and currently living a lifestyle that includes a lot of disposable single-use plastic items, then these simple actions (the "20 percent") could have the potential to reduce your plastic consumption and waste by a lot, maybe even 80 percent. These items are among the most common forms of plastic waste pollution, so removing them from your life will make a huge dent in the plastic pollution problem at the source. Go for it!

Here are six of the absolute worst plastic pollution culprits, and simple actions you can take to replace them right now with non-plastic alternatives.

SINGLE-USE DISPOSABLE PLASTIC CULPRIT	ACTION YOU CAN TAKE RIGHT NOW	MORE DETAILS
Plastic Bags	Refuse plastic bags and shop with reusable bags you carry with you: Use cloth bags or at least thick, durable plastic ones that will last indefinitely	Chapter 4, Kitchen and Grocery Shopping, page 96

SINGLE-USE DISPOSABLE PLASTIC CULPRIT	ACTION YOU CAN TAKE RIGHT NOW	MORE DETAILS
Plastic Water Bottles	Refuse disposable plastic bottles of water and carry a filled reusable water bottle with you: glass, stainless steel	Chapter 5, Restaurants and Takeout, page 139
Plastic Coffee and Tea Cups and Lids (or plastic-lined cups)	Refuse disposable cups and lids and carry your own mug with you: glass, ceramic, stainless steel	Chapter 5, Restaurants and Takeout, page 139
Plastic Food Containers	Refuse plastic food containers and carry a reusable non-plastic food container with you while on the go: glass, stainless steel, wood	Chapter 5, Restaurants and Takeout, page 139
Plastic Utensils	Refuse plastic utensils and switch to reusable non-plastic alternatives: bamboo, stainless steel, wood	Chapter 5, Restaurants and Takeout, page 139
Plastic Straws	Refuse plastic straws that are offered to you and carry your own reusable straw: bamboo, glass, stainless steel	Chapter 5, Restaurants and Takeout, page 139

Don't worry if that felt challenging. That's normal. You're in the process of changing ingrained habits and it will take time. But if that felt easy to you, try to go one step further; a step that perhaps seems simple, but, in reality, is enormously difficult: Try avoiding all single-use disposable plastics.

Try it for just one day at first, to get a taste of what it involves. We don't want you to get overwhelmed, feel discouraged and risk giving up plastic-free living altogether. But trying this out now will open your eyes wide to all the plastic in your life. It is much more difficult than it might sound to avoid single-use disposable plastics because of the biggest culprit of all: packaging.

Plastic packaging makes us want to scream! It constitutes over a quarter of all plastic produced.[1] We compost our organic waste and recycle as much as we can, so that means that the bulk of our garbage is . . . you guessed it: plastic. And practically all of that plastic waste is packaging. The municipal recycling system in our own community accepts most plastic bags, but we know that is not the solution because most of them will not actually end up being recycled (more on that in the Recycling section on page 60).

So if you are a young, eco-oriented industrial design or green chemistry student reading these words and looking for a calling, please turn your agile mind toward ways to eliminate plastic packaging. Come up with products designed without the need for packaging. Consider better package design or completely natural and compostable bioplastics without any chemical additives. The world needs more solutions in this area ASAP. But keep in mind that it is just one part of the solution, and the best way forward is to simply decrease plastic use at the source as much as possible.

The disposable plastic packaging scourge points to a problematic broader societal and cultural mindset that ranks convenient disposability above quality and durability. The whole concept of disposability is quite new, first taking off post–World War II when production and widespread adoption of plastic consumer goods went mainstream. Up until then, durability and reusability were the norm, and they influenced people's attachment to and respect for certain everyday life tools. A Merkur razor, a Zippo lighter, a Mont Blanc pen—all of these vintage, metal-based items were made to last and could be repaired relatively easily in a specialty shop or directly by the manufacturer. They might be passed down reverently from generation to generation. There is no such emotionally charged, sentimental pride of possession derived from disposable plastic Gillette razors, Bic lighters or Parker pens. They are used and tossed, and many of us may have oodles of them lying around in bathroom and office drawers, each completely indistinguishable from the other, devoid of any real meaning in our lives.

It is our hope that this book will help spark a renaissance of appreciation for durable, high quality goods that can continue to live on with pride, rather than being used a few times and disposed of with an insensitive toss into the garbage or recycling bin. When our possessions are fewer and are infused with value and meaning, we naturally take more responsibility for them—and, arguably, for other truly meaningful details in our lives—rather than seeing them as purely utilitarian plastic tools to be used a few times and discarded. We consume less, and live richer lives. And frankly, that is a key aspect of the message we are trying to get across: just consume less. Less plastic, less everything (except love, water and chocolate, of course), and focus on living more. Let experiences highlight your life.

My Plastic Free Life blogger and author Beth Terry encourages her readers to take what she calls a "Plastic Trash Challenge," which involves collecting and analyzing all your own plastic waste for at least one week—a week during which you live as you normally do.[1] This is a fabulous exercise we highly recommend; in fact, you could even do it before taking the above quick start actions if you want to have a baseline idea of your personal plastic waste profile. Regardless of when you do it, it will provide a handy reference point from which to move forward and reduce your plastic consumption.

Before we get into more step-by-step plastic-free living solutions for all aspects of your life, we're going to take a dive into the world of plastics and also give you a quick snapshot of the raw materials that make up most alternatives to plastic products. It's important that you know exactly what plastic is, why it can be hazardous to your health and the health of the planet, and what it can be replaced with.

1   Ellen MacArthur Foundation (2016) "The New Plastics Economy: Rethinking the Future of Plastics," World Economic Forum (accessed 4 March 2017: https://www.ellenmacarthurfoundation.org/publications/the-new-plastics-economy-rethinking-the-future-of-plastics).

CHAPTER 3

KNOWING YOUR PLASTICS . . . AND THE ALTERNATIVES

Our Plastic Brains: Where Did Plastic Come From and What Exactly Is It?

Plastic has infiltrated our lives from every angle, but many people don't know what it is or where it came from. We can gain some understanding of its origins from the etymology of the word plastic. It's actually an utterly gorgeous word. It derives from the Greek verb *plassein*, meaning "to mold or shape." It describes something that is malleable and flexible.

Our brains are plastic. They have the ability to mold or shape . . . to transform and change. Yes, that is how we prefer to define the word: the ability to transform and change. This deeper, more beautiful significance of the word is most evident in the world of neurology. Neuroplasticity is a hotbed of cutting-edge research investigating how the brain can transform and change.

In 2007, Jay's father had a stroke. For the first few days after the stroke, he spoke only Bengali, his mother tongue. Access to his English-speaking neurons was somehow impeded, and his brain defaulted to its original language option. A neurological reboot of sorts. These fascinating changes led Jay to a book called *The Brain That Changes Itself*, written by an innovative psychiatrist and psychoanalyst named Norman Doidge.[1] He makes clear through riveting case studies how the brain actually does have the ability to change its structure and function, even into old age. As Jay watched his father regain his English language skills, he was watching neuroplasticity in action.

The brain is truly and magnificently plastic. Now isn't that a beautiful use of the word plastic? A use that truly honors the essence of the word. We think so.

So we all have plastic brains. Hold that thought in the background of your gorgeously plastic brain until the last chapter of this book.

---

1 Norman Doidge, *The Brain That Changes Itself: Stories of Personal Triumph from the Frontiers of Brain Science*, New York: Viking Penguin, 2007.

The problem is that the word plastic does not refer only to our innate plasticity. In the early twentieth century, the term plastic was hijacked as a generic moniker to describe an emerging family of new and wondrous synthetic materials that could be molded or shaped into practically anything the human mind could conceive. The first true plastics were actually created long before the term was even appropriated to describe them.[2]

In 1855, British inventor and metallurgist Alexander Parkes used cotton-derived natural cellulose in combination with nitric acid and chemical solvents to create a gooey, transparent substance that could be molded when heated. In his patent, he dubbed it "Parkesine." An entrepreneurial New York printer named John Wesley Hyatt then snapped up the plastic creation torch, using Parkesine as his initial raw material. In 1869, his impromptu chemistry experiments produced a leather-like substance that could be flattened thin like paper or molded into shapes and hardened. It was called celluloid and used to make photographic film, billiard balls and elaborate comb, brush and mirror vanity sets marketed to rival expensive and exclusive ivory originals.

The first completely synthetic plastic—created in a lab without natural materials—was developed in 1907 by Belgian-American chemist Leo Baekeland. He combined phenol, a waste product from coal production, with formaldehyde in the presence of heat and pressure to yield a hardcore plastic he termed "Bakelite." It was used for numerous everyday products: radios, phones, appliance parts, combs, toothbrushes and cigarette holders. A 1924 *Time* magazine article with Baekeland on the cover described it as the "material of a thousand purposes."[3]

Each of these original plastics and the plastics that surround us today have a similar broad structural composition. They are all what are known in chemistry circles as *polymers*, which are long chains of repeating smaller molecular chemical units called monomers. Picture a string of beads or linked paper clips going on and on and that will give you an idea of what a polymer looks like.

Polymers can be natural or synthetic. Some common natural polymers include the cellulose in the cell walls of plants, natural rubber and the proteins comprising our muscle tissue and layers of skin. Even DNA, the spiraling ladder building block of all life, is a polymer. Many polymers have a backbone of stable carbon atoms linked primarily with hydrogen. For example, the simplest synthetic polymer structure is the plastic polyethylene, with a carbon backbone and two hydrogens coming off each carbon. Introduce other elements to the hydrocarbon spine and you can create other plastics. Nitrogen can lead to the nylon used in stockings, fluorine to the Teflon for non-stick pans, and chlorine to the polyvinyl chloride making up vinyl siding, tubing and toys.

Have you ever wondered why oil, natural gas and coal are often referred to as hydrocarbons? It's because their core polymeric structure is repeating chains of a carbon backbone with varying hydrogen side chains.

Those oil, natural gas and coal hydrocarbons are also referred to as non-renewable fossil fuels, and are the building blocks of synthetic plastics. Why are they called fossil fuels? Because their genealogy traces back millions of years to prehistoric times when the dinosaurs roamed the earth. These dense energy-rich fuels were born of the fossils of prehistoric plants and animals compacted underground and subjected to intense heat and pressure over all those years. That also is why they are non-renewable. They take millions of years to form. Once we use them up, they are gone. Forever. Shouldn't we be using them wisely then, if at all?

2   Susan Freinkel's beautifully researched book, *Plastic: A Toxic Love Story* (New York: Houghton Mifflin Harcourt, 2011) provides an entertaining review of the history of plastics.

3   As quoted in Freinkel's *Plastic: A Toxic Love Story*, p. 23.

Gift-worthy housewares help with holiday entertaining

BRIGHT...BOUNCY...UNBREAKABLE!

Gay as Christmas! Colorful housewares smoothly molded of BAKELITE Brand Polyethylene. They're wonderfully helpful with holiday parties and year 'round household chores. And they make clever, low-cost gifts.

Giant wastebasket deals handsomely with holiday clutter, is so light-weight a child can easily lift it. Tight-sealing refrigerator containers are ideal for nuts, spreads, sauces; keep foods fresh for days. Mixer-pitcher is great for juices

and festive beverages. Mixing bowl is easy to use. All are dentproof, rustproof, easy to clean.

Look for these and many other housewares made of BAKELITE Polyethylene in your favorite stores. You can recognize them by their snap-back flexibility, sturdy feel. Rigid quality controls in ultra-modern BAKELITE plants produce dependable polyethylene . . . for manufacturers to mold into housewares that are gala gifts, household helps all year.

BAKELITE
BRAND
Polyethylene Plastic

DID YOU KNOW that polyethylene film laid on the ground before concrete slab foundation is poured makes a splendid moisture barrier for today's new houses?

BAKELITE COMPANY, *A Division of Union Carbide and Carbon Corporation* UCC 30 East 42nd Street, New York 17, N. Y.
The term BAKELITE and the Trefoil Symbol are registered trade-marks of UCC

Bakelite, the first fully synthetic plastic, quickly became a staple in North American households.

The length and structural arrangement of the polymer chains in part determines the properties of the plastic. Densely packed polymers can create a rigid plastic, while loosely spaced ones can lead to a softer more pliable plastic. Polymers alone rarely have the physical qualities to be of practical value, so most plastics contain a multitude of chemical additives to facilitate the manufacturing process or produce a particular desirable property, such as flexibility, toughness, color or resistance to UV light. These additives can be dyes, fragrances, plasticizers, fillers, fluffers, hardeners, stabilizers, lubricants, fire retardants, blowing agents, antistatic chemicals and even fungicides and antibacterial agents. Imagine that, plastics eerily designed to repel insects and bacteria, just like genetically modified cotton or corn! Often it is the additives that are most harmful to our health as they may not be chemically bound to the base polymer and can easily leach from the plastic.

There is a vivid spaghetti sauce analogy that, for us, has always been a poignant illustration and personal reminder of how easily additive chemicals can leach into food and drink from plastic containers. Visualize strands of spaghetti as the long plastic polymer molecules of polyvinyl chloride (PVC), and the spaghetti sauce as the plasticizing additives—the phthalates. PVC can be up to 55 percent plasticizing additives by weight, most of which will be phthalates. When you mix the spaghetti and the sauce, they don't actually bind together; they just slide around each other like snakes in the mud. This is why the plasticizers are unstable and will leach out over time, especially with wear and tear, when heated or exposed to edible acids like lemon or tomato sauce. Yes, tomato sauce, and in that sense, our example is multifaceted. A plastic container is effectively like the spaghetti and sauce. When you add actual spaghetti and sauce to a plastic container the oily acidic sauce will interact with the additives of the plastic.

It's a personal reminder to us of all those years we used and reused—and microwaved (a definite no-no!)—plastic containers for leftover food. It always seemed so strange that we could never completely wash off the film inside the container left by microwave-heated chicken noodle soup. That's because the oily soup had become part of the container, and conversely, the container had clearly become part of us when we ate the soup. Sometimes when microwaving the soup in a plastic container it would become so hot that it would actually cause the plastic to bubble a bit as it mixed with the soup. When cooled, the result was a new permanent whitish tint and corrugated texture to the container. Knowing what we know now, we say, yikes!

As we round out our little history and chemistry lesson, it's helpful to understand that plastics can be divided into two very broad categories. This distinction is particularly useful in considering the recycling of plastics and the need to move toward a waste-free circular economy:

- Thermoplastics: Plastics that are molded with heat and will retain their shape after the heat and pressure of the mold are removed. With reheating, they will melt and can be reformed over and over several times into new shapes as they cool—this is because their polymer chains are not chemically bonded to each other. Hyatt's celluloid is considered the first thermoplastic. These plastics can be recycled and remade into new products, though generally of lower quality (i.e., down-cycled products).

- Thermosets: Plastics that form irreversible chemical bonds as they cure, so they will retain their shape indefinitely. They will not re-melt with heat like thermoplastics because their polymer chains are highly cross-linked. When heated, they will scorch and decompose and thus cannot be reformed into new shapes. Baekeland's Bakelite was the first thermoset plastic. These plastics generally cannot be recycled into new products.[4] Once they reach the end of their useful life, they essentially become landfill waste.

---

4   Researchers have recently discovered a new class of thermosets that may be recyclable: J.M. Garcia et al. (2014) "Recyclable, Strong Thermosets and Organogels via Paraformaldehyde Condensation with Diamines." *Science* 344(6185): 732–735. See also Qipeng Guo (2014) "Recycling the 'Unrecyclable': a New Class of Thermoset Plastics." TheConversation.com (accessed 4 March 2017: http://theconversation.com/recycling-the-unrecyclable-a-new-class-of-thermoset-plastics-26594).

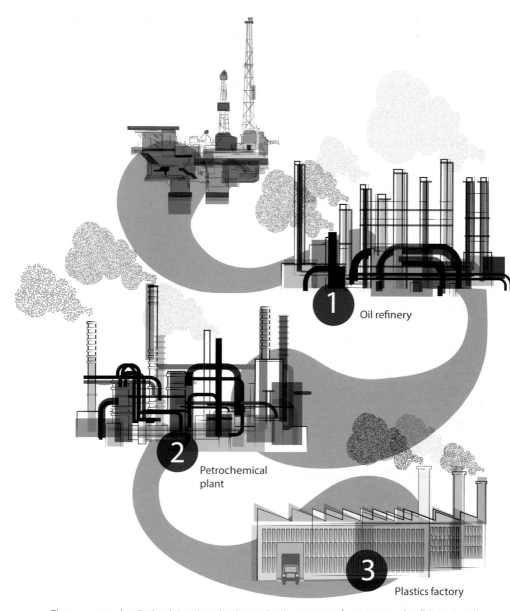

1. Oil refinery

2. Petrochemical plant

3. Plastics factory

The energy and pollution intensive plastic production process, from raw crude oil (or natural gas or coal) to 1). oil refinery to 2). chemical and additive fabrication to 3). plastic resins and finished plastic products.

Before we take a closer look at the most common plastics that populate our lives, and why they can be problematic for our health, we'll highlight some of the huge impacts plastics are having on the natural world around us, whether you look just outside your front door or venture to the ocean floor.

OUR PLANET IS HURTING AS IT BECOMES MORE PLASTIC EVERY DAY

Land. Air. Water. Do we find plastic everywhere? We'll see, but first let's look at some basic plastic production numbers.

How much plastic is produced every year? The equivalent of more than 900 Empire State Buildings. As of 2014, about 342 million tons (310 million tonnes) of plastic is produced annually, which is a twenty-fold increase since 1964.[5] Also in 2014, 33.3 million tons (30 million tonnes) of plastic waste were generated in the United States alone: that's 10 percent of the annual worldwide plastic production.[6] At current growth rates, global production is expected to double in the next twenty years and practically quadruple by 2050.

And how does that translate into fossil fuel use? About 4 percent of the petroleum consumed annually is used to make plastic resins, and another 4 percent is required to power plastic manufacturing processes.

Okay. So now how much of all that plastic is used to make packaging—the pernicious plastic pollution pariah? It's about 26 percent, or 89 million tons (81 million tonnes).[7] And of that, only about 14 percent is recycled, while 40 percent is landfilled, and a phenomenal 32 percent escapes waste management collection systems completely and becomes pollution somewhere in the world.[8] So that brings us to a whopping 28 million tons (25 million tonnes) of plastic directly polluting the global environment every year. That's a lot of plastic pollution.

The problem is visible all over the world, and especially in developing countries where waste management systems are less present or effective. Curious about what all this waste plastic looks like? All you have to do is type "plastic pollution images" into Google to get some horrifying visuals of the scale of the problem.

Keep in mind, however, it's both visible *and invisible* all over the world. A growing number of scientists argue that we have entered a new geological epoch known as the Anthropocene era.[9] It is characterized by pollution from human activities altering the Earth's geology as never before. A key marker of this geological shift is the growing sedimentary layer of plastic developing on land and in water environments all over the world, from the mythic heights of the Everest region[10] to the deepest depths of our oceans and seas.[11]

Professor Jan Zalasiewicz of Leicester University was surprised by the results of his Anthropocene research: "We were aware that humans have been making increasing amounts of different kinds of plastic—from Bakelite to polyethylene bags to PVC—over the last 70 years, but we had no idea how far it had travelled round the planet. It turns out not just to have floated across the oceans, but has sunk to the deepest parts of the sea floor. This is not a sign that our planet is in a healthy condition either . . . The planet is slowly becoming covered in plastic."[12]

5   The New Plastics Economy: Rethinking the Future of Plastics, p. 10.

6   U.S. Environmental Protection Agency (2016) "Advancing Sustainable Materials Management: 2014 Fact Sheet," Nov. 2016 (accessed 4 March 2017: https://www.epa.gov/sites/production/files/2016-11/documents/2014_smmfactsheet_508.pdf).

7   The New Plastics Economy: Rethinking the Future of Plastics, p. 10.

8   The New Plastics Economy: Rethinking the Future of Plastics, p. 12.

9   J. Zalasiewicz et al. (2016) "The Geological Cycle of Plastics and Their Use as a Stratigraphic Indicator of the Anthropocene," *Anthropocene* 13:4–17.

10   S. Goldenberg (2011) "Himalayas in Danger of Becoming a Giant Rubbish Dump," theguardian.com (accessed at: https://www.theguardian.com/environment/blog/2011/sep/12/himalayas-waste).

11   L.C. Woodall, et al. (2014) "The Deep Sea is a Major Sink for Microplastic Debris," Royal Society of Open Science rsos.140317 (accessed 4 March 2017: http://rsos.royalsocietypublishing.org/content/1/4/140317).

12   From an interview with the *Guardian*: R. Mckie (2016) "Plastic Now Pollutes Every Corner of Earth," theguardian. com (accessed at: https://www.theguardian.com/environment/2016/jan/24/plastic-new-epoch-human-damage).

Scientists studying the geology of the island of Hawaii made a startling discovery through their investigations on Kamilo Beach.[13] They announced the appearance of a new "stone" formed through the intermingling of melted plastic, beach sediment, lava fragments and organic debris. Guess what they've called this new stone?

Plastiglomerate. Welcome to the new Anthropocene era brought to you by plastiglomerate!

Is there plastic in the air? Alas, yes. BPA, the hormone disrupting chemical used to make hard clear polycarbonate plastic bottles and the epoxy resins lining food cans, has been measured in the air all over the world in urban, rural, marine and polar settings, including Antarctica.[14] The levels were highest in South Asia where the open burning of plastics was found to be a significant source of atmospheric BPA in urban regions. Land? Check. Air? Check. Water? You better believe it.

The plastic pollution problem is most vivid and disturbing in the ocean setting where plastics can float and be easily mistaken for food by birds and fish. This now enormous problem first came onto the public radar in 2001 when Captain Charles Moore of Algalita Marine Research and Education discovered a swirling soup of small plastic debris in the North Pacific Ocean gyre.[15] The media picked up on this and sensationalized it into fictional islands of floating plastic twice the size of Texas. This vast area has now carved a place in the public psyche as the "Great Pacific Garbage Patch." The plastic pollution in this area is real, but it is not a single, giant, solid, drifting island of colored plastic debris, as the media has portrayed it. There are random "raft-like" agglomerations of fishing nets, bottles, bags and other large plastics, but overall it is more of a smog of tiny plastic pieces: microplastics that are less than 5 millimeters in diameter. Captain Moore's discovery was monumental in catalyzing awareness about oceanic plastic pollution and the beginnings of activism to combat plastic pollution.[16]

Some of the most cutting-edge ocean plastic pollution research has been done by the intrepid folks at the 5 Gyres Institute. "5 Gyres" refers to the five main subtropical gyres—located in the North and South Pacific, the North and South Atlantic, and the Indian Ocean. Soon after co-founders Anna Cummins and Marcus Eriksen launched 5 Gyres, we had the honor in 2009 of sponsoring one of their initial ocean trawls to gather data about the state of plastic pollution in oceans around the world. Anna sent us little jars filled with samples of the microplastic debris they had gathered from their trawls in the South Pacific and North Atlantic gyres. As we write, these jars are sitting beside us. There are small black, white, orange, baby blue and clear chunks of plastic along with tiny feathery wisps of opaque plastic that make the jar into a disturbing snow globe when lightly shaken. Depressing, but powerful inspiration for change.

Collaborating with eight international scientists, including Captain Moore, 5 Gyres coordinated the first global estimate of plastic pollution in our oceans, and the results are jarring: 5.25 trillion pieces of *floating* plastic weighing in at 270,000 tons (245,000 tonnes).[17] A more recent inventory of data from around the world pegs the numbers even higher, somewhere between 15 and 51 trillion particles of

13   P.L Corcoran., C.J. Moore and K. Jazvac (2013) "An Anthropogenic Marker Horizon in the Future Rock Record," *GSA Today* 24(6):4–8.

14   P. Fu and K. Kawamura (2010) "Ubiquity of Bisphenol A in the Atmosphere," *Environmental Pollution* 158:3138–3143.

15   C.J. Moore, S.L. Moore, M.K. Leecaster, and S.B. Weisberg (2001) "A Comparison of Plastic and Plankton in the North Pacific Central Gyre," *Marine Pollution Bulletin* 42(12): 1297–1300. A "gyre" is a system of circulating ocean currents. These oceanic gyre systems cause plastic debris to be concentrated in a central area due to the swirling action of the currents.

16   He wrote a book about his experience, and his work, which is ongoing, has led to much more research on oceanic plastic pollution: Charles J. Moore, with Cassandra Phillips, *Plastic Ocean*. New York: Penguin (Avery), 2011.

17   M. Eriksen, et al. (2015) "Plastic Pollution in the World's Oceans: More than 5 Trillion Plastic Pieces Weighing over 250,000 Tons Afloat at Sea," *PLoS ONE* 9(12): e111913.

plastic.[18] Couple those with a seminal study indicating that about 8 million tons (7 million tonnes) of plastic waste enter the oceans from land globally each year.[19] This is the equivalent of dumping the contents of one garbage truck into the ocean per minute.[20] Another study shows 10,000 tons (9,000 tonnes) of plastic annually going into the Great Lakes alone.[21] Now consider that the amount of plastic thought to be floating in the seas constitutes only 1 percent of the plastic that is estimated to have been released into the oceans to date—the other 99 percent must be somewhere below the surface.[22] The best research available at the time of writing estimates that there are over 165 million tons (150 million tonnes) of plastic waste in the ocean today.[23] We are quite literally creating toxic plastic soups of our waterways.

What does the future hold if we don't change our wasteful plastic polluting ways? Remember those garbage trucks dumping their plastic contents into the ocean every minute? If nothing changes, that will increase to the contents of two dump trucks by 2030 and four every minute by 2050. By 2025, the ratio of plastic to fish in the ocean is expected to be one to three, as plastic stocks in the ocean are forecast to grow to 276 million tons (250 million tonnes).[24] And, without significant action, there may be more plastic than fish in the ocean, by weight, by 2050. Imagine that, more plastic than fish in the oceans of the world, and the equivalent of four garbage trucks full of plastic being emptied in the ocean every minute of every day.

Eriksen describes our current grim reality as follows:

> Much of what we know can be summarized in three conclusions: fragmented plastic is globally distributed, it is associated with a cocktail of hazardous chemicals and thus is another source of hazardous chemicals to aquatic habitats and animals, and it entangles and is ingested by hundreds of species of wildlife at every level of the food chain, including animals we consider seafood.[25]

To get an idea of how all this plastic is affecting wildlife, and by extension us, let's look at the journey of plastics through the aquatic food chain.

Plastics break down into smaller and smaller pieces quite quickly in the oceans due to degradation from light and other weathering processes. Plastics are colorful, may float and come in all shapes and sizes, so as they break down, plastics resemble edible food for fish and birds. Larger pieces of plastic are eaten by larger fish and birds, dolphins, tuna and whales, and smaller pieces by smaller fish. Those smaller fish are then eaten by the larger fish.

---

18   E. Van Sebille, et al. (2015) "A Global Inventory of Small Floating Plastic Debris," *Environmental Research Letters* 10(12):124006.

19   J.R. Jambeck, et al. (2015) "Plastic Waste Inputs from Land into the Ocean," *Science* 347(6223):768-771.

20   *The New Plastics Economy: Rethinking the Future of Plastics*, p. 14.

21   M.J. Hoffman and E. Hittinger (2017) "Inventory of Plastic Debris in the Laurentian Great Lakes," *Marine Pollution Bulletin*, (available at: http://www.sciencedirect.com/science/article/pii/S0025326X1630981X).

22   UNEP and GRID-Arendal (2016) "Marine Litter Vital Graphics," United Nations Environment Programme and GRID-Arendal, p. 41 (accessed at: http://www.unep.org/gpa/resources/marine_litter_vital_graphics.asp).

23   *The New Plastics Economy: Rethinking the Future of Plastics*, p. 14.

24   Ocean Conservancy and McKinsey Center for Business and Environment (2015) "Stemming the Tide: Land-Based Strategies for a Plastic-Free Ocean," Ocean Conservancy and McKinsey & Company, p. 11 (accessed at: http://www.oceanconservancy.org/our-work/marine-debris/stop-plastic-trash-2015.html)

25   Personal communication with Marcus Eriksen, 18 November 2016. See also UNEP (2016) "Marine Plastic Debris and Microplastics – Global Lessons and Research to Inspire Action and Guide Policy Change," United Nations Environment Programme (accessed at: http://www.unep.org/gpa/documents/publications/Marine_Plastic_Debris_and_Microplastic.pdf).

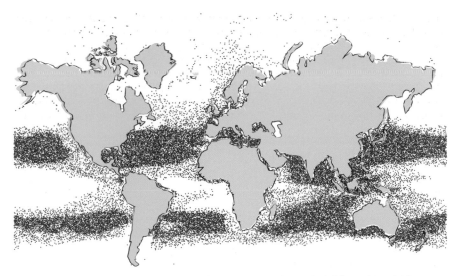

Plastic pollution in the oceans is largely a smog of microplastics invisible to the naked eye, rather than massive islands of plastic debris. (Adapted from a model created by the 5 Gyres Institute and Dumpark).

These plastics readily "adsorb" toxic pollutants—meaning the toxins attach to the plastic—that are already in the ocean; lovely things like pesticides, polychlorinated biphenyls (PCBs), dioxins, radioactive waste and heavy metals. As aquatic wildlife eat these plastics, the toxins get concentrated up the food chain in the fat tissue of each organism—a process known as bioaccumulation. This means that the fish or bird is getting exposed to not just the toxins in the plastic itself, but also any other chemicals the plastic has sopped up along the way. By the time a fish reaches the mouth of a human diner, that trout or tilapia may well contain a cocktail of accumulated toxins.

Down at the very base of the food chain are tiny microorganisms called plankton, which effectively feed everything larger than them. Plankton keep us all alive, not only because they are food for larger aquatic wildlife, but also because one particular type of plankton, phytoplankton, are little oxygen-producing machines. Through a sunlight-powered process called photosynthesis, they convert carbon dioxide into sugary energy and life-giving oxygen.

Researchers have shown that plankton are readily mistaking plastic for food, gobbling up microplastics such as microbeads that come into aquatic environments from personal care products like facial scrub and toothpaste.[26] Zooplankton have even been filmed preferentially eating tiny fluorescent polystyrene microbeads.[27]

This is serious. If the plankton go, so does the rest of the ocean ecosystem—and this would certainly have a, how shall we say, *serious* effect on the entire world because plankton supply about 50 percent of the oxygen in our global atmosphere. Marine biologist and National Geographic explorer-in-residence Sylvia Earle estimates

26   M. Cole, P. Lindeque, E. Fileman, C. Halsband, R. Goodhead, J. Moger and T.S. Galloway (2013) "Microplastic Ingestion by Zooplankton," *Environmental Science and Technology* 47(12): 6646-6655.

27   *New Scientist* (2015) "Plankton Snacking on Plastic Caught on Camera for the First Time," newscientist.com (accessed at: https://www.newscientist.com/article/dn27849-plankton-snacking-on-plastic-caught-on-camera-for-the-first-time).

that one particular type of phytoplankton—*Prochlorococcus*—provides the oxygen for one in every five breaths we take.[28] So if the plankton are replaced by plastic in the oceans, we too may be replaced by plastic down the road.

Enough said. You get the picture. Plastic pollution is serious and we need to wake up and do what we can to stop it. The purpose of this book is to help you do just that.

Now we're going to dive deeper into the specific plastics we live with day-to-day and show why they can be hazardous to our health.

THE GROWING TOXIC PROBLEM OF THE COMMON PLASTICS THAT SURROUND US

We knew we were really onto something when in 2007 we received a detailed six-page letter from a major plastics industry association taking issue with aspects of the information presented on our website. We were thrilled that our sensitization efforts had reached them and hit some chords.

They claimed we were causing "unwarranted concern" about plastics among the public through our website and various media interviews. Their key concern was our use of a table we had adapted from their website detailing the recycling symbols, properties and applications of the most common groupings of plastic resins. We had used their table verbatim (citing them and the other involved plastic industry organizations as the sources), and added on extra columns detailing our perspective on the potentially leaching chemicals from each resin, the potential health effects of these chemicals and the scientific sources upon which we based our findings. They didn't like those last three columns.

In all fairness, it was an amiable, well-written letter that raised some interesting points regarding some of the claims we made. But to this day, we stand by everything we said and say on our website. For example, we made the statement: "Plastic packaging—especially the ubiquitous plastic bag—is an enormous source of landfill waste." We were told in the letter that plastic bags account for less than 1 percent of landfill waste according to government data. Maybe, but to us even 1 percent of the waste going into landfills is an *enormous* quantity of waste given the size and number of landfills across the country, and the world for that matter.

Looking at that letter now, ten years later, and in light of the volumes of new smoking gun toxicity studies on these chemicals and the growing reams of data on global plastic pollution, those industry rebuttals to the claims we made are weak and highly unsettling—almost laughable if the situation weren't so serious—especially the disturbing defense of confirmed hormone-disrupting toxins like bisphenol A and phthalates, and the minimizing of plastic pollution harming marine life. The true toxic nature of plastics is finally being uncovered and documented by health specialists and environmental researchers all over the world.

What follows is a little tour of the most common types of plastic one might come across in everyday life. With each plastic or family of plastics we give a little description of what it is, where it may show up in your typical daily routine, and then we address the question: How toxic is it?

---

28   D. Nelson (2011) "Save the Plankton, Breathe Freely: How Do Plankton Affect the Air We Breathe?" National Geographic Society (accessed at: http://nationalgeographic.org/activity/save-the-plankton-breathe-freely).

As is evident from the title of this book, remember that it has been written from a solid *precautionary* perspective and based on the assumption that all synthetic plastics can be toxic in some way, especially when they break down into tiny microplastic particles—which is exactly what is currently happening to waste plastics all over the world.[29] These tiny pieces of plastic are being eaten, drunk, breathed in or in some way taken in by living organisms; be they you, me, a lugworm or a blue whale. These plastics all derive from oil, natural gas or coal and are full of chemical additives that can leach out, so we prefer not to give them the benefit of doubt in this global toxic experiment that is currently underway without our consent.

The key unsavory toxins—things like phthalates and BPA—we break out into sidebars to give you more detail on their noxious natures. Please be sure to read the box on endocrine-disrupting chemicals, which explains why these hormone-disruptors coming out of plastics are so problematic, even with exposure to miniscule amounts: this explanation goes to the heart of why plastics are hazardous to our health and is the focus of much of the current research on the dangers of plastics. It also explains the paramount importance of taking a precautionary approach toward plastics *now*.

THE SERIOUS PROBLEM OF PLASTICS BULLYING OUR HORMONES: ENDOCRINE-DISRUPTING CHEMICALS

In the late 1980s, a determined zoologist named Theo Colborn began studying the health of wildlife in the Great Lakes region of North America. Reviewing thousands of scientific studies about the effects of pesticides and industrial chemicals on Great Lakes wildlife ranging from bald eagles to beluga whales, she saw strange reports: herring gull chicks dying in their eggs, cormorants born with eyes missing and crossed bills and domesticated mink no longer producing pups.[30] She compiled all the data into a grid and began to see a pattern. All these uncanny effects seemed to be linked to malfunctions of the endocrine system.

Hormones are efficient chemical messenger "keys" that control most major bodily functions such as cell metabolism, reproduction, development, behavior and even intelligence. They are made in body organs known as glands and travel to receptors—little docking station "locks"—made for them throughout the body. In women, the ovaries make estrogen, testosterone and progesterone, while in men the testes produce testosterone. Glands keep tight control on body functions they regulate, and they like hormones to be in balance. This elegant, finely tuned realm of gland control center locks and hormone messenger keys is known as the body's endocrine system.

Endocrine-disrupting chemicals (EDCs) are imposters in the body, sneaking around our bloodstream imitating natural hormones—estrogen is a common target—by barging in, taking over hormone receptors and offsetting the

29   IUCN (2017) "Primary Microplastics in the Oceans: A Global Evaluation of Sources," International Union for Conservation of Nature (accessed 4 March 2017: https://portals.iucn.org/library/node/46622).

30   C.F. Kwiatkowski, A.L. Bolden, R.A. Liroff, J.R. Rochester and J.G. Vandenbergh (2016) "Twenty-Five Years of Endocrine Disruption Science: Remembering Theo Colborn," *Environmental Health Perspectives* 124:A151–A154; T.T. Shug et al. (2016) "Minireview: Endocrine Disruptors: Past Lessons and Future Directions," *Molecular Endocrinology* 30(8):833–847.

crucial balance of the endocrine system. They can wreak slow, steady, long-term havoc on our health, especially among some of the most vulnerable of us.

There are two important elements of EDCs that distinguish them from other toxic chemicals: dose and timing.[31]

About 500 years ago, Paracelsus, one of the founders of toxicology—the study of how chemicals adversely affect living organisms—developed a core toxicological principle that can be summed up as follows: the higher the dose, the greater the toxic effect. The idea is that the more one is exposed to a substance, the worse the "poisonous" reaction. That does not apply to EDCs leaching out of plastic, especially it seems for those mimicking sex hormones like estrogen or testosterone (such as bisphenol A [BPA] or phthalates). EDCs turn this logic on its head because they can cause negative effects in the body at very low concentrations.[32] Conversely, at high doses, they may turn off a response they stimulate at a low dose. Thus, long-term exposure to a tiny amount of estrogen-mimicking BPA—such as from a sippy cup or water bottle—may have a greater adverse effect on the body than if the body received a large influx of the chemical. In fact, at the higher dose, there may be no response, as though there are too many available keys so the receptor lock becomes overwhelmed and simply shuts down completely.

EDCs can be especially harmful at key periods of vulnerability, such as during pregnancy and post-birth development. Yes, children and pregnant women, both of whom have vast amounts of growth and developmental hormones coursing through their bodies, are directly affected by EDCs. Furthermore, Colborn found that adult animals often seemed to be fine, but the worst effects were showing up in their young. The impact of early exposure to EDCs may not show up until much later in life and can go on to affect future generations; EDCs may actually be reprogramming genes.

So where are these EDCs found and how are we exposed to them? Researchers have discovered almost 1000 potential EDCs falling into numerous product categories: plastics and rubbers, household products, personal care products and cosmetics, food additives, flame retardants, pesticides, antimicrobial agents, biogenic compounds, industrial additives, solvents, metal processing chemicals, reactants and medical and veterinary chemicals. In 2003, Colborn created TEDX, The Endocrine Disruption Exchange, an international nonprofit organization dedicated to compiling and disseminating scientific evidence about endocrine disruptors. The TEDX site provides a comprehensive tool for searching all these chemicals and provides details on each substance as well as the evidence indicating it is an EDC.[33] In the plastics and rubbers category alone they list 143 potential EDCs.

(continued)

---

31   TEDX: The Endocrine Disruption Exchange (2011) "Endocrine Disruption Fact Sheet," Endocrinedisruption.org (accessed 4 March 2017: http://endocrinedisruption.org/assets/media/documents/EDFactSheet11-7-11.pdf).

32   L.N. Vandenberg, et al. (2012) "Hormones and Endocrine-Disrupting Chemicals: Low-Dose Effects and Nonmonotonic Dose Responses," *Endocrine Reviews* 33(3):378-455; F.S. vom Saal and C. Hughes (2005) "An Extensive New Literature Concerning Low-Dose Effects of Bisphenol A Shows the Need for a New Risk Assessment," *Environmental Health Perspectives* 113(8):926-933.

33   TEDX List of Potential Endocrine Disruptors (accessed at: http://www.ewg.org/research/dirty-dozen-list-endocrine-disruptors). Note that this is not to be confused with TEDx, the offshoot of TED talks, which is an international community that organizes TED-style events anywhere and everywhere.

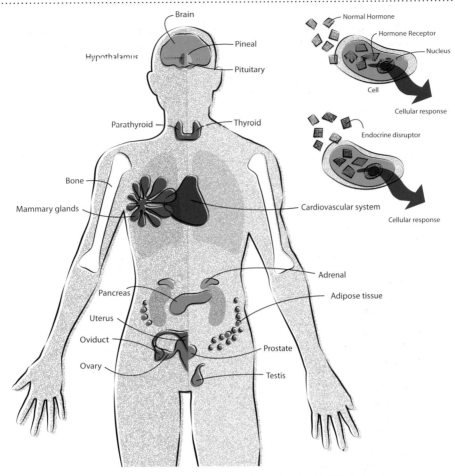

The body's major endocrine glands in females (left) and males (right). Endocrine-disrupting chemicals from plastics connect with the same hormone receptors as normal hormones, but may produce different cellular responses. (Adapted from A.C. Gore et al. (2015) "EDC-2: The Endocrine Society's Second Scientific Statement on Endocrine Disrupting Chemicals," Endocrine Reviews 36 (6): E1-E150, p. E6.)

As well, Environmental Working Group and The Keep A Breast Foundation have created a handy "Dirty Dozen" downloadable guide about the worst common endocrine disruptors, how they act, and how to avoid them: BPA, dioxin, atrazine, phthalates, perchlorate, fire retardants, lead, arsenic, mercury, perfluorinated chemicals (PFCs), organophosphate pesticides and glycol ethers.

Colborn is often referred to as "the mother of endocrine disruption." Thanks to her work, and the ongoing work of many other researchers, it is becoming clear that endocrine disruption should be seen as the new cancer. Up until her death in 2014, she argued forcefully that endocrine disruption be broadly defined, especially in new laws regulating toxic chemicals. Such laws tend to promote assessing the risk of potential toxins one at a time and according to the dated toxicological maxim that the dose makes the poison. This prescient statement on the site of TEDX sums up Colborn's view of the widespread nature of the problem, and provides thoughtful fodder to encourage us all to spread the word about the dangers of EDCs:

- It is a mistake to try to comprehend the myriad effects of endocrine-disrupting chemicals by assessing only reproductive and developmental endpoints and a few hormones. Hundreds of scientific studies have demonstrated endocrine impairment in the central nervous system, the immune and metabolic systems, and many glands and organs. Newly discovered alterations by endocrine disruptors in the gene, molecule and cell environment may have repercussions that do not manifest for decades and can be passed through many generations.

- New legislation regulating toxic chemicals that narrowly defines endocrine disruption as reproduction and development, or that addresses chemicals one at a time, or one disorder at a time, will clearly fail to protect us in the long run. Broadly defining endocrine disruption now is a gift we must give to future generations, for whom the words endocrine disruption will unfortunately be as common as the word cancer is today.[34]

We are already seeing some of the potential plastic-related effects of endocrine disruption showing up as severe allergies to plastic in individuals, even youths.

We were contacted by a young woman who is unable to eat anything that has touched or been packaged in plastic. She has been diagnosed with a severe sensitivity to plastic by allergy specialists. After years of testing based on her symptoms—including depression, attention deficit disorder (ADD) and ovarian cysts—she and her family suspect they have narrowed her condition down to a correlation with autoimmune encephalitis. It appears that the part of her brain creating natural estrogens is attacked by her immune system when synthetic estrogen-mimicking chemicals from plastics are introduced into her body. She is only in her teens. Is this the tip of the iceberg?

Where applicable in our description of plastic types that follows, we include the recycling code—officially known as the "resin identification code"—for common plastic resins to help you identify the plastic. The code is a number from 1 to 7 surrounded by chasing arrows and often found molded or printed on the bottom of plastic products. Codes 1 to 6 each refer to a specific plastic resin. Note that number 7 refers to a catch-all category for all plastics other than the first six specific resins. We'll describe this recycling code system below in more detail in the Recycling section (page 60), but for now it is sufficient to note that these codes do not indicate if the product is actually recyclable or if it is safe; the numbers are simply to aid in quickly and accurately identifying the type of plastic resin used to make a product.

The order in which we present these plastics is based very roughly on their approximate order of commonness in everyday life.[35]

34   TEDX: The Endocrine Disruption Exchange (2017) "Defining Endocrine Disruption," Endocrinedisruption.org (accessed at: http://endocrinedisruption.org/endocrine-disruption/introduction/defining-endocrine-disruption).

35   This ordering follows to some extent the order set out by Susan Freinkel in her book *Plastic: A Toxic Love Story*, New York: Houghton Mifflin Harcourt, 2011, pp. 236–239. Her firsthand, extensive research into the characteristics and applications of many common plastics also plays into our descriptions, as does the practical research of Beth Terry in her book *Plastic Free: How I Kicked the Plastic Habit and How You Can Too*, New York: Skyhorse, 2015, pp. 19–30. The American Chemistry Council's table of Plastic Packaging Resins was also a helpful source (accessed at: https://plastics.americanchemistry.com/Plastic-Resin-Codes-PDF). Please note, however, that these descriptions and their organization are ours alone, including the opinions on toxicity, and are not necessarily endorsed by Susan Freinkel, Beth Terry or the American Chemistry Council.

Polyethylene Terephthalate (PET or PETE, #1): From Disposable Water Bottles to Polyester Fleeces

PET—aka polyester—is one of the packaging workhorses. All those single-use water bottles lying on the beach are the offspring of PET. You'll also find capless or pierced ones at the bottom of the ocean because PET is denser than water and sinks like a rock. It's much-loved as a packaging material due to its see-through clarity and ability to create an impermeable liquid-gas barrier, sealing in the carbonated fizz of your ginger ale while keeping out the oxygen that could prematurely spoil your salad dressing. PET is also used to make food containers for peanut butter, jams, jellies and pickles. It's multi-talented: much of the PET produced is used to fashion polyester textiles, such as wrinkle-proof clothing, fleeces and carpeting. It might also be the padding and insulation for your pillow and comforter.

HOW TOXIC IS POLYETHYLENE TEREPHTHALATE?

We consider it one to avoid, especially for food and drink contact. A chemical called antimony trioxide is used as a catalyst and flame retardant in making PET, and this antimony additive is considered a possible carcinogen—cancer-causing agent—for humans.[36] In normal conditions, the amount of that antimony coming out of a single-use water bottle is likely minimal, but research has shown that the leaching increases significantly as the temperature increases—think water bottles or food containers out in the sun or stored in the car on hot summer days.[37] Not good. There is research showing that PET may leach phthalates too, even though the plastics industry says that phthalates are not required to make PET.[38] In a study of military packaged water, the researchers exposed bottled water to temperatures ranging from a normal spring day to scorching desert sunshine for up to 120 days and found that at the higher temperatures antimony and phthalates were being released.[39]

We hear a lot about people's experiences with plastic. A few years ago we were contacted by a thirty-something woman from Southern California who had been diagnosed with stage 1 breast cancer. She had no family history of breast cancer, and said that in terms of diet and exercise she did everything right. She was convinced that her cancer developed from years of exposure to toxins leaching out of the plastic single-use water bottles she stored in her car trunk in the heat and drank from daily. It's obviously anecdotal evidence based on her intuition, and neither she nor we have any way of proving her hypothesis, but it raises the question: Why take the chance when there are alternatives? Why not take a precautionary approach?

The Polyethylenes: The Most Popular Packaging Plastics Out There (HDPE, #2 and LDPE, #4)

It almost sounds like we're describing a hit band from the '60s. Well, this sub-group of versatile plastics actually are about as popular as the Beatles, whether those of us using them realize it or not. As the most widely used plastics in the world, they dominate the packaging landscape. The polyethylene polymer has the simplest basic chemical structure of any polymer, making it easy to process and thus extremely popular for low value, high volume applications. It's strong and flexible, as well as

36   S. Sundar and S. Chakravarty (2010) "Antimony Toxicity," *International Journal of Environmental Research and Public Health* 7(12):4267–4277.

37   P. Westerhoff, P. Prapaipong, E. Shock and A. Hillaireau (2007) "Antimony Leaching from Polyethylene Terephthalate (PET) Plastic Used for Bottled Drinking Water," *Water Research* 42(3):551–556.

38   L. Sax (2009) "Polyethylene Terephthalate May Yield Endocrine Disruptors," *Environmental Health Perspectives* 118(4):445–448.

39   M. Greifenstein, D.W. White, A. Stubner, J. Hout and A.J. Whelton (2013) "Impact of Temperature and Storage Duration on the Chemical and Odor Quality of Military Packaged Water in Polyethylene Terephthalate Bottles," *Science of the Total Environment* 456-457:376–383.

moisture-resistant and relatively transparent, so you can see why it's a favorite for packaging. Wondering what your milk carton or disposable beverage cup is coated with? Think polyethylene. The most common polyethylene resins are:

- Low Density Polyethylene (LDPE, #4) and Linear Low Density Polyethylene (LLDPE, #4): They are used mostly for a lot of thin filmy applications, including all kinds of bags (dry cleaning, newspapers, bread, frozen foods, fresh produce and home garbage), shrink wrap, coatings for cartons and cups, but also for sturdier products like container lids, squeezable bottles for things like honey and mustard, wire and cable covering. LLDPE is slightly more flexible and stretchy and is also used for toys and tubing.

- High Density Polyethylene (HDPE, #2): As the name suggests, it's a heavier tougher form of polyethylene and it's commonly used for grocery bags, Tyvek insulation, cereal box liners and for a variety of sturdier bottles (milk, water, juice, bleach, shampoo, dish and laundry detergents, household cleaners and medicines). You can also find it in plumbing pipes, plastic-wood composites and wire and cable covering.

HOW TOXIC ARE POLYETHYLENES?

We consider polyethylenes to be "safer" plastics for food and drink use, primarily because they are relatively strong and stable compared to some of the other common plastics. This is partly why they are so popular for packaging. That said, there is research showing they can release endocrine-disrupting chemicals, especially when exposed to the sun (ultraviolet light).[40] The main leaching culprits are estrogen-mimicking nonylphenols and octylphenols, which are added to polyethylene as stabilizers and plasticizers.[41]

Polypropylene (PP, #5): Safer Than Many, But Still Questionable

Also a packaging maven, you could say polypropylene is a step up in quality and stability from polyethylene. It better resists heat and chemicals—making it desirable for hot liquids and foods—and it's just plain stronger, so it works well for bottle caps and closures subjected to significant pressure. Many of the bottles we carry in our store have polypropylene caps because a similarly stable and tough non-plastic alternative has not yet emerged. You'll find it as medicine bottles, and food containers for ketchup, yogurt, cottage cheese, syrup, margarine and takeout meals. Those sturdy Rubbermaid storage bins and the lids and filter casing for Brita water pitchers are polypropylene. Most cars are filled with plastic, including polypropylene, which is used for bumpers, carpets and various interior parts. It's even a component of the body panels on Elon Musk's elegant Teslas, sandwiched between layers of carbon fiber and encased in epoxy resin.

HOW TOXIC IS POLYPROPYLENE?

Polypropylene is also a "relatively safe" plastic in our opinion, because of its strength and stability. Nonetheless, it too has been shown to leach plastic additives, in particular the synthetic lubricating agent oleamide and antibacterial chemicals. This discovery came about by accident when Canadian researchers using disposable polypropylene test tubes, pipettes and culture plates were baffled by strange results

40   C.Z. Yang, S.I. Yaniger, V.C. Jordan, D.J. Klein and G.D. Bittner (2011) "Most Plastic Products Release Estrogenic Chemicals: A Potential Health Problem That Can Be Solved," *Environmental Health Perspectives* 119(7):989–996.

41   A. Guart, F. Bobo-Blay, F. Borrell and S. Lacorte (2011) "Migration of Plasticizers Phthalates, Bisphenol A and Alkylphenols from Plastic Containers and Evaluation of Risk," *Food Additives & Contaminants: Part A* 28(5):676-685; J.E. Loyo-Rosales, G.C. Rosales-Rivera, A.M. Lynch, C.P. Rice and A. Torrents (2004) "Migration of Nonylphenol from Plastic Containers to Water and a Milk Surrogate," *Journal of Agricultural and Food Chemistry* 52(7):2016–2020.

in their experiments.[42] They found that the additives in the polypropylene were "biologically active" and were affecting their results. Oleamide occurs naturally in the human body, so one can rationally assume that synthetic oleamide could have the potential to confuse biological systems; this is pure speculation on our part, but may be the case in the same way endocrine-disrupting chemicals confuse hormonal systems. Research is ongoing in this area.

Polyvinyl Chloride (PVC, #3): The Everyday "Poison" Plastic

PVC—aka vinyl—is used in a wide array of consumer products covering numerous aspects of everyday life, from school supplies to showers to medical care to homebuilding. You could call it the shapeshifting plastic because of its ability to adopt all kinds of personas—from flexible to rigid—depending on the chemical additive mixture used to make it. It's such a dizzying array of applications, we're just going to do a straight-out list of some of them:

*   Flexible: bags for bedding and medical use (IV, blood), medical tubing, shrink wrap, shower curtains, toys (think rubber duck), lunch boxes, purses, loose leaf binders, rainwear, "pleather" clothing, Naugahyde upholstery, hoses, wire and cable insulation, carpet backing, flooring, squeeze bottles and bottles for shampoo, mouthwash, cooking oil, peanut butter, detergent and window cleaner.

*   Rigid: blister packs and clamshell packaging, credit cards, plumbing piping, vinyl siding, window frames, fencing, decking, railing and other construction materials.

HOW TOXIC IS PVC?

In our opinion, it is among the worst consumer product plastics—quite possibly *the* worst—and one to avoid whenever and wherever possible. It is often referred to as the most toxic consumer plastic for our health and the environment because of the range of dangerous chemicals it may release during its life cycle, including cancer-causing dioxins, endocrine-disrupting phthalates and bisphenol A (see the sidebars for more details on these, and tips on avoiding them, on pages 34 and 39, respectively), and heavy metals like lead, mercury and cadmium.[43] The problem with PVC is that its base monomer building block is vinyl chloride, which is highly toxic and unstable, thus requiring lots of additives to calm it down and make it usable. But even in its final "stabilized" form, PVC is not very stable. The additives are just so eager to leach out, and they do.

PVC often makes us think of shower curtains. Years ago, before we became "plastic-aware" we purchased a PVC shower curtain. When we opened the sealed plastic bag holding the curtain, we were hit hard by a blistering wave of noxious chemicals. It stunned us, but we still hung up that curtain and used it for a bit until we realized it was literally making us feel nauseous and stinging our eyes. In 2008, several years after our curtain experience, the Center for Health, Environment and Justice did a fascinating study where they tested five PVC shower curtains purchased at big box retailers.[44] All of the curtains contained cancer-causing volatile organic compounds, phthalates, organotins (nervous system toxicants) and one or more of the heavy metals lead, cadmium, mercury and chromium. Yikes! So that's what we were smelling and breathing in. And while we're in the bathroom, don't forget the cute little rubber ducky; it may well be phthalate-infused PVC.

---

42   G.R. McDonald et al. (2008) "Bioactive Contaminants Leach from Disposable Laboratory Plasticware," *Science* 322(5903):917.

43   M. Belliveau and S. Lester (2004) "PVC Bad News Comes in 3s: The Poison Plastic, Health Hazards and the Looming Waste Crisis," Center for Health, Environment and Justice & Environmental Health Strategy Center (accessed 4 March 2017: http://chej.org/polyvinyl-chloride-pvc).

44   S. Lester, M. Schade and C. Weigand (2008) "Volatile Vinyl: The New Shower Curtain's Chemical Smell," Center for Health, Environment and Justice (accessed 4 March 2017: http://chej.org/polyvinyl-chloride-pvc).

Another PVC application that disturbs us deeply is soft, pliable medical tubing, blood bags and catheters in hospital and other medical settings. Given that the tubing is used for such medical equipment as intravenous lines, it is a direct link to the recipient's bloodstream. Soft PVC can be composed of over 50 percent phthalates by weight. These phthalates are not chemically bound to the PVC. When you have an intravenous salt solution or precious blood supply—not to mention a potent cocktail of pharmaceuticals—going through this tubing and straight into the bloodstream of a person, it is virtually certain the liquid is laced with free-roaming phthalates.

On April 1, 2016—though this was no April Fool's joke—a new peer-reviewed study was presented at the annual meeting of the Endocrine Society, the world's oldest and largest organization of scientists devoted to hormone research. For four years, the presenting Belgian researchers had tracked over 400 children who were initially treated for a critical illness in pediatric intensive care units. They found that the children's direct exposure to the phthalate DEHP (di(2-ethylhexyl)phthalate) leaching from medical devices during their treatment contributed to them experiencing long-term attention deficit.[45] Step back and consider the full context of this revelatory discovery: Here you have critically ill children suffering later in life from attention deficit disorder because they were exposed to hormonally-active, brain-altering plastic chemicals as a result of the supposedly lifesaving treatment they were receiving at one of the most vulnerable moments of their lives. How utterly mixed up and sad is that? This is classic endocrine disruption at work where the effects of early life exposure to the hormone-disrupting chemical may not manifest until later in life (see the sidebar on Endocrine-Disrupting Chemicals on page 27).

PHTHALATES: TIME TO "BOY"COTT THEM

In 2005, Dr. Shanna Swan of the University of Rochester published a now seminal study that led to a family of chemicals known as phthalates being catapulted into the limelight—at least the limelights of the scientific community and the chemical industry. The former lauded the research, finding it compelling and disturbing. The latter pilloried it, labeling it flawed and premature. Swan and her team found that baby boys whose mothers were exposed to phthalate chemicals showed disturbing effects that could be termed "demasculinization" or "feminization" of the boys: smaller penis size, undescended testicles and scrotums that were described as "not distinct from surrounding tissue."[46] The effects were amplified when the exposure was to multiple phthalates.

What are phthalates? They are synthetic chemicals used primarily as softening agents, or "plasticizers," in plastic polymers—in particular polyvinyl chloride (PVC)—and as solvents in other products; for example, to dissolve and carry fragrances in cosmetic and personal care products. You can find them in food packaging, plastic wraps, children's toys, inflatable toys, lunchbags, school supplies (pencil cases, binders, folders), modeling clay, glow sticks, raincoats, shower curtains, garden hoses, vinyl tiles, wallpaper and flooring, adhesives, detergents, lubricating oils and

45   S. Verstraete, I. Vanhorebeek, A. Covaci, F. Guiza, G. Malarvannan, P.G. Jorens and G. Van den Berghe (2016) "Circulating Phthalates During Critical Illness in Children are Associated with Long-Term Attention Deficit," *Intensive Care Medicine* 42(3):379–392.

46   S.H. Swan et al. (2005) "Decrease in Anogenital Distance among Male Infants with Prenatal Phthalate Exposure," *Environmental Health Perspectives* 113(8):1056–1061.

paints, pharmaceuticals and medical tubing and IV bags (be sure to see our PVC section on page 33 about how these medical uses are extremely worrisome). As for personal care and cosmetic products, phthalates tend to lurk in soaps, shampoos, deodorant, hair spray, nail polish and lotions. And "lurk" is the right word because they may not be indicated on the label, having been lumped into the broad term of "fragrance" on the product ingredients list.[47]

One of the problems with phthalates is that they move around easily and a lot, and we're exposed to them in a myriad of ways—mostly by eating and drinking foods that have been in contact with phthalates in food packaging and containers, but also by inhaling them in the air from "fragrances"; they can also be present in house dust, water sources and sediment.[48] They have been detected in human urine, blood and breast milk.[49] They do not bind to the plastic polymer in PVC so they easily leach out of food containers and packaging, especially when heated and in the presence of oils. And those fruity shampoo scents or flower fresh hair spray smells may be infused with volatile, toxic, "fragrance"-carrying phthalates we are breathing in. Children are more susceptible to picking them up in the home environment while playing on the floor where phthalate dust settles.

Remember how BPA appears to be present in the bodies of most human beings? Same deal with phthalates. The U.S. Centers for Disease Control and Prevention have found measurable levels of many phthalates across the general American population, thus indicating widespread exposure.[50]

The core problem is the possible effects of phthalates on our health and the health of our children. Like BPA, phthalates are endocrine disruptors and in addition to Swan's chilling discovery of their potential effects on development of young boys, phthalates have been linked to several other health issues, including asthma, neurodevelopmental problems in newborns, fertility issues, liver damage, obesity and possibly breast cancer.[51] DEHP is "reasonably anticipated" to be a human carcinogen based on evidence from animal studies.[52] More research needs to be done, but like all endocrine disruptors the effects of exposure may not show up for years, and we think that is reason enough to take a precautionary approach and minimize our exposure to phthalates. Governments seem to think so too.

47   In a positive development, Unilever recently announced that it intends to voluntarily disclose detailed information on fragrance ingredients for all products in its portfolio of personal care brands by 2018: http://www.treehugger.com/organic-beauty/unilevers-game-changing-decision-reveal-fragrance-ingredients.html (accessed 4 March 2017).

48   U.S. Centers for Disease Control and Prevention (2016) "Biomonitoring Summary: Phthalates Overview: Di-2-ethylhexyl Phthalate," National Biomonitoring Program (accessed 4 March 2017: https://www.cdc.gov/biomonitoring/DEHP_BiomonitoringSummary.html).

49   E.P. Hines, A.M. Calafat, M.J. Silva, P. Mendola and S.E. Fenton (2009) "Concentrations of Phthalate Metabolites in Milk, Urine, Saliva and Serum of Lactating North Carolina Women," Environmental Health Perspectives 117(1):86–92.

50   U.S. Centers for Disease Control and Prevention (2015) "National Report on Human Exposure to Environmental Chemicals: Updated Tables, February 2015," Fourth National Report on Human Exposure to Environmental Chemicals (accessed 4 March 2017 at: https://www.cdc.gov/exposurereport).

51   U.S. Department of Health and Human Services (2016) "Phthalates," ToxTown, U.S. National Library of Medicine, National Institutes of Health (accessed 4 March 2017: https://toxtown.nlm.nih.gov/text_version/chemicals.php?id=24); Breast Cancer Fund (2012) "The State of the Evidence on Phthalates" (accessed 4 March 2017: http://www.breastcancerfund.org/clear-science/radiation-chemicals-and-breast-cancer/phthalates.html); L. López-Carrill et al. (2010) "Exposure to Phthalates and Breast Cancer Risk in Northern Mexico," Environmental Health Perspectives 118(4):539–544; S.H. Swan (2008) "Environmental Phthalate Exposure in Relation to Reproductive Outcomes and Other Health Endpoints in Humans," Environmental Research 108(2):177–184.

52   U.S. Department of Health and Human Services (2016) "Di(2-ethylhexyl) Phthalate," Report on Carcinogens, Fourteenth Edition, National Toxicology Program, National Institutes of Health (accessed 4 March 2017: https://ntp.niehs.nih.gov/ntp/roc/content/profiles/diethylhexylphthalate.pdf).

Six commonly used phthalates have been banned above certain levels in toys and childcare products in various parts of the world, including Canada, the United States and Europe: di-2-ethyl hexyl phthalate (DEHP), dibutyl phthalate (DBP) and benzyl butyl phthalate (BBP), di-isononyl phthalate (DINP), di-isodecyl phthalate (DIDP) and di-n-octyl phthalate (DNOP). A childcare product is considered to be any product intended to facilitate the sleep, relaxation, hygiene, feeding and sucking or teething of a child. But these two product categories represent only a tiny fraction of the phthalates out in our world and day-to-day products, and millions of tons of phthalates are produced annually.

TIPS FOR REDUCING EXPOSURE TO PHTHALATES:

- Avoid plastic containers, plastic wraps, children's toys, garden hoses, raincoats and anything else made of PVC (recycling symbol #3). Opt for glass or stainless steel, or, if you must use a plastic food container, go for a safe, more stable one like polypropylene or high density polyethylene.

- Be sure to check your children's toys, especially ones they put directly in the mouth, and if you suspect one may be PVC but there is no indication of the type of plastic, ask the manufacturer. If it is PVC, recycle it.

- Don't microwave plastics, or use oily or acidic foods in plastic containers as this can increase leaching.

- Avoid personal care and cosmetic products (soaps, shampoos and hair sprays) that may contain phthalates. Read the labels, though it's unlikely phthalates will be listed on the label. If the label simply says "fragrance," there is a distinct possibility it contains phthalates. You can check products and find phthalate-free personal care products using the Environmental Working Group's comprehensive Skin Deep database: www.ewg.org/skindeep/ (at the time of writing, it listed 64,471 products).

- Vacuum and mop your floors and wet wipe other surfaces—especially where children are—to regularly remove phthalate-containing dust. Ventilating regularly—ideally, daily—to freshen up the air in your home will also help: open windows and doors, use a ceiling fan or air exchanger. Note that this is helpful not just for phthalates, but also for other toxins coming out of plastics, such as polybrominated diphenyl ether (PBDE) flame retardants (see the Other Chemicals side bar on page 47).

- Have your children play on a blanket or cotton or wool carpet rather than the bare floor if the floor is dusty.

Polystyrene (PS, #6): Nice as an Insulator, But Not for Your Coffee Cup

As previously mentioned, we live in Wakefield, an idyllic, picturesque rural Quebec town with the pristine Gatineau River winding through it. We settled here years ago for the natural beauty and progressive, eco-friendly community. It was rather ironic when a few years later a company called Styro Rail arrived and set up a sprawling expanded polystyrene (EPS) insulation manufacturing facility. They regularly belch out volatile pentane gas used in the manufacture of EPS—sometimes day and night—and produce tons and tons of EPS. Now every time we pass their facility on the highway—which used to be a pristine field of green—we behold a sea of EPS partially shrink-wrapped in weather-beaten tattered blue plastic (likely a member of the polyethylene family) and left for months on end in their massive outdoor storage area.

The EPS we just described—commonly referred to via its trade name, Styrofoam—is perhaps the most recognizable form of polystyrene. It creates a solid moisture barrier and is used ubiquitously for clamshell takeout food containers and drinking cups, egg cartons, packing trays for everything from ground beef to peeled oranges, bike helmets, home insulation and packing peanuts to keep shipments safe in transit. It can also take on a rigid form that might be clear or opaque and is channeled into single-use food containers and cutlery, CD and DVD cases, video cassette cartridges and disposable razors. It is also combined with rubber to create an opaque high impact polystyrene used for model assembly kits, coat hangers, electronic housings, license plate frames, aspirin bottles and medical and lab equipment, including test tubes and petri dishes.

HOW TOXIC IS POLYSTYRENE?

This is another one we avoid whenever possible, especially for food and drink use. One might think that polystyrene, foamy and commonly used as an insulating material, would be ideal for coffee and tea cups: it keeps the drink warm and prevents the cup from being too hot to handle with naked hands. Unfortunately, this is exactly how it is marketed and used. But those polystyrene cups leach styrene, especially when exposed to hot temperatures.[53] The problem with styrene is that it is "reasonably anticipated to be a carcinogen,"[54] which is conservative "science speak" meaning that there is research pointing directly to links with cancer. With long-term exposure, styrene is also considered a brain and nervous system toxicant, and animal studies have shown it to cause genetic damage and to have negative effects on the lungs, liver and immune system.[55]

It is popular as a home insulation material, and truth be known, the insulation under our basement radiant floor is polystyrene foam (not from Styro Rail, mind you, which wasn't even on our radar when our house was built). Long-term leaching into the ground does concern us, though it's a bit late for us to reconsider that one. For food and drink, however, we definitely steer clear of the stuff.

53   M. Ahmad and A.S. Bajahlan (2007) "Leaching of Styrene and Other Aromatic Compounds in Drinking Water from PS Bottles," *Journal of Environmental Sciences* 19(4):421–426. The study also looked at styrene leaching from Styrofoam cups and found temperature significantly increased the leaching.

54   Agency for Toxic Substances and Disease Registry (2012) "ToxFAQs for Styrene," U.S. Department of Health and Human Services (accessed 4 March 2017: https://www.atsdr.cdc.gov/ToxProfiles/TP.asp?id=421&tid=74).

55   U.S. Department of Health and Human Services (2016) "Styrene," Report on Carcinogens, Fourteenth Edition, National Toxicology Program, National Institutes of Health (accessed 4 March 2017: https://ntp.niehs.nih.gov/ntp/roc/content/profiles/styrene.pdf); V.A. Beningnus, A.M. Geller, W.K. Boyes and P.J. Bushnell (2005) "Human Neurobehavioural Effects of Long-Term Exposure to Styrene: A Meta-Analysis," *Environmental Health Perspectives* 113(5):532–538.

The Polyurethanes: Supporting Your Downward Dog and Nightly Slumber

The polyurethane plastic family is a large and diverse one that ranges from flexible foams (mattresses, spray foam insulation, carpet underlay and cushioning in furniture cars and shoes) to rigid solids (hoses, tubing, gaskets and seals), to thin films or coatings (adhesives for food packaging, coating on silicone breast implants, condoms), to stretchy fibers (sportswear, bras and wetsuits). You might be sleeping on a polyurethane mattress, but you're likely most familiar with polyurethane in its sporty fiber personas as the trademarked Spandex and Lycra used for athletic and yoga gear, and in tights and socks galore. Venture beyond a local farmer's market and it's not easy to find 100 percent pure wool socks anymore. Most "wool" socks contain a percentage of elasticizing Spandex or Lycra.

HOW TOXIC ARE POLYURETHANES?

We think they are worth avoiding whenever possible. Polyurethanes are made of toxic chemicals known as isocyanates, which are the leading cause of occupational asthma—and thus a real risk for workers in the polyurethane industry, as well as chemically sensitive individuals.[56] As for our day-to-day use, polyurethanes have also been linked to a skin irritation known as contact dermatitis through direct contact with such polyurethane items as a toilet seat, jewelry and Spandex tape sewn into underwear.[57]

Another aspect of its toxicity to keep in mind: polyurethane is a highly flammable base resin and may well contain a host of toxic flame retardant additives, though it is extremely difficult to know which ones. Mattress manufacturers consider their flame retardant formulas a trade secret and are loath to divulge them.[58] Given that we spend about a third of our lives with our bodies directly against our mattresses breathing in whatever they may be off-gassing, we think that industry secrecy is reason enough to take precaution and switch to a non-plastic mattress such as cotton or natural rubber (more on this in the Bedroom section on page 121).

Then there is polyurethane spray foam insulation, which builders may argue is safe once it is sprayed on and has cured (although that still puts the sprayer at risk of exposure to volatile chemicals, and we also still have the flame retardant additive issue). The fact is, it is not necessarily safe even when cured because the isocyanate methylene diphenyl diisocyanate (MDI) commonly used in such insulation can off-gas from the insulation, and has been linked to asthma, lung damage and even death.[59] Yes, we need to be vigilant even about what goes into our walls intending to keep us warm and cozy.

---

56   D. Bello et al. (2007) "Skin Exposure to Isocyanates: Reasons for Concern" *Environmental Health Perspectives* 115(3):328–335.

57   H. Turan et al. (2011) "Polyurethane Toilet Seat Contact Dermatitis," *Pediatric Dermatology* 28(6):731–732; S. Hellig et al. (2011) "Persistant Allergic Contact Dermatitis to Plastic Toilet Seats," *Pediatric Dermatology* 28(5):587–590; R. Nguyen and A. Lee (2012) "Allergic Contact Dermatitis Caused by Isocyanates in Resin Jewellry," *Contact Dermatitis* 67(1):56–57; K. Arisu et al. (1992) "Tinuvin P in a Spandex Tape as a Cause of Clothing Dermatitis," *Contact Dermatitis* 26(5):311–316.

58   H. Wallace (2008) "Should You Ditch Your Chemical Mattress?" *Mother Jones*, March-April 2008 (accessed 4 March 2017: http://www.motherjones.com/politics/2008/03/should-you-ditch-your-chemical-mattress).

59   Earthtalk (2015) "Ward Off Chemical Exposure: Alternatives to Methylene Diphenyl Diisocyanate are More Expensive but Perhaps Safer for your Lungs and More," *Scientific American* (accessed 4 March 2017: https://www.scientificamerican.com/article/better-home-insulation-needed-to-ward-off-chemical-exposure); U.S. National Institute for Occupational Safety and Health (1996) "Preventing Asthma and Death from Diisocyanate Exposure DHHS," Centers for Disease Control and Prevention (accessed 4 March 2017: https://www.cdc.gov/niosh/docs/96-111).

Polycarbonate (PC, #7): The BPA-Laden Black Sheep

In the consumer product context, polycarbonate is widely and negatively associated with its core constituent, the endocrine disruptor bisphenol A (BPA). As such, its use for food and drink contact purposes has decreased significantly in recent years. But polycarbonate is in practice an engineering plastic—originally created to compete with die-cast metal—with numerous industrial applications like gears and equipment housing. Strong, transparent and shatter-proof, it was considered a lightweight replacement for glass, which is why it was so popular for sports water bottles and baby bottles. It is still a favorite for rigid products including CDs and DVDs, eyeglass lenses, dental sealants, lab equipment, snowboards, car parts and housing for cell phones, computers and power tools. As well, and despite the issues with BPA, polycarbonate is still used widely to make the large, blue three- and five-gallon (11- and 19-L) water bottles that are so common in office coolers and home water stations.

HOW TOXIC IS POLYCARBONATE?

Given its connection to BPA, we consider polycarbonate one to avoid whenever possible, and especially for food and drink contact. Please read the box below, which provides an overview of health problems associated with BPA, based on the latest research at the time of writing.

BISPHENOL A (BPA): IT'S HERE, IT'S THERE, IT'S EVERYWHERE

We explained earlier that BPA—the endocrine-disrupting chemical used to make hard polycarbonate plastic and epoxy resins—is in the air all over the world. Well, guess what? It's likely in all of our bodies too. Researchers surmise that humans all over the world—adults, adolescents and children—likely have a measurable amount of BPA in their blood, urine or body tissue.[60] Several government studies have detected BPA in large portions of the population:

- In Canada, 91% of the population aged 6 to 79.

- In the United States, 93% of the population aged 6 and older.

- In Germany, 99% of 3 to 14 year olds.[61]

We are most exposed to it through our diet. It leaches out of polycarbonate products such as food containers and large water jugs, as well as from the epoxy lining of aluminum and steel cans used to package pretty much any canned food or drink you can imagine, from crushed tomatoes and creamed corn to beer and ginger ale. The leaching increases with acidic and oily foods and high temperatures.

60   L.N. Vandenberg et al. (2010) "Urinary, Circulating, and Tissue Biomonitoring Studies Indicate Widespread Exposure to Bisphenol A," *Environmental Health Perspectives* 118(8):1055–1070.

61   Statistics Canada (2010) "Bisphenol A Concentrations in the Canadian Population, 2007 to 2009," Canadian Health Measures Survey (accessed 4 March 2017: http://www.statcan.gc.ca/pub/82-625-x/2010002/article/11327-eng.htm).

BPA is also present in high quantities as a print developer on thermal paper cash receipts. It comes off on your fingers and is absorbed deep enough into your skin that it can't be washed off.[62] In fact, hand sanitizers and other skin care products contain a mixture of dermal penetration–enhancing chemicals that can increase by up to 100 fold the skin's absorption of BPA. In a recent study, researchers found that when men and women held thermal receipt paper immediately after using a hand sanitizer with penetration-enhancing chemicals, BPA was transferred to their hands and then to French fries that they ate—this combination of BPA going into the body through the skin and the mouth led to a rapid and dramatic increase in the BPA level in their blood and urine.[63]

It is an endocrine-disrupting chemical and comprehensive reviews of the scientific literature have found that BPA can be harmful to humans at levels found in the average person well below those considered safe by government regulatory bodies.[64] Some of the strongest associations researchers have made are between early life BPA exposure and altered behavior, including disrupted brain development in children, along with increased probability of childhood wheeze and asthma. BPA is considered a "reproductive toxicant" because it impacts female reproduction and has the potential to affect male reproductive systems in humans and animals.[65] The now voluminous body of peer-reviewed scientific literature associates BPA with numerous health problems including early puberty, obesity, infertility, insulin inhibition, hyperactivity and learning disabilities, as well as possible increased risk of breast and prostate cancer, heart disease and type II diabetes.[66]

ARE BPA-FREE PLASTICS SAFER?

Perhaps you've seen a baby bottle or sippy cup or water bottle in a store with a label rejoicing "BPA-Free." Don't get too excited. Given the public distrust of BPA, and bans on BPA in baby bottles in some parts of the world (Canada, Europe, some U.S. states), manufacturers have been replacing BPA with other chemicals from the diverse bisphenol family—substances with unimaginative names like bisphenol AF, bisphenol B, bisphenol C, bisphenol E, bisphenol F and bisphenol S. The names are similar for a reason—their chemical structures are practically identical and they seem to have the same endocrine disruption bullying tendencies. Research has shown that many such replacements are also exhibiting hormone disrupting activity—sometimes even more so than cousin BPA—thus carrying on the toxic legacy of this sinister family.[67]

---

62   S. Lunder, D. Andrews and J. Houlihan (2010) "BPA Coats Cash Register Receipts," EWG.org (accessed 4 March 2017: http://www.ewg.org/research/bpa-in-store-receipts).

63   A.M. Hormann, F.S. Vom Saal, S.C. Nagel et al. (2014) "Holding Thermal Receipt Paper and Eating Food after Using Hand Sanitizer Results in High Serum Bioactive and Urine Total Levels of Bisphenol A (BPA)," *PLoS One* 9(10):e110509.

64   J.R. Rochester (2013) "Bisphenol A and Human Health: A review of the literature," *Reproductive Toxicology* 42:132–155.

65   J. Peretz, L. Vrooman, W.A. Ricke, P.A. Hunt et al. (2014) "Bisphenol A and Reproductive Health: Update of Experimental and Human Evidence, 2007–2013," *Environmental Health Perspectives* 122:775–786.

66   H.A. Tilson (2012) "Bisphenol A: Collection," *Environmental Health Perspectives* January 2007-December 2011; Breast Cancer Fund (2012) "The State of the Evidence on Bisphenol A (BPA)," Breastcancerfund.org (accessed 4 March 2017: http://www.breastcancerfund.org/clear-science/radiation-chemicals-and-breast-cancer/bisphenol-a.html).

67   J.R. Rochester and A.L. Bolden (2015) "Bisphenol S and F: A Systematic Review and Comparison of the Hormonal Activity of Bisphenol A Substitutes," *Environmental Health Perspectives* 123(7):643-650 (accessed 4 March 2017: https://ehp.niehs.nih.gov/1408989/).

TIPS TO REDUCE YOUR EXPOSURE TO BISPHENOLS

- Avoid polycarbonate plastic products and BPA-free plastic products, especially for food and drink purposes (marked "PC" with recycling symbol #7; but note that this is a catch-all category containing all plastics other than the specific ones indicated by numbers 1 to 6).

- If you must use them—for example the common large blue water jugs for water transport and storage and water coolers—try and minimize the time the water is in contact with the bottle. Transfer it to another container, such as glass or stainless steel, as soon as possible. Recycle or replace scratched or worn polycarbonate or BPA-free plastic containers (they start to look cloudy and harder to see through when wearing out). BPA leaching increases as the polycarbonate becomes scratched and worn out.

- Avoid heating food or drink (especially in the microwave) in polycarbonate or BPA-free plastic products. Avoid putting oily or acidic food or drink in them (e.g., lemon and tomato). Heat, oils and acidic substances can increase the leaching of bisphenols.

- Avoid canned foods as much as possible. The lining of most cans is a BPA-containing epoxy. Look for fresh organic foods as much as possible.

- Refuse cash register receipts, unless you absolutely need them. Don't let children handle receipts. Avoid handling receipts after using hand sanitizer or hand skin creams. Wash your hands as soon as possible after touching receipts.

Epoxies: From Super Glues to Food Can Lining

Epoxy resins are a hardcore broad polymer group with properties like high strength, low weight, and temperature and chemical resistance, making them popular for numerous consumer and industrial applications including high-performance adhesives, coatings, paints, sealants, insulators, car-boat-plane parts, wind turbine blades, fiber optics and electrical circuit boards. They also form the interior lining of most canned foods. You might find them on high-performance decorative terrazzo flooring or used by painters and sculptors to create glossy protective finishes and psychedelic shapes in their artwork.

HOW TOXIC ARE EPOXIES?

As common and handy as they are for various aspects of everyday life, we try and avoid them where possible, especially for contact with food and drink. Most epoxies are made with bisphenol A (see the box devoted to BPA on page 39) and another toxin called epichlorohydrin, which has been associated with blood, respiratory and liver damage and is considered a probable human carcinogen.[68]

---

68 U.S. Environmental Protection Agency (2000) "Epichlorohydrin (1-Chloro-2-3-Epoxypropane) - CAS 106-89-8," Health Effects Notebook for Hazardous Air Pollutants (accessed 4 March 2017: https://www.epa.gov/haps/health-effects-notebook-hazardous-air-pollutants).

The possibility of being exposed to low levels of BPA and epichlorohydrin from the linings of cans is real.[69]

The Acrylics: Bulletproof LEGO, Anyone?

The acrylic family of plastics is about as tough, resilient and diverse as they come. Being rigid thermoplastics, they can withstand enormous physical stress and return to their original size and shape unchanged. They can be as clear and see-through as glass, and remarkably strong—yes, even bulletproof—making them popular in the world of high-security applications; think the Popemobile's transparent walls, the windows on limousines for transporting heads of state and bank teller windows (note that polycarbonate and polyurethanes may also be used in making bulletproof glass, which consists of multiple layers of clear plastic resins). Acrylic resins are used to make cataract replacement lenses and for various dental applications, including fillings and removable dentures. You'll also find them as plane windows, outdoor signs, car light casing, aquariums and shower doors.

Three of the most common acrylics are acrylonitrile butadiene styrene (ABS) and styrene acrylonitrile (SAN) and polyacrylonitrile (PAN). Given their toughness and stability they may be used in place of polystyrene; for example, SAN is used to make more durable dishware.

The added stability comes at a cost as these acrylics are about twice the cost of polycarbonate to manufacture. ABS plays into a wide variety of household items including hard molded toys like LEGO, musical instruments (recorders and clarinets), luggage, golf club heads, furniture edging and helmets. And in the industrial world you'll find ABS in appliance casings, car body parts, boats, mobile homes and pipelines. As for PAN, if you see the word "acrylic" on your clothing label, it's some form of PAN, which is most commonly used in its fiber form to make textiles ranging from socks and sweaters to tents and sails.

HOW TOXIC ARE ACRYLICS?

Given their strength, rigidity and stability, we consider acrylics to be "relatively safe" plastics. You'll notice that both ABS and SAN include styrene as core ingredients in their manufacture, and that we described styrene above under polystyrene as extremely toxic. The final ABS and SAN polymers are stable enough that there should not be free styrene leaching, but like all plastics, we still try and avoid acrylics for food and drink contact. ABS polymers destined for applications that could present a fire hazard—such as electronics and appliances—may have added flame retardants, and these could pose toxicity issues.

Acrylic methacrylate resins used to make dental fillings, crowns, bridges and dentures have been shown to be cytotoxic—meaning they are toxic at the cellular level, rather than, say, being toxic to a particular organ—due to the leaching of toxic chemicals that include formaldehyde and methyl methacrylate.[70] Studies have indicated cytotoxicity in denture base resins, including reports of mucosal irritation and inner mouth sensitivity due to the substances leaching out of acrylic dentures.[71]

---

69   Environment Canada & Health Canada (2008) "Oxirane, (chloromethyl)-(Epichlorohydrin)," Screening Assessment for the Challenge (accessed 4 March 2017: http://www.ec.gc.ca/ese-ees/default. asp?lang=En&n=BA416AA1-1).

70   M.E. Saravi, M. Vojdani, F. and Bahrani (2012) "Evaluation of Cellular Toxicity of Three Denture Base Acrylic Resins," *Journal of Dentistry* (Tehran) 9(4):180–188.

71   J.H. Jorge, E.T. Giampaolo, A.L. Machado and C.E. Vergani (2003) "Cytotoxicity of Denture Base Acrylic Resins: A Literature Review," *Journal of Prosthetic Dentistry* 90(2):190–193.

The Polyamides: From Nylon Stockings and Velcro to Kevlar Super Clothing

There are natural polyamides, such as silk and wool, and then there are synthetic ones like nylon and Kevlar born not of Mother Nature, but of chemical manufacturing giant DuPont. Another uber-versatile plastics family—coveted for their strength, durability and elasticity—polyamides can be fibers for weaving textiles, or solids for sports equipment and car parts. DuPont researchers came up with nylon in the 1930s when seeking a synthetic replacement for silk. Kevlar was discovered by accident in the 1960s by a DuPont chemist looking for a new fiber for strong lightweight tires. Let's break them out a bit to show just how widespread these common polyamides are:

- Nylon fibers: clothes and stockings, toothbrush and hairbrush bristles, Velcro, rope, musical instrument strings, tents, parachutes, carpets and tires.

- Nylon solids and films: food packaging, combs, boat propellers, skateboard wheels, mechanical screws and gears, automotive parts (engine casing, fuel lines, fuel tanks).

- Kevlar: About five times as strong as steel, it is popular with the military and security sets, especially for body armor and helmets. It's also used for other heavy duty clothing (chaps, motorcycle gear, fencing equipment), shoes, sports racquet strings, racing sails, canoes and kayaks, musical instruments (drumheads and bows), non-stick frying pan coating (replacement for Teflon), rope, cable, sheath coating for fiber optic cable, joints, hoses and car brakes.

HOW TOXIC ARE POLYAMIDES?

As a family of plastic resins, polyamides are relatively safe, given their strength and stability. Our concern lies primarily with the wide range of synthetic clothing they are used to make, and in particular with the multitude of additives that may have been added to such textiles. We talk about this in the Fabrics and Textiles section (page 46).

Polytetrafluoroethylene (PTFE): Teflon Is in a Toxic Category of Its Own

PTFE is a strong non-reactive thermoplastic fluoropolymer commonly known to the world as Teflon, the trade name given to it by DuPont, which discovered it in 1938. Like Kevlar, its creation was an accident by a DuPont chemist, this time experimenting with refrigerants. It is by far most well known as the super slippery non-stick coating on Teflon cookware such as frying pans and bakeware. It is also used as an industrial lubricant to keep gears and machinery running smoothly. In its expanded form, PTFE is used to make surgical grafts for implanting in the human body, electronic cables used on space voyages and the popular waterproof and breathable Gore-Tex fabric used on expeditions to the summit of Mount Everest.

HOW TOXIC IS POLYTETRAFLUOROETHYLENE?

We consider it one to avoid for cookware and bakeware. We also prefer to avoid related disposable food packaging for oily foods. Up until very recently, Teflon has been manufactured using a surfactant additive called perfluorooctanoic acid (PFOA), one of the poster children of a vicious family of carcinogenic and persistent environmental pollutants known as perfluorinated compounds (PFCs). Apart from cancers, PFOA has been linked to heart attack and stroke and serious negative effects on the endocrine system, immune system, liver and pituitary gland.[72]

72   Environmental Working Group (2007) "EWG Assessment of EPA Draft Human Health Risk Assessment for the Teflon Chemical PFOA," EWG.org (accessed 4 March 2017: http://www.ewg.org/research/ewg-assessment-epa-draft-human-health-risk-assessment-teflon-chemical-pfoa).

PFCs are all over the place and have been used widely to make fluoropolymers like PTFE for not just non-stick cookware, but a wide range of products including clothing, cosmetics, carpet adhesives, wire insulation and food packaging where resistance to oily, greasy, stain-causing foods is desired—here we're talking about paper wrappers for burgers and sandwiches, butter, pizza boxes and popcorn bags being lined with PFCs. That might help explain why four common PFCs, including PFOA and its toxic sibling perfluorooctane sulfonate (PFOS), are estimated to be in the blood of 98 percent of the U.S. population, and why researchers think this exposure is ubiquitous and chronic.[73]

In PFOA-containing Teflon, toxic PFOA fumes can be released when the pans are heated to high temperatures. This "Teflon toxicosis" was discovered when pets—in particular birds—were found to be dying from these fumes in the presence of not just hot non-stick frying pans, but also toaster ovens, cookie sheets, pizza pans, self-cleaning ovens, heat lamps, oven interiors with non-stick coatings, irons and space heaters, as well as carpet glues and new sofas.[74]

DuPont states that as of January 1, 2012, they have stopped using PFOA to make the non-stick coatings in Teflon cookware and bakeware, but they do not disclose what is being used in its place.[75] Is it another PFC? Who knows? But given DuPont's weak track record for transparency and taking responsibility for health and environmental damage caused by PFOA toxicity, we prefer to heed precaution and pass on anything Teflon.[76]

Melamine: From Dishware to Protein Replacement? Not!

During the 1950s and 1960s post–World War II plastics boom, melamine tableware was fashionable and in demand. You can still find lots of vintage retro Melmac melamine dishes on eBay in festive multi-colored designs. You can also still buy lots of brand new melamine. It's a thermoset resin made by polymerizing the nitrogen-rich, white, powdery, synthetic, toxic chemical melamine with formaldehyde, a toxic and volatile carcinogen. You can see where we're headed with this one as well. But you must understand there are two elements here: melamine resin, and the precursor chemical, also called melamine, which is used to make the resin. Apart from dishes, melamine resin is used to make cutlery, dry erase boards and high-pressure laminates common in countertops—with trade names like Formica and Arborite—flooring and cabinets.

HOW TOXIC IS MELAMINE?

It is yet another plastic resin that we prefer to avoid. The chemical melamine can leach out of melamine dishware and cutlery into food, especially with acidic foods, and when heated—melamine tableware should definitely not be put in the microwave![77] While the amounts being released may be miniscule, research directly links the chemical to serious kidney damage. Certain bacteria in the human gut

73   U.S. National Biomonitoring Program (2016) "Fact Sheet: Perfluorochemicals," Centers for Disease Control and Prevention (accessed 4 March 2017: https://www.cdc.gov/biomonitoring/PFCs_FactSheet.html); D. Trudel et al. (2008) "Estimating Consumer Exposure to PFOS and PFOA," *Risk Analysis* 28(2) 251–269.

74   Rick Smith and Bruce Lourie (2009) *Slow Death by Rubber Duck: How the Toxic Chemistry of Everyday Life Affects Our Health*, Toronto: Alfred A. Knopf Canada, p. 85.

75   Chemours (2017) "Teflon: Key Safety Questions About Teflon Nonstick Coatings" Chemours.com (accessed 4 March 2017: https://www.chemours.com/Teflon/en_US/products/safety/key_questions.html#q2).

76   Legal actions have held DuPont liable for causing cancer in residents near their factories due to DuPont-derived PFOA being knowingly and negligently released into local drinking water; see S. Kelly (2016) "Teflon's Toxic Legacy: DuPont Knew for Decades It Was Contaminating Water Supplies," Earth Island Journal-EcoWatch (accessed 4 March 2017: http://www.ecowatch.com/teflons-toxic-legacy-dupont-knew-for-decades-it-was-contaminating-wate-1882142514.html).

77   U.S. Department of Health and Human Services (2014) "Melamine in Tableware: Questions and Answers," U.S. Food and Drug Administration (accessed 4 March 2017: http://www.fda.gov/Food/ResourcesForYou/Consumers/ucm199525.htm).

seem to metabolize the chemical melamine into cyanuric acid, which is thought to contribute to the formation of stones in the kidney, ureter and bladder.[78]

The chemical melamine was put squarely on the global toxicity map in 2008 when some Chinese milk producers illegally added the nitrogen-rich toxin to milk and infant formula as a filler and to falsely elevate the protein content. By November 2008, 294,000 Chinese infants had been affected, which included 50,000 being hospitalized and six deaths due to kidney damage.[79] Using melamine dishes is not going to risk exposure to anywhere near such levels of the chemical melamine, but why would you want *any* of such a chemical going into your body?

The Rubber Clan: From Latex Soothers to Foamy Neoprene

Now why would we include rubber in a list of common plastics? Because, whether they are natural or synthetic, rubbers look, feel and act like plastics, and frankly, in our experience, a lot of folks simply consider them another form of plastic. Plus, they are common in all kinds of consumer products—including many for children— and they can have allergy or toxicity issues.

What makes something a rubber? In chemistry circles, rubbers are known as elastomers, and elastomers are polymers that have the qualities of being both viscous and elastic. A viscous substance is thick, like honey or syrup, while water, on the other hand, has a very low viscosity. And rubbers are elastic because no matter what direction they may be pushed or pulled they will always return to their original shape and size. Earlier we talked about ABS and SAN, which are considered rigid rubbers, but here we're talking about softer rubbers that are used in everyday life, latex rubber and neoprene in particular.

Natural latex is extracted as a milky liquid from trees, with most commercial natural latex coming from the Pará rubber tree (*Hevea brasiliensis*) found in Africa and Southeast Asia. Synthetic rubber, just like traditional plastics, is made from petroleum-based sources and the building block of synthetic rubbers is a monomer called butadiene.

You'll find natural and synthetic latex rubber used to make all kinds of day-to-day consumer products: baby bottle nipples, soothers, dish gloves, shoes, toys, mattresses, tires, balls, balloons, carpeting, hot water bottles, disposable diapers, sanitary pads, rubber bands, erasers, swimming goggles, racket handles, motorcycle and bicycle handgrips, condoms, diaphragms, tires, hoses, belts, car mats and flooring. It is also popular in the medical setting for blood pressure cuffs, stethoscopes, intravenous tubing, syringes, respirators, electrode pads, surgical masks and gloves.

Then there are neoprenes, which are a tougher synthetic rubber family, resisting degradation more than natural and synthetic latex. They are especially common in breathable water resistant consumer products like lunch bags, laptop sleeves, clothing and the buoyant foam insulation for wetsuits.

HOW TOXIC IS RUBBER?

It depends. We prefer to avoid synthetic latex rubbers and neoprene. And we are conscious of the possibility of allergies to natural rubber, but otherwise consider it safe.

---

78   X. Zheng et al. (2013) "Melamine-Induced Renal Toxicity is Mediated by the Gut Microbiota," *Science Translational Medicine* 5(172):172ra22; B. Weinhold (2013) "Gut Bacteria and Melamine Toxicity," *Environmental Health Perspectives* 121:A149.

79   World Health Organization (2009) "Toxicological and Health Aspects of Melamine and Cyanuric Acid," Report of a WHO Expert Meeting in Collaboration with FAO, supported by Health Canada, 1-4 December 2008, Geneva: World Health Organization (accessed 4 March 2017: http://www.who.int/foodsafety/publications/chem/Melamine_report09.pdf).

The issue with synthetic rubber products is that they may be manufactured using plasticizing softeners known as nitrosamines, which are reasonably anticipated to be carcinogens and which can leach out of common products such as nipples, pacifiers, balloons and condoms.[80] While some countries—including Canada, the European Union and the United States—have put limits on the amount of nitrosamines that can be used in certain products like baby nipples and soothers, these children's products may still contain some nitrosamines. For that reason, we consider natural rubber or silicone nipples and soothers to be a safer choice.

Certain proteins present in natural rubber latex can cause an allergic reaction. These allergies are relatively common and could include symptoms ranging from sneezing or a runny nose to, in rare cases, life-threatening anaphylactic shock. Being well understood, such allergies can be quickly diagnosed, so if you suspect you might be sensitive, best to avoid natural rubber latex products and have an allergy test done. One well-known example is disposable natural rubber latex gloves—often used in hospital and lab settings—which in a sensitive person may trigger an allergic reaction in the form of contact dermatitis, essentially a dry, itchy skin rash.[81]

It is possible during the manufacturing of a natural rubber product to remove the problem protein that can elicit a latex allergy, for example in children's products like nipples and soothers.[82]

Neoprene too is an allergen, potentially causing skin inflammation symptoms like eczema or contact dermatitis. In one study, a patient using neoprene hip waders (presumably for fishing) had to be hospitalized because of the reaction.[83] The catalysts for such reactions are additives called thioureas, used to accelerate the rubber vulcanization process in making neoprene. Ethylene thiourea is a key culprit, and in addition to its skin annoying properties it's considered a probable human carcinogen.[84]

Fabrics and Textiles: Why Non-Synthetic Clothing Makes a Lot of Sense

As we've made our way through the most common plastics, you may have noticed that many of them, such as acrylic and nylon, have a fabric form that may be used for some types of clothing, and that there may be toxins built into some plastic fabrics: hormone-disrupting phthalates in polyvinyl chloride, potentially skin-irritating isocyanates in polyurethanes like Spandex and Lycra, possibly cancer-causing antimony in polyester, and probable carcinogens thioureas in neoprene.

In 2013, Greenpeace commissioned comprehensive testing of textile products sold in countries around the world—including children's clothing and shoes—and detected a variety of hazardous chemicals in them, notably numerous endocrine

80   U.S. Department of Health and Human Services (2016) "Nitrosamines," Report on Carcinogens, Fourteenth Edition, National Toxicology Program, National Institutes of Health (accessed 4 March 2017: https://ntp.niehs.nih.gov/ntp/roc/content/profiles/nitrosamines.pdf); W. Altkofer, S. Braune, K. Ellendt, M. Kettl-Gromminger, and G. Steiner (2005) "Migration of Nitrosamines from Rubber Products—Are Ballons and Condoms Harmful to the Human Health?" *Molecular Nutrition and Food Research* 49(3):235–238.

81   Centers for Disease Control and Prevention (2013) "Frequently Asked Questions—Contact Dermatitis and Latex Allergy," Oral Health (accessed 4 March 2017: https://www.cdc.gov/oralhealth/infectioncontrol/faq/latex.htm).

82   For example, this is the case with soothers and nipples made by the Danish company Natursutten. The company also states, however, that they would "never recommend using a product made from natural rubber for a child with a diagnosed latex allergy" (accessed 4 March 2017: http://www.natursutten.com/faq/faq-pacifiers).

83   M.C. Martinez-Gonzalez, J.J. Goday-Bujan, M. Almagro and E. Fonseca (2009) "Allergic Contact Dermatitis to Diethylthiourea in a Neoprene Wader," *Actas dermo-sifiliográficas* 100(4):317–320.

84   U.S. Environmental Protection Agency (2000) "Ethylene Thiourea - CAS 96-45-7," Health Effects Notebook for Hazardous Air Pollutants (accessed 4 March 2017: https://www.epa.gov/haps/health-effects-notebook-hazardous-air-pollutants).

disruptors and carcinogens.[85] These chemicals are found in the finished products either because they are included as an actual ingredient of the product or as a residue from a particular process used in making the item. The fact is, they are there, but we don't necessarily know if they are coming out of the clothing and directly affecting our health.

So there is the issue of these toxins possibly leaching out and affecting our health whether we realize it or not, and potentially contributing to a condition that develops over a long period of time, such as cancer. This sort of slow, ongoing exposure makes it very difficult to trace it back to a particular source when the health condition finally manifests with physical symptoms. This is one reason why we choose a precautionary approach and try to avoid synthetic clothing (see our Clothing section on page 124 for some ideas on how to go about this, and Clothing in the Resources section at page 180 for a few product suggestions).

Here's another issue: The ocean microplastic pollution problem is directly impacted by plastic textiles and fabrics. As these textiles are used and washed, tiny pieces of synthetic microplastic debris are released into the air or the wash water. We may breathe them or they may settle in house dust or outside in the environment, but also they go down the drain with the wash water and eventually end up in rivers and oceans because they are too small to be caught by municipal wastewater systems. Researchers estimate that a single garment can produce more than 1,900 microplastic fibers per wash—and in areas that receive sewage discharges they have found polyester and acrylic fibers resembling those in clothing.[86]

All these tiny microplastics then become food for wildlife unable to discriminate between what is real food and what is plastic. And so, the plastics and their toxins make their way throughout the ecosystem and up the food chain, concentrating more toxins as they go.

ARE THERE OTHER CHEMICALS COMING OUT OF PLASTICS?

The short answer: an unequivocal yes. Most plastic additives are not chemically bound to the plastic polymer, so they can move around and leach out easily. The next logical question is: what are these chemicals? The short answer: who knows? It is impossible to know without asking the manufacturer for a complete list of all ingredients. It's definitely worth a try, but don't be surprised if you're told it is confidential business information. Just keep trying, because the more people that ask, the more manufacturers will realize it is an issue of public, that is, customer, concern. And if there is one thing that companies increasingly respond to—especially in this day and age of lightning quick viral social media posts demanding corporate accountability—it is customers requesting answers and explanations and talking publicly about non-responsiveness, especially when the health of babies and pregnant women is at increased risk because of their products.

85   K. Brigden, S. Hetherington, M. Wang, D. Santillo and P. Johnston (2013) "Hazardous Chemicals in Branded Textile Products on Sale in 25 Countries/Regions During 2013," Greenpeace Research Laboratories Technical Report 06/2013 (accessed 4 March 2017: http://www.greenpeace.org/eastasia/publications/reports/toxics/2014/little-story-monsters-closet/).

86   M.A. Browne, P. Crump, S.J. Nivens, E. Teutens, A. Tonkin, T. Galloway and R. Thompson (2011) "Accumulation of Microplastic on Shorelines Worldwide: Sources and Sinks," Environmental Science & Technology 45(21):9175–9179.

The other option is to have the product tested in a chemistry lab for its composition. Such testing, however, is extremely expensive and may not detect every single chemical ingredient.

One of the core problems affecting the public's awareness of chemicals in consumer products is the fact that manufacturers are not required in most countries, including Canada and the United States, to disclose all of the ingredients in a product. If a chemical produces noticeable adverse effects on human health or the environment and there is sufficient scientific evidence of these effects, governments may begin to take action to ban or limit its manufacture and use, but even if and when they do, governments by nature tend to move very slowly—and are subject to unpredictable political forces and personalities—so a lot of harm to human health and the environment can be done in the interim.

Apart from the endocrine-disrupting chemicals we've highlighted in previous boxes—phthalates and the bisphenols—and the myriad of chemicals we have already described above, here are some other chemical toxins that are found in various common plastics, and which might have the potential to leach out:

- FLAME RETARDANTS: Plastic manufacturers don't want their volatile, petroleum-derived plastic products going up in flames, so they add flame retardants to many plastic resins. Flame retardants can be a good thing and save lives—nobody wants their polyester shirt to ignite while adding a log to the fire. The most commonly used ones are polybrominated diphenyl ethers (PBDEs) and organophosphates (abbreviations for some of the worst culprits are TDCIPP, TPHP and TBPP)—and they are not a good thing. They are highly toxic and they persist in the environment for a long time. Studies have shown them to be endocrine disruptors and link them to various problems ranging from altered thyroid function to reduced fertility and other reproductive and developmental health issues—they are especially an issue for pregnant women and infants.[87] The irony is research has shown that chemical flame retardants are ineffective in preventing furniture fires, and even firefighters are actively opposed to the use of flame retardants because of the toxic gases and smoke they can produce.[88] California used to have a law in place that encouraged the use of flame retardants in upholstered furniture, but in 2014, for the reasons just stated, this standard was changed to eliminate the need for such flame retardants—and as of 2015, California law requires all new upholstered furniture sold in the state to include a visible label stating whether flame retardant chemicals (but not which chemicals) were added.

- ANTIMICROBIALS: Synthetic antimicrobial agents—which is essentially a sanitized, marketing-friendly way of saying "pesticides"—are being added not only to things like mouthwash, toothpaste, deodorant, soaps,

87   Endocrine Disruptors Action Group (2016) "Toxic by Design: Eliminating Harmful Flame Retardant Chemicals from Our Bodies, Bomes, & Communities," White Paper (Accessed 4 March 2017 at: https://endocrinedisruptorsaction. org/2016/10/11/toxic-by-design/); L. Feng et al. (2016) "Levels of Urinary Metabolites of Organophosphate Flame Retardants, TDCIPP, and TPHP, in Pregnant Women in Shanghai," *Journal of Environmental and Public Health* 2016:9416054 (accessed 4 March 2017: https://www.hindawi.com/journals/jeph/2016/9416054).

88   Endocrine Disruptors Action Group (2016) "Why Flame Retardants Don't Stop Fires," Endocrinedisruptorsaction. org (accessed 4 March 2017: https://endocrinedisruptorsaction.org/2016/11/15/why-flame-retardants-dont-stop-fires).

hand sanitizer and cosmetics. You'll also find them in all kinds of plastics used to make household consumer products like food containers, cutting boards, toothbrushes, medical devices, sports equipment, clothing, appliances—even toys. Why do there need to be antibacterial agents in plastics? Untreated plastics can be susceptible to degradation, discoloration and unpleasant odors caused by bacteria, fungi, algae, yeast, mildew and other microbes. The plastic manufacturer's solution? Add a highly toxic synthetic biocide to the plastic while it is being molded into shape so it completely impregnates the plastic. One of the most common and pernicious of those biocides is triclosan, which can be found built into those products listed above. It can pass directly through the skin, and being an endocrine disruptor has some serious health risks associated with it: impaired thyroid function and possible adverse effects on male and female reproductive function.[89] Plus, its widespread use contributes to the development of antibiotic-resistant germs or "superbugs," which decreases the effectiveness of antibiotics. Triclosan accumulates in the environment and in wildlife tissue, and can become even more toxic: as it degrades in surface water exposed to sunlight it can transform into highly carcinogenic dioxin, and, in drinking water it may react with chlorine to become carcinogenic chloroform.[90] On top of all that, it is no more effective than standard soap and water. It has been banned in soaps and hand washes in the United States and Europe, but it's still widely present in all manner of consumer products, many of them plastics.

- HEAVY METALS: Here we're talking primarily about lead, cadmium, mercury and arsenic, which are commonly used as stabilizing additives in the making of the highly toxic plastic polyvinyl chloride (PVC). Mercury is also used as a catalyst in the making of vinyl chloride, the building block of PVC. Remember that PVC is the plastic we described as likely the most toxic consumer product plastic in existence. These heavy metals are one reason why (for the other reasons, see the PVC section on page 33). As noted above, PVC is used to make a broad range of products, but let's just highlight here that it is still—incredibly—used in children's toys. So why are these heavy metals problematic? Here's a quick run-down:

  - LEAD is a potent nervous system toxicant that can severely damage the brain and kidneys. Children are more sensitive to lead and can experience long-term developmental effects. Lead is reasonably anticipated to be a human carcinogen.[91]

89   R.J. Witorsch (2014) "Critical Analysis of Endocrine Disruptive Activity of Triclosan and Its Relevance to Human Exposure Through the Use of Personal Care Products," *Critical Reviews in Toxicology* 44(6):535–555; H. Huang et al. (2014) "The In vitro Estrogenic Activities of Triclosan and Triclocarban," *Journal of Applied Toxicology* 34(9):1060–1067.

90   K. Lah, M.M. Williams and M. Mergel (2016) "Triclosan," Toxipedia (accessed 3 March 2017: http://www.toxipedia.org/display/toxipedia/Triclosan); E. MacDonald and K. Mitchell (2016) "Canada is Behind the Times on Triclosan," Ecojustice (accessed 3 March 2017: https://www.ecojustice.ca/canada-behind-times-triclosan).

91   Agency for Toxic Substances & Disease Registry (2007) "Public Health Statement for Lead" CAS# 7439-92-1 (accessed 3 March 2017: https://www.atsdr.cdc.gov/PHS/PHS.asp?id=92&tid=22); see also P.B. Tchounwou, C.G. Yedjou, A.K. Patlolla and D.J. Sutton (2012) "Heavy Metals Toxicity and the Environment," in A. Luch ed., *Molecular, Clinical and Environmental Toxicology*, Volume 3: Environmental Toxicology, Basel: Springer, 2012, pp. 133–164 (accessed 3 March 2017: https://www.ncbi.nlm.nih.gov/pmc/articles/PMC4144270).

- CADMIUM is a known human carcinogen and can cause serious long-term damage to the lungs and kidneys.[92]

- MERCURY, like lead, is seriously toxic to the nervous system, brain and kidneys, and can also damage the stomach and intestines. It is a possible human carcinogen.[93]

- ARSENIC is a known human carcinogen and has long been recognized as a human poison that can severely affect the skin, stomach, intestines, liver, bladder, kidney and lungs.[94]

Do we really need any more reasons to avoid PVC? The amounts of these heavy metals being released from plastic products may be at trace levels, if at all, but we prefer to take a precautionary approach and avoid plastics as much as possible because we believe there are no safe levels of such toxicants—especially where children are concerned.

- ADDITIVES, ADDITIVES AND MORE ADDITIVES! Here are some categories of plastic additives for you to ponder: antimicrobials, antioxidants, antistatic agents, biodegradable plasticizers, blowing agents, colorants, curing agents, dyes, extenders, external lubricants, fillers, flame retardants, fluffers, foaming agents, fragrances, heat stabilizers, impact modifiers, initiators, internal lubricants, light stabilizers, optical brighteners, pigments, plasticizers, process aids, reinforcements, slipping agents and solvents.[95] And these are just the categories. Within each category are scores, even hundreds or thousands, of possible chemicals that could be used. Here's one example that underlines the highly processed nature of plastics in extremely harsh conditions: heat stabilizers prevent plastic polymers from decomposing (literally falling apart) as they are being processed at standard temperatures well above 350°F (180°C). A chemical used to prevent the plastic from falling apart in such conditions must itself be pretty harsh. Because most additives do not appear on product labels, we have no way of knowing exactly what chemicals are in that plastic cup or shirt or toy stuffed animal.

The best approach in the face of such uncertainty regarding what is coming out of the plastics that surround us is a precautionary one: avoid additive-ridden plastics whenever possible.

92   U.S. Agency for Toxic Substances & Disease Registry (2012) "Public Health Statement for Cadmium" CAS# 7440-43-9 (accessed 3 March 2017: https://www.atsdr.cdc.gov/PHS/PHS.asp?id=46&tid=15).

93   U.S. Agency for Toxic Substances & Disease Registry (2012) "Public Health Statement for Mercury" CAS# 7439-97-6 (accessed 3 March 2017: https://www.atsdr.cdc.gov/toxfaqs/tf.asp?id=1195&tid=24).

94   U.S. Agency for Toxic Substances & Disease Registry (2012) "Public Health Statement for Arsenic" CAS# 7440-38-2 (accessed 3 March 2017: https://www.atsdr.cdc.gov/PHS/PHS.asp?id=18&tid=3).

95   British Plastics Federation (2016) "Plastics Additives," Plastipedia.co.uk (accessed 3 March 2017: http://www.bpf.co.uk/plastipedia/additives/default.aspx).

Is Silicone a Plastic? Is it Safe?

Silicones have become enormously popular in recent years and are constantly marketed as safe replacements for traditional plastics. We see them everywhere—baby bottle nipples, utensils, toys, mugs, food containers, seals on bottles and containers. They're even proudly used in cookie sheets and muffin trays that will be subjected to high temperatures for the oven, and ice cube molds destined for the freezer. For years, Jay's mom had a set of silicone poached egg molds that would be in direct contact with boiling water. This always made Jay cringe—but he did still eat Mom's eggs (sometimes you really have to choose your battles; she has since migrated to a metal poached egg cooker).

You'll also find silicones used in cosmetics and various personal care products to make them soft and smooth. In more industrial contexts they are commonly used for insulation, sealants, adhesives, lubricants, gaskets, filters, medical applications (e.g. tubing) and casing for electrical components.

Are silicones plastic? Silicones—or siloxanes as they are also known—are something of a hybrid between synthetic rubbers and synthetic plastic polymers. They can take on different forms and be used to make malleable rubber-like items, hard plastic-like resins and thick spreadable fluids.

We treat silicones as plastics like any other, given that they have all these plastic-like properties: flexibility, malleability, clarity, temperature resistance and water resistance. Like plastic, they can be shaped or formed, and softened or hardened into practically anything. While they are water resistant, they are also highly gas permeable, making them useful for medical or industrial applications where airflow is required. Being easy to clean, non-stick and non-staining makes them popular for cookware and kitchen utensils.

So, what *exactly* are they? Many people seem to think they are a natural material derived directly from sand. Not so. Like any plastic polymer, silicones are synthetic and include a mix of chemical additives derived from fossil fuels. The key difference from all the carbon-based plastics we described above is that silicones have a backbone made of silicon. It's important to get the terminology right here, and there are three distinct related substances to understand:

- Silica: When people say silicones are made of sand, they are not incorrect, though that's too simplistic a description. Silica—or silicon dioxide—is what they are referring to. Silica is the raw material used to make silicone resins. Beach sand is practically pure silica, as is quartz.

- Silicon: This is the base element that makes up silica, but silicon is not generally found in nature in this elemental form. It is made by heating silica at very high temperatures with carbon in an industrial furnace.

- Silicone (siloxane): The silicon is then reacted with fossil fuel–derived hydrocarbons to create siloxane monomers which are bonded together into polymers to form the final silicone resin. The quality of these silicones can vary greatly depending on the level of purification done. For example, the silicones used to make computer chips are highly purified.

HOW TOXIC ARE SILICONES?

This is the big question, and there is not yet a clear answer. They are very stable polymers with strong temperature and chemical resistance, so we consider them relatively safe. A number of the products we offer in our store—such as stainless steel or glass food containers and bottles—include silicone seals or gaskets to make them airtight and watertight. At this point, we are not aware of a better durable alternative for such applications, apart from perhaps natural rubber for things like soothers and bottle nipples, as long as there is no risk of rubber allergy.

Many experts and authorities consider silicones to be non-toxic and safe for contact with food and drink. For example, Health Canada states: "There are no known health hazards associated with use of silicone cookware. Silicone rubber does not react with food or beverages, or produce any hazardous fumes."[96] Consumer advocate and toxin-free living expert Debra Lynn Dadd takes a cautious view toward silicones and continues to assess new research, but she is not willing to give up her silicone cookware just yet, as she considers it safer than non-stick alternatives with perfluorinated chemical coatings.[97]

While the research indicates that silicones are certainly very stable, they are not completely inert and non-leaching; some silicones have demonstrated biological effects, such as causing tissue irritation.[98] There are studies indicating the possibility of leaching from silicone. For example, one study tested the release of siloxanes from silicone nipples and bakeware into milk, baby formula and a simulant solution of alcohol and water. Nothing was released into the milk or formula after six hours, but after 72 hours in the alcohol solution several siloxanes were detected.[99] Siloxanes are considered potential endocrine disruptors and some have been linked to cancers.[100] Being so widely used in the making of silicone polymers and household products, siloxanes are present at detectable levels in land, air and water, and given their durability, they tend to persist in the environment for a long time.[101]

The upshot is that the scientific evidence is weak in pointing a smoking gun at silicones, but the questions and uncertainty are there, so it's worth keeping a close eye on them—especially given the growing concerns about endocrine-disrupting chemicals that might produce health problems a generation after a miniscule exposure.

RECYCLABILITY OF SILICONE

Apart from the health aspects described above, silicone poses an environmental threat because it is rarely recycled. Although silicone products can be collected by specialized recycling companies that will typically down-cycle it into oil used as lubricant for industrial machines, it is rarely accepted in municipal curbside recycling programs. Therefore, just like plastics, not only can silicone only be down-cycled, but most of it just ends up in landfills where it won't biodegrade for hundreds of years.

---

96   Health Canada (2015) "The Safe Use of Cookware," healthycanadians.gc.ca (accessed 4 March 2017: http://www. healthycanadians.gc.ca/product-safety-securite-produits/consumer-consommation/education/household-menagers/cook-cuisinier-eng.php#si).

97   Debra Lynn Dadd (2016) "Silica, Silicon, Silicone," Toxc Free Q&A (accessed 4 March 2017: http://www.debralynndadd.com/q-a/silica-silicon-and-silicone/).

98   S. Bondurant, V. Ernster and R. Herdman, eds., *Safety of Silicone Breast Implants*, Institute of Medicine, Committee on the Safety of Silicone Breast Implants, Washington D.C.: National Academies Press, 1999.

99   K. Zhang et al. (2012) "Determination of Siloxanes in Silicone Products and Potential Migration to Milk, Formula and Liquid Simulants," *Food Additives & Contaminants. Part A, Chemistry, Analysis, Control, Exposure & Risk Assessment* 29(8):1311-1321.

100   TEDX List of Potential Endocrine Disruptors (accessed 4 March 2017: http://www.endocrinedisruption.org/endocrine-disruption/tedx-list-of-potential-endocrine-disruptors/chemicalsearch); C. Lassen, C.L. Hansen, S.H. Mikkelsen and J. Maag (2005) "Siloxanes - Consumption, Toxicity and Alternatives" Danish Environmental Protection Agency, Environmental Project No. 1031 2005 (accessed 4 March 2017: http://www2.mst.dk/Udgiv/publications/2005/87-7614-756-8/pdf/87-7614-757-6.pdf).

101   D. Wang et al. (2013) "Review of Recent Advances in Research on the Toxicity, Detection, Occurrence and Fate of Cyclic Volatile Methyl Siloxanes in the Environment," *Chemosphere* 93(5):711-725.

SOME FINAL BASIC TIPS FOR USING SILICONE:

Given our precautionary approach, we prefer to avoid silicones when there are better alternatives. That said, here are a few silicone-use tips if you do decide to make them part of your life:

- The silicone should be high quality, ideally "medical grade," but at least "food grade." The higher the quality, the less the possibility of leaching chemicals.

- You can test a silicone product for chemical fillers by pinching and twisting a flat surface of it to see if any white shows through. If you see white, a filler likely has been used because pure silicone should not change color at all. If it has fillers, the product may not be uniformly heat resistant and may impart an odor to food. But most importantly, you will have no idea what the filler is and it may leach unknown chemicals into the food. For all you know, the filler may be a silicone of low quality or not silicone at all.

- Bottle nipples and pacifiers should be safe, but best not to put them in the dishwasher, and if they get cloudy or worn out, replace them (ideally, they should be replaced every six to eight weeks). Natural rubber is another option, as long as your child does not have an allergy to natural rubber latex.

- For cookware, we prefer to avoid silicone completely. There are excellent glass, ceramic and stainless steel options for cooking and baking. Yes, we do consider silicones a safer alternative to Teflon and similar non-stick cookware that may have perfluorinated chemicals, but we would opt to use it only when there is really no other choice. We just don't like the idea of it being subjected to such extreme temperatures while in direct contact with food (often oily food).

- Things like silicone oven mitts, utensils (spatulas, spoons), splatter guards and pot holders should be fine given the minimal amount of time they are in contact with food. But again, we prefer to avoid them for direct food use where possible. We get rather queasy about leaving a silicone spoon soaking in a simmering batch of tomato chili, or a spatula flipping burgers on a hot, oily griddle or flaming barbecue.

Bioplastics

While writing this section, we watched a video about bioplastic bags manufactured in Bali, Indonesia by a social enterprise called Avani. The founder of the company takes a piece of one of their light green bags, derived from renewable cassava root (a staple food crop in Asia and Africa), places it in a cup of warm water, stirs it for about a minute until it dissolves, and then drinks it.[102] It's dramatic and makes one wonder if all of our current fossil fuel-based plastics will one day be replaced by "safe" biodegradable bioplastics. Interestingly, the video has been removed from the web without a trace—we suspect Avani understandably doesn't want to be seen to be encouraging people to drink their bags. And we sure don't recommend trying that at home with your bioplastic bags.

Are bioplastics the solution to our plastic toxicity and pollution problems? Are they safe, viable alternatives to traditional plastics? It's simplistic and inaccurate to think that replacing all the traditional plastics with bioplastics that have equivalent properties and are completely biodegradable is going to happen right away, but things are moving. The world of bioplastics is new and complex and it is growing fast. They currently account only for about 1.4 percent of global plastics production:

102   Accessed 9 January 2017: http://inhabitat.com/dissolvable-bioplastic-bags-from-bali-are-safe-enough-to-drink. See also www.avanieco.com.

about 4.6 million tons (4.2 million tonnes) of bioplastics in 2016,[103] compared with 300+ million tons (272 million tonnes) of traditional plastics in 2015.[104] However, this is expected to jump over 50 percent by 2021 to 6.7 million tons (6.1 million tonnes), and some experts predict bioplastics could eventually replace 90 percent of the traditional fossil fuel–based plastics surrounding us today.[105]

We think bioplastics will be one part of the solution—the core solution is preventing plastic use and demand in general—and then only under certain conditions that prevent us from ending up with the same or even worse problems than we are faced with in dealing with traditional fossil fuel-based plastics. What do we mean? Well, some bioplastics are made with fossil fuel–based plastics. Some are not biodegradable or recyclable. Some contain a slew of toxic chemical additives. To understand what we're getting at here, you need to have a basic understanding of bioplastics. So, take a deep breath, and here goes. . . .

What exactly are they? Bioplastics can be broadly defined as plastics that are bio-based or biodegradable, or exhibit both these properties. What in the world does that mean? Don't worry, we'll explain.

Let's get some bioplastics-related terminology straight—the real definitions of words you might have heard bandied about in the media or seen on product labels: bio-based, biodegradable, degradable and compostable. You can think of these words as describing different stages and aspects of the life cycle of *certain* bioplastics, because they don't necessarily apply to all bioplastics.

Bio-based focuses on the "beginning of life" of the product, that is, the origin of what the plastic is made from.[106] Bio-based plastics are made, at least in part, from renewable, naturally occurring materials, usually plant biomass—such as corn/maize, wheat, potatoes, soy, tapioca, coconut, cassava, sugar cane, wood and pine needles—but also more adventurous things like shrimp shells or insect bodies. This is in contrast to traditional fossil fuel–derived plastics made from non-renewable carbon sources such as petroleum, natural gas or coal. Upshot: in bioplastics, the carbon source is natural and renewable.

Biodegradable refers to the "end of life" of the plastic; that is, what happens to the product when disposed of after its useful life. A bioplastic product is considered biodegradable if it breaks down completely in the natural environment through the action of naturally occurring microorganisms such as bacteria, fungi and algae. These tiny microorganisms are able to use the elements of the bioplastic, principally the carbon and nitrogen, as food. Note that to be biodegradable, there is no requirement for the plastic to break down in a specific amount of time, nor that it leave no toxic residue. But the breakdown must be complete within a reasonable amount of time (about one growing season); not partial and not "eventually."[107]

Degradable means that the plastic will undergo a significant change in its chemical structure under specific environmental conditions resulting in a loss of some properties. Essentially, it means the plastic is capable of breaking down into smaller pieces. As you can tell, it's rather meaningless as a product marketing ploy because pretty much any and all plastics are capable of being broken down into smaller

103   Plastics News Europe (2016) "Global bioplastics industry growing steadily," Plasticsnews.com (accessed 9 January 2017: http://www.plasticsnews.com/article/20161130/NEWS/312019999/global-bioplastics-industry-growing-steadily).

104   G. Gourmelon (2015) "Vital Signs: Global Plastic Production Rises, Recycling Lags," Worldwatch Institute.

105   L. Shen et al. (2010) "Present and Future Development in Plastics from Biomass," *Biofpor* 4(1):25–40.

106   R. Narayan (2013) "A Faculty Entrepreneur's Experience on the Impact of Standards in Shaping Bioplastics Technology and Business," Presentation at World Standards Cooperation Roundtable, Washington, D.C., 26 June 2013.

107   R. Narayan (2009) "Biodegradability," *bioplastics MAGAZINE* 4(1):28–31.

pieces. And given the global microplastics problem we are faced with, making plastics easier to break down is not a good thing if the plastics in question are in whole or in part fossil fuel–derived. There are catchy twists on this one: photodegradable (capable of breaking down by sunlight) and hydrodegradable (capable of breaking down by water). And then there's oxo-degradable or oxo-biodegradable (capable of breaking down by exposure to oxygen, i.e., air), which are in a whole suspicion-raising category of their own that we'll talk about more below. But note for now that fossil fuel–based plastics are degradable, but not biodegradable. Bioplastics are degradable, and *may* be biodegradable.

Compostable also refers to a bioplastic's "end of life" and, in particular, whether or not it will biodegrade in a composting environment. ASTM International (formerly American Society for Testing and Materials) and the International Organization for Standardization (ISO), the two main international standard-setting bodies, define a compostable plastic as one that "undergoes degradation by biological processes during composting to yield carbon dioxide, water, inorganic compounds and biomass at a rate consistent with other known, compostable materials and leaves no visually distinguishable or toxic residue."[108] A couple of key distinctions to make with this added layer of knowledge: A bioplastic may be biodegradable, but not compostable; all compostable bioplastics are biodegradable. Upshot: To be compostable, a plastic must break down completely to basic natural substances and leave no trace of anything toxic.

So, if a takeout food container is labeled "compostable," I can just throw it in my home composter and look forward to its harmless nutrients feeding my new crop of homegrown arugula next season, right? Not necessarily. There are two broad categories of composting: that home composter in your backyard, or a large-scale industrial composting facility.

Commercial industrial composting facilities have set levels of heat, aeration and moisture to maximize the activity of the oxygen-requiring microorganisms breaking down the compost. A key criterion for a plastic to be called compostable according to most international standards is that 60 percent of the resin biodegrade within 180 days. And a typical industrial composting process runs for twelve weeks with temperatures constantly above 122°F (50°C).[109]

Home composting is obviously less controlled and generally it will take much longer for things to break down. But some bioplastics are home compostable, and as a general rule, home composting is one of the best ways to significantly decrease your organic waste. If you can find some way to set up a home composting system, it will play a key role in your personal waste reduction.

Both of these composting methods are in contrast to a landfill, which is an anaerobic (oxygen-free) environment. In a landfill, bioplastics—or pretty much anything, for that matter—will not readily break down if not exposed to oxygen. And the bioplastics in a landfill that do break down will cause release of the potent greenhouse gas methane, which is produced by the anaerobic bacteria breaking down the material.

This brings up a key "pro" of bioplastics: Because they are fundamentally derived from newly formed renewable resources, they have a lower carbon footprint than fossil fuel-based plastics derived from carbon that is millions of years old. And even though a lot of energy goes into all the processes required to make them,

108   R. Narayan and C.A. Pettigrew (1999) "ASTM Standards Help Define and Grow a New Biodegradable Plastics Industry," *ASTM Standardization News*, December 1999.

109   J.H. Song, R.J. Murphy, R. Narayan and G.B.H. Davies (2009) "Biodegradable and compostable alternatives to Conventional Plastics," *Philosophical Transactions of the Royal Society* B 364(1526):2127–2139.

renowned bioplastics expert Dr. Ramani Narayan from Michigan State University says that plastics made from renewable, bio-based raw materials still come out ahead as long as their carbon footprint is the same as or better than the carbon footprint of fossil fuel–based plastics.[110]

On the other hand, an environmental "con" of bioplastics is that much of the base feedstock currently derives primarily from energy-intensive, biodiversity-stunting monocrops of corn, some of it genetically modified. Natureworks, the largest producer of corn-based bioplastics in the world, states that in their processing of the bioplastic polymer all traces of genetic material are removed—maybe, but the GM (genetic modification) industry is still being promoted. And this is an industry that can be very ruthless against smaller farmers in enforcing its GM patents and striving to dominate the global food supply with GM foods that may have serious long-term health risks to humans.[111]

Now let's get into the nitty gritty detail that greenwashing stakeholders in the bioplastics industry really don't want you to know.

The key point: Many bioplastics are not 100 percent made of natural biomass. To be called a bioplastic, they generally have to be at least 20 percent derived from natural sources. What about that other 80 percent? Excellent question. Many bioplastics contain fossil fuel–based plastic resins and numerous synthetic additives—such as fillers, softeners and flame retardants—just like conventional plastics.

Earlier we mentioned the suspicions surrounding a group of bioplastics known as oxo-biodegradable plastics. These are traditional fossil fuel–based plastics—such as polyethylene, polypropylene, polystyrene, polyethylene terephthalate and sometimes also polyvinyl chloride—that have been combined with what are called transition metals—for example, cobalt, manganese and iron—which cause fragmentation of the plastic when triggered by UV radiation or heat. The additives make the plastic break down faster. Oxo-biodegradable plastics are included in the bioplastics category and are often touted by the industry—especially the vocal Oxo-Biodegradable Plastics Association—as biodegradable *eventually*, but whether they really break down completely in the natural environment in the time frames quoted is questioned by experts and much of the core bioplastics industry, which distances itself from the oxo-biodegradable plastics industry. Oxo-biodegradables are often marketed to countries with minimal waste management infrastructure as a quick solution, but they remain in the environment causing serious plastic pollution issues.

Here's an example of the problem with oxo-biodegradable plastics. In 2008, Discover began offering a biodegradable credit card made of a special form of PVC. You'll recall from our common plastics lessons earlier on that PVC is considered one of the most toxic consumer plastics in existence, but it is still used to make most credit cards. This special "BioPVC" is manufactured with an additive (the formulation is a trade secret) which makes the card easy to be broken down by microbes. Discover claimed the BioPVC "allows 99 percent of the card plastic to be safely absorbed when exposed to landfill conditions. The card plastic will begin to break down in soil, water, compost or wherever microorganisms are present; with it fully degrading within five years."[112]

110   Terry, *My Plastic Free Life*, p. 167; from her conversation with Dr. Narayan.

111   A. Dean and J. Armstrong (2009) "Genetically Modified Foods," Statement of the American Academy of Environmental Medicine (accessed 4 March 2017: http://www.aaemonline.org/gmo.php).

112   Discover Financial Services (2008) "Discover Financial Services Introduces Biodegradable Discover Card" Press Release, 9 December 2008 (accessed 4 March 2017: https://investorrelations.discover.com/newsroom/press-releases/press-release-details/2008/Discover-Financial-Services-Introduces-Biodegradable-DiscoverR-Card/default.aspx).

Experts considered this idea of PVC breaking down naturally and harmlessly as extremely dubious, and even "a load of hooey."[113] The expert we met earlier, Dr. Narayan, tested the claims and found that microorganisms only consume about 13 percent of the card before the breakdown process plateaus.

The "un-greenwashed" reality: This "BioPVC" marketed as a "biodegradable" plastic is still the same old toxic, petroleum-based PVC, simply blended with an extra chemical additive that attracts microorganisms to break it down faster. While it might just barely make it into the broad definition of bioplastics because it breaks down faster—though even that is clearly questionable—it certainly is not bio-based, compostable or in any way eco-friendly. It is still toxic, fossil fuel–based plastic. And in fact, it could be significantly more harmful than normal PVC because its faster breakdown rate makes it more quickly available in smaller pieces to be eaten by wildlife.

Is your head spinning after all that? Bioplastics is a complex area, but with this knowledge you are empowering yourself to overcome the rampant greenwashing going on in the current marketplace.

The complexity of this fast-moving, murky field makes it a veritable playground for bioplastic products portrayed as "biodegradable" when in fact they are made in part from synthetic, petroleum-based ingredients that may not actually biodegrade quickly, completely, or at all.

Here are a few of the most common bioplastics used in consumer products these days:

- Polylactic acid or polylactide (PLA) is a bio-based plastic (a biopolyester, in particular) made from lactic acid, a fermentation product of corn or cane sugars. It may be made in part from GM corn. PLA is by far currently the most commonly used bioplastic. Most PLA consumer products are made using Ingeo, a branded PLA produced by Natureworks LLC. Products made with Ingeo can include clothing, bottles, gift and credit cards, bags, food packaging, fabrics, fiber fill for pillows and comforters, diapers, wipes and disposable dishes. Ingeo PLA is certified compostable in an industrial composting facility by various third party certification bodies. It is not biodegradable in home composters or the marine environment.

- Mater-Bi is another common branded sugar-based resin, and it is partially bio-based. It is made by Novamont of Italy from various sources of starch, and contains vegetable ingredients such as cellulose, glycerin and natural fillers, but it also contains biodegradable fossil fuel–derived raw materials. It is certified for industrial and home composting by various certifications and Novamont claims it is not made with genetically modified feedstock. For consumer products, Mater-Bi is used primarily to make films, bags, and tableware.

- Natural fibers such as sugarcane or sorghum (bagasse), wheat, bulrush, bamboo, reed, palm and wood. Fiber-based products are not bioplastics, but we mention them in our bioplastics section because of how they are pulped and molded into compostable food containers. There are now even palm leaf and banana leaf–derived plates, which also are obviously not bioplastics, but just show how natural fibers are being increasingly used to replace plastics. One area that is really gaining steam is that of wood fiber as companies like Pulpworks in the United States and ecoXpac in Denmark lead the way with replacements for plastic blister packaging. EcoXpac has partnered with Carlsberg to create the first fiber-based beer bottle. New York–based Ecovative has developed home-compostable mushroom packaging as a replacement for polystyrene.

113   Freinkel, *Plastic: A Toxic Love Story*, pp. 207, 220. From her conversations with Tim Greiner and Ramani Narayan, respectively.

SO HOW CAN ONE KNOW IF A BIOPLASTIC PRODUCT IS REALLY BIODEGRADABLE AND COMPOSTABLE?

With all this grey area regarding what is realistically "biodegradable," the best way to know if a product you are considering is biodegradable or not is to check if it has a certification label of biodegradability or compostability.

There are now several key third party certifications for bioplastics, which are based on controlled tests done in accordance with internationally recognized standards set out by ISO and ASTM. For example, ASTM D6400 is the key standard determining whether or not a plastic can be composted in municipal or industrial facilities.[114] The certifications most likely to be encountered in North America are reviewed briefly here, but there are various other systems around the world.

Probably the most common compostability certification in North America is from the Biodegradable Products Institute (BPI), and products meeting this certification sport the logo above on the left (note that this does not mean the item can be composted in a home composter, only an industrial facility). There is a unique certification number in the lower right hand corner, allowing you to identify the manufacturer or distributor of an approved product. The BPI website (www.bpiworld.org) provides an excellent database of 3300+ compostable products currently on the market. If you don't see a label, or just want more information on the biodegradability or compostability of a product, this is an excellent place to start.

In Canada, the "Compostable" certification for compostable bags (logo above in the center) follows norms set out by the Bureau de Normalisation du Quebec (BNQ) and the Standards Council of Canada for speed of disintegration and biodegradation, metal content and the absence of negative effects on the ability of the resulting compost to foster plant growth. This indicates compostability in an industrial composting facility, but not a home composter.

There are several certifications that derive from Europe, but are well established and now recognized all over the world. The European Bioplastics "Seedling" logo (above on the right) is a certification of industrial, but not home, compostability.

Two separate European organizations—Vinçotte from Belgium and DIN CERTCO from Germany—administer the "Seedling" compostability certification, and also provide their own specific certifications.

---

114   ASTM D6400-12 (2012) "Standard Specification for Labeling of Plastics Designed to be Aerobically Composted in Municipal or Industrial Facilities," ASTM International: West Conshohocken, PA (accessed 4 March 2017: https://www.astm.org/Standards/D6400.htm).

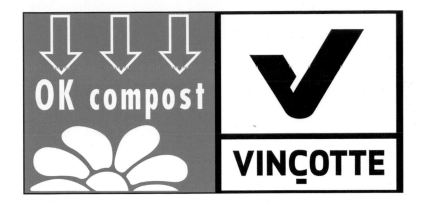

With its distinct OK logos, Vinçotte (www.okcompost.be/en/) provides a range of certifications for bio-based content, compostability and biodegradibility:

- Bio-based content: See the logo above on the top left—the number of stars indicates the percentage of bio-based material (1 star = 20 to 40 percent; 2 stars = 40 to 60 percent; 3 stars = 60 to 80 percent; 4 stars = over 80 percent).

- Compostability: The logo above on the top right indicates the product is compostable in an industrial facility. There is a separate logo, including the word "HOME," for products that will completely biodegrade in a home composting system.

- Biodegradability: Vinçotte offers a range of specific certifications for biodegradability in various media:

  - OK biodegradable SOIL: Guarantees the product will completely biodegrade in the soil without adversely affecting the environment.

  - OK biodegradable WATER: Guarantees the product will completely biodegrade in a natural freshwater environment.

  - OK biodegradable MARINE: New since 2015, this certification guarantees the product will completely biodegrade in a marine environment, such as saltwater seas and oceans. It is an especially important development given the growth of marine plastic pollution in recent years. At the time of writing, it is the only such marine biodegradability certification we are aware of.

Germany's DIN CERTCO (www.dincertco.de/en/), offers a similar range of specific certifications for bio-based content, compostability and biodegradability.

One of the unique DIN CERTCO certifications is for products containing additives that are harmless to the composting process. This provides bioplastic manufacturers a way to show their products are suitable for composting because the additives are completely biodegradable; it includes additives such as printing inks, pigments, dyes, glues, coatings and processing aids.

The Key Takeaway About Bioplastics: They are **NOT** the solution to plastic pollution and toxicity problems. They will likely play a role, but given their mixed character and the chemical additives most of them contain, relying on them is not a replacement for making a concerted effort to reduce all plastic use at the source (whether fossil fuel– or bio-based).

- Be wary of claims that include the words "natural," "bio-based," "plant-based," "biodegradable" and "compostable." Ask the manufacturer for proof to back up claims.

- Avoid oxo-biodegradable products, which are simply conventional fossil fuel–based plastics chemically altered to break down into smaller pieces faster.

- Try and determine exactly what kind of bioplastic resin the product is made of, and if it is not in one of the categories we have mentioned above, try to find out more about it by contacting the manufacturer and asking if it is bio-based (if so, what percentage?), if it is fully biodegradable, if it is compostable (if so, in an industrial or home composter?). Ask what additives have been mixed with the resin to make the final product (e.g., fillers, flame retardants, softeners and colors).

- Look for a third-party certification label to determine if the product actually is bio-based, biodegradable and compostable (and if it is compostable, whether in an industrial composting system only, or a home composter as well, or in a freshwater or marine environment).

- Even if a product is made with a bioplastic resin that you know is certified compostable, be sure to check if there is a certification label for the final product. The core resin might be compostable, but the processing of it to make the final product could have included additives that now prevent it from biodegrading fully and being compostable.

- Check if your municipality accepts bioplastics for recycling or composting, and if so, which ones and in what types of products. If your municipality does not, then you may be able to find a facility near you using Biocycle's online database of composting, anaerobic digestion, and organics collection services in the United States and Canada (www.findacomposter.com). Note, however, that organic composting services will likely not accept bioplastics.

- A useful resource is the Sustainable Biomaterials Collaborative (www.sustainablebiomaterials.org/), which provides all kinds of information on bioplastics.

- Most important of all: Try to avoid all disposables, but if you absolutely must use a disposable item, try to make it a bio-based, home compostable one with biodegradable additives.

THE RECYCLING MYTH

The recycling myth is one big monster that activists for a plastic-free planet must face every single day when trying to help people understand the importance of reducing one's plastic consumption. Thanks to the intelligent strategy that the plastic industry came up with in the early 1980s of imprinting a recycling code on the most commonly consumed plastic items, a large majority of consumers think that the bulk of the plastics they consume are recyclable and actually do get recycled through their local curbside recycling program. In reality, only a small percentage of the contents of a recycling box is recycled.

We discovered how hard-wired this myth is early on when participating in consumer trade shows for Life Without Plastic. People would approach us and say something like, "But what's the problem with plastics? I recycle almost all of my plastics." We would reply that unfortunately most plastics do not get recycled. In fact, only 9.4 percent of all discarded plastics were recycled in the United States

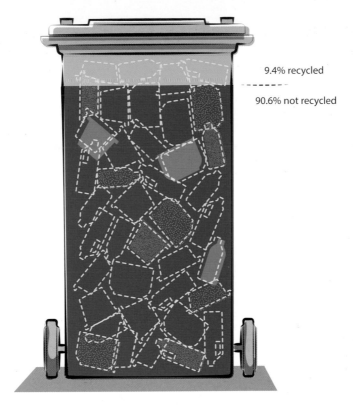

9.4% recycled

90.6% not recycled

Plastic waste generated in the United States (2014)

in 2014[115] (3.12 million tons out of 33.3 million tons) (2.83 million tonnes out of 30.2 million tonnes)—or down-cycled, that is, as plastics generally can be remade only into lower value products. The solution to our plastic problem is not to recycle more, it is to consume less plastic.

If you are purchasing products with plastic packaging, it's important to know what packaging materials are most likely to be recycled to be able to make informed, recycling-friendly purchasing decisions. It's also helpful—hopefully as an incentive to minimize consumption of plastics—to understand the complex, expensive and energy-intensive recycling process. What really happens to that single-use disposable water bottle you toss in your recycling bin?

The Recycling Process

Here is a brief explanation of how a typical recycling sorting plant selects the materials it deems worthy of recycling (see page 63):

1. Recyclables collected from the municipality are dumped in a pile at the sorting plant. A loader then moves the material up onto a conveyor belt.

2. Workers then proceed to remove trash, bulky items and plastic bags, which can clog the system.

3. Using rotating discs, cardboard is separated from the pile while smaller objects fall through and continue on.

---

115   U.S. Environmental Protection Agency, Municipal Solid Waste in the U.S.: 2014 Facts & Figures (November 2016).

4. The remaining pile lands on another conveyor belt where workers then remove leftover trash or pieces of cardboard they can find.

5. A screen separates out paper (2-D objects) while the rest of the pile falls through and continues on.

6. At the next step, a giant magnet removes steel from the stream and separates it into a holding bin.

7. Glass bottles and jars are broken up into pieces and fall below while aluminum cans and foil pass through an eddy current separator (with an electrical charge), which transfers them to another holding area.

8. The remaining pile consisting of plastics and trash passes through a TiTech PolySort, which is a device that uses ultraviolet light to scan the composition of each item and sorts out the plastic pieces to be recycled, according to desirable resin types.

From this process, one can see that paper and cardboard, steel, aluminum and glass are the most likely to be recycled. Even a small piece of aluminum foil packaging is worth throwing in the recycling bin because it will get picked up through a mechanical process using a current charge. Not only are paper, metal and glass more likely to be picked as recyclables through the sorting process, but these materials can be made into new recycled products that are pretty much the same as the original, and the recycling cycle for these materials can potentially never end.

Plastics, on the other hand, can only be down-cycled into products of inferior quality or functionality. For example, food packaging cannot return to life as food packaging. It will return as something that can't be in contact with food. As the plastic resin moves through the plastic production process and cycles of recycling, it becomes unrecyclable relatively quickly and ends up in a landfill as a plastic fossil for hundreds of years. Virgin plastic will continue to be required for food packaging, and this perpetuates the production of more plastic. Contrary to glass or metal, which potentially can be recycled an infinite number of times, plastic is not part of such a closed-loop, cradle-to-cradle cycle.

You should inquire with your municipality about which items are accepted in your curbside program.

The following categories of materials generally are not recyclable and should be avoided as much as possible when shopping:

- Plastic bags
- Aseptic packages (such as Tetra Pak), which are made of several layers of various materials such as plastic, aluminum and cardboard
- Clamshell and styrofoam packaging
- Bioplastics (though they may be home or industrially compostable)
- Plastics without a recycling arrow number
- Plastics made with a combination of many different plastics, for example plastic toys that contain many different parts
- Plastic with the recycling arrow numbers 3, 4, 6 and 7

In a nutshell, only plastics #1 (PETE or PET), plastic # 2 (HDPE) and plastic #5 (PP) are good candidates for recycling. The table on page 64 illustrates the various types of plastic according to their recycling resin code and how to recognize them.

THE RECYCLING PROCESS

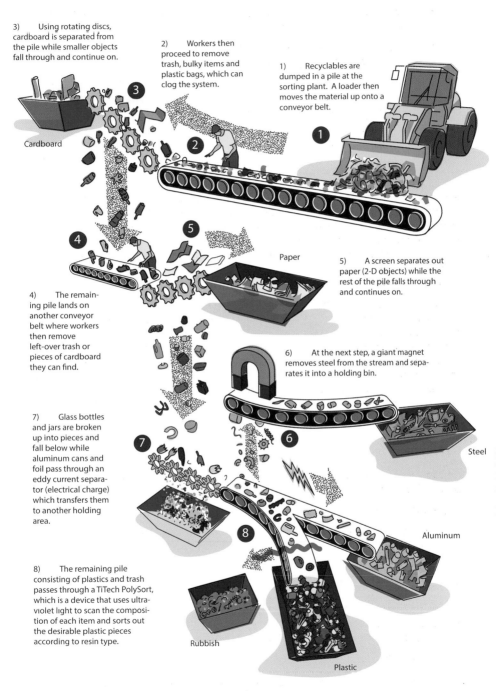

3)   Using rotating discs, cardboard is separated from the pile while smaller objects fall through and continue on.

2)   Workers then proceed to remove trash, bulky items and plastic bags, which can clog the system.

1)   Recyclables are dumped in a pile at the sorting plant. A loader then moves the material up onto a conveyor belt.

Cardboard

Paper

5)   A screen separates out paper (2-D objects) while the rest of the pile falls through and continues on.

4)   The remaining pile lands on another conveyor belt where workers then remove left-over trash or pieces of cardboard they can find.

6)   At the next step, a giant magnet removes steel from the stream and separates it into a holding bin.

Steel

7)   Glass bottles and jars are broken up into pieces and fall below while aluminum cans and foil pass through an eddy current separator (electrical charge) which transfers them to another holding area.

Glass

Aluminum

8)   The remaining pile consisting of plastics and trash passes through a TiTech PolySort, which is a device that uses ultraviolet light to scan the composition of each item and sorts out the desirable plastic pieces according to resin type.

Rubbish

Plastic

PLASTIC TYPE	HOW TO RECOGNIZE IT	RECYCLABILITY
Polyethylene Terephthalate— PETE or PET	Clear plastic bottles for soft drinks and water, plastic food jars and condiments, polyester fabric	Good
High Density Polyethylene—HDPE	Opaque milk bottles, oil and vinegar bottles, ice cream containers and bottles for shampoos, toiletries and cleaning products, some plastic bags	Good
Polyvinyl Chloride—V or PVC	Cling wraps, squeeze bottles, soft toys, shower curtains, blood bags, diaper covers	Low
Low Density Polyethylene—LDPE	Plastic bags, cling wrap, flexible containers, coating for milk cartons, baby bottles, frozen food bags	Low
Polypropylene—PP	Baby bottles, yogurt, margarine and deli containers, toys, reusable food containers	Good
Polystyrene—PS	Disposable plastic cutlery, coffee cups and lids, food containers, packing peanuts, egg containers	Very low
Others—O	Catch-all category. Includes products made of Bisphenol A (BPA), bioplastics and other plastic resins such as melamine	Very low

It is important to consider the kind of materials that are most likely to be recycled when making purchases. Unfortunately, plastic packaging of grocery items is increasing rather than decreasing. More and more, product packaging is being switched from readily recyclable packaging, such as a glass jar, to non-recyclables like plastic-lined Tetra Pak containers. Such plastic packaging generates savings for manufacturers, and because customers don't complain about them and find them rather convenient, they become the norm. At the grocery store, for example, customers will often purchase pre-packaged and processed products packaged in plastic out of convenience and as a time saver. We are all busy people and it is normal to seek convenient ways to save time. Fortunately, plastic is not the only convenient way to purchase packaged products.

For example, someone who needs a cake for a special event may not realize various options exist that have varying degrees of impact on the planet. The pre-made cake in a transparent polystyrene plastic casing may appear to be the most convenient in terms of preparation and planning, but other, more sustainable options are almost as convenient. You can request the cake be packaged in a plush cardboard box, which is both compostable and recyclable (if it is not soiled). Another option is to bring your own cake box and skip the packaging altogether.

The point is, options do exist, and knowing what packaging is less damaging to the environment can turn your purchase into an eco-responsible and even efficient one.

In order to maximize the chances that the items you put in your recycling bin will actually be recycled, here is a list of steps you can take to prepare your products. They only take a bit of your time, but make a big difference.

HOW TO SELECT AND PREP YOUR RECYCLABLES

- Check with your municipality about which materials are recyclable; print the list and keep it close to your recycling bin.

- Rinse all your recyclable items. Sorting workers will appreciate it.

- Separate lids from bottles because they are usually made of different types of plastics.

- Remove and separate paper labels from metal cans.

- Use soiled cardboard or paper, like pizza boxes, as a fire starter (if you have a fireplace or woodstove) instead of throwing them in the recycling bin—they are unlikely to be recycled.

- Unless you are absolutely certain that your town recycles plastic bags, do not add them to your recycling bin as they can get stuck in the conveyor belts at the sorting plant.

- If plastic bags are accepted as a recyclable item, gather them together and stuff them all into one bag and tie it closed with a knot.

- Do not put various recyclables in plastic bags.

- Flatten cardboard boxes.

The Externalization of the Real Plastic Packaging Cost

Running a recycling program is expensive, and most product manufacturers do not contribute to these costs. This means the costs associated with the disposal or recycling of plastic packaging are externalized and end up being paid by all customers through their municipal taxes, including those who make valiant efforts to limit their consumption of plastic products and packaging.

What's needed are creative incentives put in place by local and national governments to encourage more sustainable packaging practices, such as:

1. Re-using packaging rather than automatically recycling it (consignment systems).

2. A packaging design revolution toward more sustainable, plant-based, compostable and additive-free packaging.[116]

3. Incentives for the recycling of plastic products. For example: cash.

Germany has been at the forefront of creative packaging waste management for more than 30 years. In 1993, the German government passed a packaging ordinance to make manufacturers responsible for taking back the packaging of their products. The ordinance covered glass, aluminum and plastic drink containers. A refundable deposit on these containers was put in place offering generous incentives as high as 25 euros (about $29) for a "one-way" plastic bottle. In 2011, the recovery rate of PET (recycling symbol #1) bottles as a result of the implementation of this program was 98.5 percent.[117]

More recently, the city of Freiburg in Germany created an innovative program to tackle waste generated by non-recyclable, disposable coffee cups. Takeout cups are generally impossible to recycle because the cardboard of the cup is fused with polyethylene to make it waterproof. The resulting material cannot be easily separated in recycling facilities. In Freiburg, coffee retailers like bakeries, coffee shops and restaurants buy reusable cups and serve their customers with these cups as an alternative to disposable cups. Customers pay a deposit of one euro for that cup, which they receive back when they return the cup to any participating establishment.[118] So you can grab a coffee to-go in a reusable mug at one java hut, and after a stroll to the other side of town drop it off at another. The cups are washed by these establishments and can be reused indefinitely. A beautiful example of a simple community effort to tackle a serious waste issue.

A Downside of Plastic Recycling

In February 2017, the non-profit organization The Story of Stuff launched a campaign against microfibers and released a short film explaining some serious issues relating to microplastic fibers.[119] The film explains that while it is cool that companies are using recycled water bottles to create new clothing, it actually creates two problems: 1) it encourages consumers to use more plastic bottles by thinking that they will be recycled into something useful; 2) the clothing made out of recycled plastic bottles releases hundreds to thousands of microfibers every time it is washed. These microfibers are so tiny that they aren't caught by municipal water treatment plants and they end up in our waterways. They then bond with toxins and harsh chemicals, which are concentrated up the food chain, being eaten by small fish, bigger fish and then humans. It's estimated that our oceans currently contain up to 1.4 million trillion microfibers, which is the equivalent of 200 million microfibers per person on this planet.[120]

---

116   Movement in this direction is being led by the Ellen MacArthur Foundation through its new Plastics Economy Initiative: https://newplasticseconomy.org (accessed 5 March 2017).

117   See Ordinance on the Avoidance and Recovery of Packaging Wastes (Packaging Ordinance - Verpackungsverordnung - VerpackV) of 21 August 1998 (Federal Law Gazette I p. 2379) as last amended by the Fifth Amending Ordinance of 2 April 2008 (Federal Law Gazette I p. 531) (accessed 5 March 2017: http://www.bottlebill. org/assets/pdfs/legis/world/germany2009.pdf). See also http://www.bottlebill.org/legislation/world/germany.htm (accessed 5 March 2017).

118   See BBC (2016) "Germany Wakes Up to the Issue of Waste with Reusable Coffee Cups" BBC.com, 22 November 2016 (accessed 5 March 2017: http://www.bbc.com/news/world-europe-38066528).

119   The Story of Microfibers (accessed 5 March 2017: http://storyofstuff.org/movies/story-of-microfibers).

120   These numbers are extrapolated from a study by C.M. Rochman, E. Hoh, T. Korube and S.J. Teh (2013) "Ingested Plastic Transfers Hazardous Chemicals to Fish and Induces Hepatic Stress" *Scientific Reports* 3(3263).

Recycling and Reusing the Other Stuff

Specialized programs exist for recycling or reusing certain specific items. For example, in Chapter 5 in Sports at the Gym and in the Great Outdoors (page 150), we discuss ways to recycle and reuse running shoes, which are a tough one to deal with.

There is one organization that really stands out far above the rest by encouraging creativity in finding ways to recycle and reuse all kinds of items that usually become trash destined for a landfill: Terra Cycle (www.terracycle.com). They aim to recycle the "non-recyclable." Their Zero Waste Box programs make it simple for individuals, businesses and community groups—anyone or any organization—to collect difficult-to-recycle waste and be certain it will be actually recycled or reused. You order a box online and fill it with things that are very hard to recycle. The cost includes return shipping and waste re-purposing. Options include athletic balls (including tennis balls—which makes tennis-loving Chantal very happy), shoes and footwear, bottle caps, candy wrappers and baby food pouches. At the time of writing, there were 81 active programs. If you feel bad about a wasteful activity you just can't give up, at least you can get one of these boxes to ensure recycling or reuse—and encourage your "partners in crime" to contribute to the cost!

PLASTIC ALTERNATIVES

In the following table, we've listed some core alternatives we tend to gravitate toward when looking for a replacement material for a product that is commonly in plastic. For each alternative, we tell you some of its uses and a bit about why we think it's a worthy alternative to plastic. Note that some of the materials are animal-derived. In all cases, it's obviously important to obtain such materials without harming the animal, or at least as a by-product of another activity such that the animal parts would have been otherwise discarded.

ALTERNATIVE TO PLASTIC	STORY OF WORTHINESS
Glass	Glass is a favorite of ours. It's inert, non-leaching, doesn't absorb smells or flavors, is easy to clean and can be produced relatively inexpensively as the raw materials are plentiful and largely naturally occurring. And it's 100% recyclable. There are the issues of it being fragile and heavy and somewhat energy intensive to produce and transport, but when you balance those with the negatives of plastic, we think glass is far superior for many uses. Derived from raw silica, the two most common types of consumer glass are soda lime and borosilicate, with the latter being slightly more durable and shock resistant. You do want to avoid leaded glass, which is common in antiques. It may be sparkly, but it can release neurotoxic lead.

(continued)

ALTERNATIVE TO PLASTIC	STORY OF WORTHINESS
Ceramic	Our feelings about ceramic are similar to those for glass. Love it and its elegant inert nature as a fine replacement to plastics in pottery, porcelain, floor tiles and sculptures. With ceramics as well, lead can be an issue; not from the ceramic itself, but some glazes applied to ceramics may contain lead or cadmium. This not likely a concern with ceramics made in North America and Europe for food contact, but it's worth checking to be sure.
Stainless Steel	One of our core staples: a tough, non-rusting, relatively lightweight and safe replacement for plastics. It's used for a myriad of daily doings: food containers, water bottles, dishes, utensils, razors, pens, straws, kettles and frying pans. The composition of its most common consumer forms (there are hundreds of different grades) is: an alloy or mix of primarily iron (about 70 percent) and chromium (around 18 percent), with nickel (8 to 10 percent) added to further improve corrosion resistance and durability at temperature extremes. Hence the terms 18-8 or 18-10 stainless steel. Both of these fall within the 304 grade, which is a high quality stainless steel grade used for most food contact applications. A lovely feature is that it's self-repairing if scratched, which is why it won't rust. Some people may have an allergy to nickel, and if that's the case, best to avoid it. It is 100% recyclable and should never ever end up in a landfill!
Cast Iron	Best known for those heavy black workhorse frying pans often passed down through generations. Cast iron is an alloy of iron and primarily silicon and carbon. It can be heated to high temperatures and retains the heat for a long time. The surface requires "seasoning" with oil to prevent it from rusting and to create an effective non-stick surface. It will release iron into the food, which the body needs, but this can be a toxicity issue for young children (under six) or if one has an iron-related allergy or illness; for anemic folks it can actually be a helpful way to reduce your iron deficiency.

ALTERNATIVE TO PLASTIC	STORY OF WORTHINESS
Aluminum	Aluminum is a light, widely used metal for applications ranging from food packaging and deodorants to planes, trains and automobiles. It is not a preferred alternative of ours, and we mention it because it is common in everyday life and one to be wary of. It is the material used to make most metal beverage cans, which are generally coated on the interior with a layer of plastic, often BPA. The coating is necessary because aluminum reacts with food and drink: without the coating, corrosion may occur. Aluminum is considered by many researchers to be highly toxic to the central nervous system in humans and animals, and a neurotoxin possibly linked to the development of Alzheimer's disease.[121] Something to keep in mind when using aluminum foil: try and avoid it touching the food.
Copper	Common uses of this essential element include cookware, ornamental dishware, wiring, plumbing pipes, roofing, additive to fungicides and pesticides, antimicrobial agent for fixtures (bedrails, bathroom fixtures), and as a preservative for wood, leather and fabrics. Yes, the body needs it, but not from your cookware, which can leach significant amounts with acidic foods (copper cookware is usually coated with another metal like stainless steel). Got copper water pipes? Better than plastic we think. But if you have soft water (tending toward acidity) flushing the pipes daily avoids copper buildup. Copper is 100% recyclable—it should never ever be trashed.
Tin (Pewter, Bronze, Brass)	Pure tin is now very uncommon for food applications. It was common as pewter tableware (85 to 99% tin, with other variations of metals like copper, antimony, lead, bismuth) in ancient times. You'll find a bit in bronze, which is 80 to 90% copper, and some in brass, which is mostly copper and zinc. These days the common consumer use of these metals is for ornamental items, not tableware intended for actual use with food and drink. You've likely heard of the generic term "tin" for a container that might hold cookies or candy. These decorative "biscuit tins" are usually made of steel with a thin coating of tin, and are best used for ornamental or dry food use.

(continued)

121   C.A. Shaw et al. (2014) "Aluminum-Induced Entropy in Biological Systems: Implications for Neurological Disease," *Journal of Toxicology* 2014:491316; C.A. Shaw and L. Tomljenovic (2013) "Aluminum in the Central Nervous System (CNS): Toxicity in Humans and Animals, Vaccine Adjuvants, and Autoimmunity," *Immunologic Research* 56(2–3):304–316.

ALTERNATIVE TO PLASTIC	STORY OF WORTHINESS
Titanium	Tough titanium is gaining popularity. Here's why: it can be extremely strong (especially in certain alloys), is corrosion-resistant even in salty seawater and it's uber lightweight. As you might have guessed, those qualities make it a favorite with explorers, adventurers, backpackers and athletes. It's also resistant to acids and chlorine, and often used for medical applications like prostheses and orthopedic implants. It is considered safe for food and drink. All this comes at a price: it is expensive, close to double the cost of high quality stainless steel.
Organic Cotton	Organic cotton makes us smile; it's soft, breathable and durable for everything from clothing to diapers to bed sheets to lunch bags to towels. Why organic? Because conventional cotton crops are generally drenched in pesticides and chemical fertilizers or may be genetically modified so the cotton plant produces pesticides specific to certain insects.
Rayon	Rayon is a generic term for a semi-synthetic polymer made of cellulose that can be derived from practically any plant or tree source. The problem is, harsh chemical solvents are required to break down these cellulose pulp fibers into a usable material for clothing. Viscose rayon, a common form, is generally made from wood pulp treated with toxic carbon disulphide to create the fabric. There are, however, much less toxic rayons out there: Lyocell (branded as Tencel) is made in a closed loop production method that uses way less chemicals and can be applied to any form of cellulose.
Wool (Alpaca, Angora, Cashmere, Merino, Mohair)	Wool has magnificent properties that include being water-resistant, naturally anti-fungal and anti-bacterial. It's a fabulous insulator that holds heat when wet. Compare wearing wet wool socks in winter with wet cotton ones. We go into more detail about wool in the Clothing section on page 124.

ALTERNATIVE TO PLASTIC	STORY OF WORTHINESS
Bamboo	Bamboo is a fast-growing plant that is part of the grass family. Certain species of bamboo can grow up to 3 feet (1 m) in 24 hours making it a sustainable product. Bamboo has a high compressive strength and is almost as strong as steel. It is an excellent alternative to plastic as long as it is not varnished, which is unnecessary for most applications. Be leery of bamboo fabric clothing that doesn't have a Lyocell or Tencel label on it, as it may be drenched in toxic chemicals (see Rayon on page 70 for details).
Hemp	Hemp is a strong natural fiber that requires much less water to grow— and no pesticides—compared to other traditional crops. Its seeds and flowers are used in food and body care. Its fibers and stalks are used in clothing, construction materials and even paper. Hemp and marijuana come from the same cannabis species, but are genetically distinct, so hemp does not have the same psychoactive effect.
Silk	Smooth sleek silk is a lustrous luxurious alternative to plastic textiles. It is usually derived from the cocoons of the larvae of the mulberry silkworm (*Bombyx mori*), which produces long thin threads of fiber to construct the cocoon. Silk is most common as a material for clothing, but is also used for rugs, sheets, parachutes, surgical sutures and tooth floss. There is an alternative form of wild silk called "peace silk" that does not require the worm to be killed.
Leather	Leather is used to make various goods including clothing, bookbinding and furniture covering. It is generally fabricated out of cattle skin and needs to be tanned to be suitable for commercial applications. We go into more detail about leather in the Clothing section on page 124.
Wood	When you compare a plastic toy to a wooden toy, the soothing living energy of the wood contrasts starkly with the empty chemical nature of synthetic plastic. Wood is a natural, organic, carbon-based material made of a firm web-like structure of cellulose fibers fixed in a rigid matrix of lignin polymers. Upshot: it's firm and fibrous. Floors, buildings, fences, furniture, utensils, dishes, toys, tools—its applications are endless. Our main concern with wood is if and how it may have been treated—possibly to protect it from weathering, insects or rot, or to change its appearance. We opt for non-chemical treatments such as linseed oil or beeswax, especially for food contact applications like cutting boards, toothbrushes and utensils.

(continued)

ALTERNATIVE TO PLASTIC	STORY OF WORTHINESS
Cork	Cork is an aesthetically attractive natural material with powerful properties: impermeability, buoyancy, elasticity, flame retardancy. Most commercially-used cork derives from the bark of the Cork oak tree (*Quercus suber*) found primarily in southwest Europe and northwest Africa. It is sustainably harvested by stripping the bark from the trees—usually on a nine to twelve year cycle—in a way that the tree continues to live and grow, and they can live up to 300 years! Apart from bottle stoppers and drink coasters, it has become popular as a sustainable flooring alternative and in consumer products ranging from bags to jewelry.
Natural Rubber	We've discussed this one in more detail in our overview of common plastics on page 45. Rubber is not a plastic, but because it looks, feels and acts like a plastic and has a synthetic form, we thought it best to address it with our discussion of the whole rubber family. Our verdict: It's a good alternative for products like mattresses, toys, baby soothers and bottle nipples, as long as you don't have a rubber allergy (though it is possible in the making of natural rubber products to remove the allergy-causing protein).
Plant Fibers: Tampico, Coco and Palmyra	Tampico fibers come from a type of agave and have a high degree of shape retention and high heat resistance. They work well for scrubbing brushes. Coco fibers can grow up to a foot (30 cm) long and are used as bristles for brooms and brushes. Palmyra fibers are used with a blend of other fibers for mops and scrubbers.
Animal Hair: Pig, Horse and Badger	Pig bristles come from a wild variety of pig with long hair. They are thicker and harder at the root than at the tip and can be used for hard or soft brushes. Horse hair from the tail and the mane is used extensively by natural brush makers, in particular for brooms and hand brushes. Badger hair is typically used for shaving brushes because it has a rounded tip, which prevents irritation of the face. Unfortunately, badger meat does not have much commercial value and therefore badgers are grown solely for their hair. Pig bristles are a more humane alternative for shaving brushes.

CHAPTER 4

REMOVING PLASTIC FROM YOUR PERSONAL SPACE
How to Create a Healthier Home

We sometimes sense when people come into our home for the first time that they are looking around very closely with an eagle eye, expecting not to find any plastic anywhere. That's just not the case. Yes, we are the "Life Without Plastic" people, as they sometimes call us, but we're not zero plastic, nor are we zero waste. We are, however, hyper aware of the plastic that surrounds us and comes into our life, and we are always looking for ways to decrease our plastic footprint. That awareness is like a little filter overlaying our decision-making, helping us to always try and opt for quality and durability over cheaply made disposability. In our home, you do see a lot of wood, a lot of stainless steel and a lot of mason jars. We love mason jars. You'll also find some older secondhand, solidly made items, like the vintage Vitamix blender we purchased on eBay.

So now it's your turn, if you're game. Time to assess where you're at on your plastic-free journey. The Personal Plastic Audit laid out below flows from one we created with Travis Bays of Bodhi Surf & Yoga Camp and Amy Work of Geoporter to help Bodhi and others in Bahia Ballena, Costa Rica decrease their plastic use. It will help provide you with a structure in assessing your current state of plastic use.

BECOME AWARE OF THE PLASTIC IN YOUR HOME: HOW TO DO A PERSONAL PLASTIC AUDIT

Most people are somewhat stunned when they realize just how much plastic has infiltrated all parts of their lives. Conducting your own Personal Plastic Audit in your home or organization* will give you a baseline reference point for where you stand in terms of your current plastic footprint. By the way, children make excellent, passionate auditors with a keen eye for detail! A plastic audit can be a powerful and eye-opening family activity and office team-building exercise.

(*Note: The following template described is oriented toward a residential home, but could be easily adapted to any organizational setting.)

Preliminary preparations

Timing: You'll need to figure out what works best for your current life situation, but we suggest at least a two-week period to begin.

TOOLS

- A way to record the audit. It can be a pencil and a physical notebook, ideally lined to make it easier to list items. Or it could be a smartphone or electronic pad or tablet. Or it could be your laptop or desktop computer. Mobile is handy. If you're using a desktop computer, that's just fine, but you will also need a separate notebook and pencil or a mobile electronic device to record things on the go as you are going through your house.

- Or, use a camera to take photos of items instead of listing them.

- A medium-sized cardboard box or wooden crate, or, ahem, plastic bin (plastic does have its uses!), or a large cloth or durable plastic bag. This is for spontaneous purges. (See Step 3 on page 75).

- Eagle-eyed enthusiasm. Seriously. Part of this is the attitude you bring to it. Are you ready to ask some hard questions of yourself and your belongings?

STEP 1: DIVIDE YOUR HOME INTO SMALLER AREAS

Break it down into manageable chunks so you are not tackling the whole home at once, which may feel overwhelming and simply never happen. Write down the "chunks," that is, the rooms or areas of the house, in a simple list in the order that you would naturally walk through them. This is necessary to get a more specific and organized view of the situation. It will provide a solid basis to work from in the later evaluation part of the audit. Consider carefully how you live, and try to section your home according to the natural divisions that reflect your lifestyle flows and daily rhythms. For example, natural obvious delineations may be the kitchen area, the living area, the bathroom area, the sleeping area, the garden area, the garage. You get the picture—and it's helpful that the layout be a set of images you visualize in your head.

The time spent on this part of the audit should be spread over about two days— one day to write out your list the way it first comes to mind, time to think and sleep on it, and a final review of the divisions to ensure they represent the way you actually do live.

STEP 2: CREATE YOUR AUDIT TABLE—OR NOT

Using your list from Step 1, create a simple table on paper or as a spreadsheet on your electronic device with the first (left) column including a row for each home area on your list, going down in the order of your flow in moving through your home. And then add in columns going from left to right with the following headings: Plastic Item, Possible Alternatives, Notes (Repurpose, Reinvent, Redistribute, Recycle).

Home Area	Plastic Items	Possible Alternatives	Notes (Repurpose, Reinvent, Redistribute, Recycle)
Kitchen			
Living Room			
Bathroom			
Bedroom			
Garden			
Garage			

Each of the columns will be explained as we go through the process.

One thing: If creating a table like this seems overwhelming, too time-consuming or unnecessary, don't do it. Simply crack open a new page in your notebook, or a new note or document on your mobile device, and move on to the next step. The main thing is that you are recording the results of your Step 3 evaluation somewhere.

STEP 3: ACTION TIME! EVALUATE YOUR HOME—FIND AND RECORD THE PLASTICS

Time to get moving and see what plastics you can find. This is the heart of the plastic audit and requires you to look really hard at your living environment and notice all the plastics that surround you. You will likely be surprised to discover just how much plastic is in your life.

When products have been identified, they need to be logged into your electronic spreadsheet or jotted down in your notebook. If you're using a notebook, try and leave some space for notes beside each item.

If you are feeling especially ambitious and know what type of plastic the item is made of (e.g. by checking if it has a recycling number on it), add that detail to your spreadsheet in brackets after the item. This will be helpful in safely and effectively recycling or disposing of the plastic items you will be replacing. Overviews of the most common types of plastic and how to identify them are set out above in the Common Plastic Types and Recycling sections (on pages 31 and 60, respectively).

As you are doing this evaluation, if you have immediate ideas for how you could replace an item with a non-plastic item, jot down your replacement idea in the "Possible Alternatives" column of your spreadsheet. But don't get bogged down in thinking too much about this. Stay in the flow.

Remember that box or carton or bag we asked you to bring along? It may come in handy now. If you come across a plastic item that you know you don't need or it so disgusts and annoys you that you want to get rid of it right away, throw it in the bag or box. We call these spontaneous purges. How you deal with them is described in the next step.

The suggested time for this part of the audit is a few days. You might want to do an area a day or set aside a few hours or a day and do the whole shebang at once. Again, go with your life's flow. A substantial amount of time is required because you're going to find things you never even noticed were plastic before you stopped and took this long hard look at them.

In your evaluation, be mindful of the space itself. Look at the floors, the carpets, the curtains and the fixtures. Your floor may be made of plastic laminate that looks like wood and you don't even realize it.

STEP 4: PLASTANALYSIS—WHAT STAYS? WHAT GOES?

You've gone through your entire home and have a complete spreadsheet or list documenting all the plastic items you've identified. Awesome! Congratulations— that's a huge awareness-building step.

Now it's time to do your *plastanalysis*: Go through all that data by asking a few questions about each item you've identified. You need to determine what happens next, and here are a few questions to help guide you in deciding whether or not to remove or replace an item (see the flowchart below as well):

- Is this item made of high quality plastic and still serving a valid purpose in my life?

- Is this an item that should be removed or replaced?

  - Is it an unstable plastic and in direct contact with food or drink, or does it pose a direct threat to human health (e.g. a plastic toy a child might put in their mouth)?

    - Is it in such a degraded state that it needs immediate removal or replacement?

- Can I repurpose or reinvent it into a new, safer use? If so, mark this in the final Notes column of the spreadsheet.

- Can I redistribute it by passing it on to someone else who can put the item to good use without it causing harm? If so, mark this in the final Notes column of the spreadsheet.

If the item still serves a useful purpose in your life and is not creating direct harm, there is no need to replace it right away. The aim of this exercise is definitely not to create unnecessary waste or expense. Remember that currently most plastic waste is going into a landfill or being incinerated or ending up as plastic pollution somewhere in the world, quite possibly an ocean. Many plastics are not recycled, and of those that do enter the recycling stream, only a low proportion actually become usable new raw plastic material—generally only about 30 percent at best for plastic resins in demand.[1] Furthermore, recycled plastics are generally "down-cycled," meaning that they can be used only to make products of lower quality or reduced functionality.

You want to do whatever you can to avoid disposing in the trash any of the plastic items you are not keeping. Reusing, repurposing / reinventing and redistributing are best, and then recycling.

Not only would blind replacement of everything plastic in your home be an exercise in profound wastefulness, it would be hugely expensive. And it would completely miss the point we are trying to get across with this audit exercise, and this book, which is that *awareness* is the catalyst for behavior and habit changes.

The suggested time for this part of the audit is a few days. Once again, you might want to do an area a day, or set aside a few hours or a full day and plastanalyze everything at once.

STEP 5: ALTERNANALYSIS—CAN I FIND A NON-PLASTIC ALTERNATIVE?

Finding non-plastic alternatives for items you have determined that you need to replace may require some research on your part. As you come across possible alternatives, add them to the Possible Alternatives column of your spreadsheet. When seeking alternatives, go back in time and consider how your ancestors lived without plastic—plastic entered mainstream life only about 75 years ago! For example, there are numerous untold ways the ubiquitous and essentially free mason jar can be used throughout the home for food and office uses. (Note: The lid interiors generally are lined with bisphenol A, so if you are using the mason jar for food use and the contents will touch the lid, consider changing the lid for a stainless-steel one; options available in the Resources section on page 175.) Making your own cleaning or personal care products may be a fun option for you that can not only eliminate a lot of ongoing plastic waste, but possibly also decrease your exposure to toxic chemicals, depending on what products you are using.

The rest of this book is devoted to helping you with this task of finding ways to avoid plastic. Helpful curated suggestions for suppliers of non-plastic products are included in the Resources section at the end of the book (page 175). And remember, it may not be an actual alternative item that you need, but rather an alternative way of doing things. Sometimes a little behavior shift or life hack can eliminate a whole slew of plastic in your life. For example, deciding to use vinegar, baking soda and essential oils for cleaning purposes, rather than cleaning products purchased in plastic containers.

The suggested time for this step is the rest of your life—lol!—but if you'd like to put a set time frame around it, try a week of focused research and decision-making. The reality is that finding suitable alternatives is likely to be an ongoing process depending on your budget, your lifestyle and the extent you decide to replace the plastics in your home.

---

1   For example, in 2015 the recycling rate in the U.S. for polyethylene terephtholate (recycling symbol #1), which is used to make single-use water bottles, was 30.1 percent. Recycling Today (2016) "U.S. PET Recycling Rate Dips" (accessed 3 March 2017: http://www.recyclingtoday.com/article/2015-us-pet-recycling-rate).

The most valuable part of this whole exercise is that you are now more aware than ever before of the plastics in your life, and attuned to looking for alternatives.

CAREFULLY CHOOSING WHAT COMES INTO YOUR HOME

Here are a few tips to follow as you assess new items coming into your home:

Tip #1: Read the product labels

This is important for everything—it just makes sense to know as much as possible about what you are buying, whether it's food or clothing or personal care products.

Tip #2: Purchase in bulk

This is a biggie for food and cleaning supplies especially. In both cases, you can bring your own containers to the store and have them weighed before filling them up with what you need (this is called taring). The underlying goal is to avoid the largest source of plastic waste: packaging.

Tip #3: Buy quality, buy smart

In our experience, you generally do get what you pay for. High quality and durability often come at a price. But you have to keep in mind that a larger up front investment may give you enormous savings over time. For example, purchasing a set of reusable diapers when baby is born will save you oodles over disposable diapers during baby's diaper-wearing months.

You can significantly reduce the cost of a quality purchase by doing your research first and shopping around. There are lots of helpful product review sites out there. Embrace Google or another search engine for this. As you are sifting through online stores, be sure to check customer reviews of products that interest you. This is how you learn subtle things about a product that a seller or manufacturer may not mention in an enticing product description, or simply may not be aware of.

Tip# 4: Buy secondhand

In our community, there is a legendary secondhand store called the Rupert Nearly New, located in Rupert, Quebec. This place is a treasure trove of unique, inexpensive delights. You can find pretty much anything at "the Nearly New," as the locals call it.

There are garage and yard sales, flea markets, antique shops, vintage clothing shops and consignment shops (often great for clothes and toys!). Buying secondhand can be an excellent way to minimize the cost of a high-quality item. If you know exactly what you are looking for and have done your research, you will know a deal when you see one. And you can find incredible deals for all manner of things on various secondhand sites such as Craigslist and Kijiji, or auction sites like eBay.com and eBid.net, and the amazing Etsy for homemade goods.

A big benefit of buying used or homemade is that it is much easier to avoid plastic packaging. If you are buying online, be sure to ask the seller to not use plastic packaging if at all possible.

Tip #5: Tap into your local community

In our local community of Wakefield, Quebec, there are vibrant email and Facebook groups where folks regularly post things for sale or requests for very specific items. Maybe there are similar online community groups in your area? Check with friends and at local community centers and hangouts.

Tip #6: Minimize plastic packaging when ordering online and shipping packages

When ordering online, choose retailers you can trust. When retailers offer little description about their products, it might be a sign that they don't know much about their products and don't care to find out. One important piece of information that is often missing is the country of origin. If you know where the product comes from, it may give you an idea of the quality.

Another piece of information that is often missing is the description of the packaging. For example, it's important to know if the packaging has a plastic window or if it is in a PVC clamshell. If it's not indicated, ask. This tells the retailer it is important, and needs to be added to the product information on their website.

If there is room for comments upon checkout, make sure you request no plastic packaging. The comments inserted at checkout are usually read by packers and they are generally acted upon. Unfortunately, despite their greatest efforts to ship without plastic, chances are your parcel will have plastic tape on it. Rare are the online retailers that use paper or cellulose tape.

Having these general tips percolating in the back of your mind is helpful as we now move into more specific household changes and areas of the home. We'll begin by considering personal care products, which affect numerous aspects of our lives in the most intimate ways.

PERSONAL CARE PRODUCTS

Take a look around your bathroom at personal care products you may have: shampoo, conditioner, rinse, gel, hairspray, deodorant, hand soap, makeup, toothbrushes, toothpaste, dental floss, mouthwash, razors, shaving cream, aftershave and feminine hygiene products. A fair bit of plastic, eh? Personal care is an area where it can be extremely difficult to avoid plastic packaging. But it's worth making the effort, not only to minimize the packaging waste, but also to avoid the multitude of synthetic chemicals that are added to most mainstream commercial personal care products.

Two excellent ways to avoid or minimize plastic in personal care products is to buy them in bulk by bringing your reusable container to the bulk store, or to make your own. These days, making your own couldn't be easier. There are oodles of recipes out there. Just do a quick search on Google or Pinterest with keywords like "homemade" or "do-it-yourself" and the item you are looking for. The natural and healthy ingredients are easy to source in bulk—things like baking soda, cornstarch and essential oils—and you can store your creations in reusable glass jars or tins.

Soap

We tend to have no shortage of natural soaps floating around our two bathrooms. Many arrived as gifts or samples, or from our local Saturday farmer's market where the most lovely, creamy goat milk soaps are available.

Soap bars are really the way to go as they can replace a variety of personal care products—liquid hand soap, shower and body gels, shampoo and shaving cream—and be completely plastic-free if purchased at local markets or with paper packaging. A good staple soap to have around is a castile soap. It has a low pH compared to commercial soaps, making it ideal for anybody with sensitive skin (e.g., babies) and it can be used for practically any cleaning task.

If you prefer liquid soap, it's not hard at all to make your own, and you will save a lot of money and plastic. A gallon of top-of-the-line liquid castile soap goes for about $60 and comes in a big plastic jug. Or you could buy a couple of bars of castile soap packaged in paper for less than $5 each and make that same gallon of liquid soap yourself.

Here's what you do:

- Grate up about a cup and a half (180 g) of castile bar soap, using a standard cheese grater.
- Fill a large stockpot or bucket (ideally metal, given our goal of living without plastic) with one gallon (3.8 L) of hot tap water (or you could boil the water on the stove).
- Combine the grated soap with the hot water and stir until it's dissolved.
- Let it sit overnight.
- The next morning it will be thick gel. Blend it up using an immersion blender.
- Transfer it into a gallon jar or into reusable pump containers for easy dispensing.

You can use any type of bar soap you have to make a corresponding liquid soap—you can even save up all your bits and pieces of soap bars and use them to make a truly unique liquid soap mixture. It may not be as smooth or pure as the store-bought version, but it will work just fine for all kinds of uses: hands, dishes and general house cleaning.

If you decide you are going to buy soap, whether bulk or bottled, do try to avoid the antibacterial ones, as they likely contain the endocrine-disrupting preservative and antibacterial agent triclosan. Also watch out for sodium laureth sulphate (SLS), which is often contaminated with the carcinogenic 1,4-Dioxane. And as a final toxicity note, remember our crash course on endocrine-disrupting phthalates earlier on? If you see the word "fragrance," it's often industry speak for phthalate-laden chemical soup.

Shampoo

Like soap bars, there are also shampoo and conditioner bars, specifically formulated to clean hair. Does it seem strange to think of using a bar for your hair? Just try it. You simply lather it up in your hands as you would normal soap, and then spread it through your hair and lather away as usual. Or you can rub the bar directly on your hair and scalp—whatever works for you. They often come in paper or possibly no packaging if you get them at a market or natural product store bulk section.

If you really prefer liquid shampoo, then try a bulk store near you where you can bring your own reusable container (mason jar!) and fill it up with a bulk liquid shampoo. If they have only a standard unscented shampoo, and you like your hair to smell like a field of spring flowers, don't be afraid to add in a few drops of your preferred essential oils such as lavender, rose and chamomile . . .

The "No Poo" Movement

Nope, nothing to do with bowel movements. Everything to do with not using traditional commercial shampoo. The "No Poo" hair care method (www.nopoomethod.com) is a movement referring to shampoo-free healthy hair. It's a bit hardcore, but may be just the thing for you—and of course, it eliminates the need for conventional shampoo in plastic bottles.

The idea is this: Daily shampooing, especially with synthetic shampoos, strips away the naturally conditioning oils in our hair and damages the hair. The No Poo method advocates using a gentler cleaning ritual as follows:

- Shampoo with baking soda: Wash your hair first with a mix of baking soda and water. You can make paste of it and massage it into your scalp, or mix a tablespoon (15 ml) with a cup (237 ml) of water and pour it over your head and work it into your hair and scalp until it feels smooth. It won't lather, because there is no soap base. When done, rinse it off with warm water.

- Condition with apple cider vinegar (ACV): Rinse with an ACV water mix. About a quarter of a cup (59 ml) ACV, or white vinegar if you prefer, to a cup (237 ml) of warm water. Just pour it over your head (eyes closed!) and massage it in. Then do a final rinse with warm water. The vinegar smell will go away quite quickly, and you can speed it along by adding a few drops of an essential oil you like to the vinegar rinse mix.

It may take a couple of weeks for your hair to adjust, with it initially seeming more oily than usual, but eventually your locks should end up looking and feeling lush and healthy. Beth Terry of My Plastic Free Life swears by this method and has been using it with excellent results for years. To make it less burdensome, she mixes up the two solutions in advance and keeps them in repurposed plastic sports bottles in her shower.

Skincare

We make a lot of our own coconut oil–based skin creams as a natural, plastic-free alternative to conventional lotions. They are super easy to make. All you need are two ingredients and heat:

- Heat coconut oil on your stove until it melts.

- Add a few drops of your favorite essential oil.

- Let it cool, and then you can apply it.

Some folks prefer and swear by olive oil, just used straight on the skin as is, or with added essential oils. The downside of these lotions is that they are, well, oily and it takes a bit of time for them to absorb into your skin. If you are applying the oil all over your body it could stain certain clothes if it's not fully absorbed. For those of us living where there is a long, cold, dry, skin-parching winter, this has not been a problem as the oil tends to absorb into our skin quite quickly, but it's something to consider.

Skin lotions are often available in bulk at health food stores where you can bring your own reusable container (a repurposed pump bottle or a mason jar). Just be sure to check the label so you know what you are getting and can avoid harmful synthetic ingredients like vitamin A compounds (retinyl palmitate, retinyl acetate and retinol). While vitamin A is an essential nutrient, such compounds can increase skin sensitivity, especially when exposed to the sun.

Deodorant

Deodorants get personal. There is no single plastic-free deodorant that will work across the board for all. Some people swear by simply powdering on pure baking soda, maybe with added essential oils, while others find it irritates their skin and leaves white marks that may be visible when wearing a sleeveless shirt. If you do want to go the baking soda route but find it itchy, try adding some cornstarch, which may eliminate the irritation. If your skin is super sensitive and the cornstarch doesn't help, try using some arrowroot powder instead.

There are tons of homemade deodorant recipes out there, and they tend to have a few basic ingredients: a base oil, baking soda, cornstarch and essential oils.

The one we've seen around that we prefer comes via Katherine Martinko at Treehugger and adds in shea butter, which seems to make a difference.[2] It goes like this:

- 3 tablespoons (44 ml) virgin coconut oil
- 2 tablespoons (30 ml) shea butter
- 3 tablespoons (44 ml) baking soda
- 2 tablespoons (30 ml) cornstarch
- 5 drops essential oil of your choice (e.g., lavender, sage, lemon, honeysuckle)

Bring water to a simmer in a double boiler (you can make a simple double boiler by putting a small mason jar in the middle of a pot of water). Add the coconut oil and shea butter to the jar and let them melt. Turn off the heat and add the baking soda and cornstarch. Stir until everything is mixed together into a smooth cream. Blend in your chosen essential oil or oils. Let the mixture cool until it hardens, which it will as long as your room temperature is below 76°F (24°C). To use it, just scoop up a bit (about a teaspoon [5 ml]) in your fingers and rub it under your armpits. The warmth of your body will fully melt and absorb it. If you don't like applying it by hand, you could transfer it to an old deodorant bottle.

Keep in mind that we're talking about deodorants here, which kill body-derived, odor-causing bacteria. Conventional synthetic *antiperspirants* generally contain potentially toxic aluminum-based compounds that temporarily block pores to prevent sweating; store-bought antiperspirants may also include endocrine-disrupting parabens and triclosan.

Cosmetics

This is an area where you should begin to tackle the plastic elimination aspect by deeply rethinking what you most need. Most makeup containers are made of plastic, though there are now a few brands using glass or metal containers. Again, you can go into DIY mode and make your own working from the masses of recipes available online. (See Personal Care Products in the Resources section on page 175).

2 Accessible at: http://www.treehugger.com/organic-beauty/recipe-homemade-deodorant-really-works.html.

Homemade and natural are worth considering when it comes to cosmetics, not just for the obvious plastic packaging reduction benefits, but also because of the vast range of toxic synthetic chemicals used in commercial cosmetics. You can learn more about these chemicals of concern on the comprehensive Campaign for Safe Chemicals website: www.safecosmetics.org/get-the-facts/chemicals of concern/.

Feminine Hygiene

If you're a woman, your ability to decrease your disposable plastics and avoid dangerous synthetic chemicals is high when it comes to that time of the month. Yes, opting to avoid synthetic disposable sanitary pads and tampons will not only decrease your contributions to landfill waste—the average woman will use about 16,800 pads and tampons in her lifetime[3]—but you will also decrease your exposure to a soup of toxic chemicals potentially present in synthetic pads and tampons.

Most pads and tampons are made of bleached cotton, viscose rayon or a combination of both. Viscose rayon is a semi-synthetic polymer made from cellulose derived from wood pulp. Wood pulp, you say? That sounds good. Hang on. Both the cellulose and the cotton may be bleached using dioxin-creating chlorine,[4] and carcinogenic dioxins are among the most toxic chemicals out there. There may also be pesticide residues present.

And there's more. These products perform so effectively because they also generally contain strips of super absorbent polymers (SAPs; yup, plastic—acrylics in particular), synthetic gels with surfactants, and polyethylene dry weave plastic backings (alas, more plastic). The possible health and environmental effects of all these chemical ingredients is the subject of ongoing debate, but here are a few of the potential health hazards associated with feminine care products: allergic rash, endometriosis, infertility, cervical cancer, ovarian cancer, breast cancer, immune system deficiencies, pelvic inflammatory disease and toxic shock syndrome.[5]

So, what are the safer options, both for you and the environment?

- Reusable Cloth Pads and Liners: Widely available online and in health food stores, they can be used and washed over and over. Expect them to last three to five years if well cared for. Find masses of beautiful homemade options on Etsy with the search "cloth menstrual pads." Got an old organic cotton flannel shirt lying around? You can make your own pads and liners with simple patterns easily found using the Google search "DIY menstrual pads."

- Reusable Knitted Tampons: Seriously, it's done; Etsy or Google it. There are hand crocheted ones made of bamboo and cotton; bamboo fabric is apparently much more absorbent than cotton. In both cases, organic is best to avoid chemicals used in processing the fabric.

3   K. Mok (2014) 7 "Powerful Reasons Why You Should Switch to Reusable Menstrual Products," Treehugger.com (accessed 4 March 2017: http://www.treehugger.com/health/reasons-why-you-should-switch-to-reusable-menstrual-products.html).

4   Feminine product manufacturers are supposed to be using non-chlorine bleaching processes - the U.S. Food and Drug Administration has found trace levels of dioxins in tampons. We take a zero tolerance approach to dioxins because they are just too plain dangerous. See U.S. Food and Drug Administration (2015) "Tampons and Asbestos, Dioxin and Toxic Shock Syndrome," as cited in S. Dudley (2016) "Tampon Safety" (accessed 4 March 2017: http://center4research.org/i-saw-it-on-the-internet/tampon-safety). See also W. Nicole (2014) "A Question for Women's Health: Chemicals in Feminine Hygiene Products and Personal Lubricants," *Environmental Health Perspectives* 122:A70–A75; U.S. Food and Drug Administration (2009) "Dioxin in Tampons" (accessed 4 March 2017: http://www.fda.gov/scienceresearch/specialtopics/womenshealthresearch/ucm134825.htm).

5   A. Scranton (2013) "Chem Fatale: Potential Health Effects of Feminine Care Products," Women's Voices for the Earth (accessed 4 March 2017: http://www.womensvoices.org/wp-content/uploads/2013/11/Chem-Fatale-Report.pdf).

- A Reusable Menstrual Cup: More and more women swear by these flexible little cups which are placed in the vagina to fill up with menstrual blood. You then empty it out, give it a gentle soapy wash and re-insert it. Yes, we are reticent about inserting anything silicone or natural rubber into such a sensitive absorbent part of the body (read our take on silicone on page 51), but it's safer than a toxic tampon, and if it's high quality medical-grade silicone or natural rubber, it's going to be very stable. The waste reduction benefits are so huge and health risk so minimal. If you suspect you may have a rubber latex allergy, definitely opt for silicone.

- Sea Sponge Tampons: A completely natural option. These renewable, sustainably harvested sea sponges come from the sea where they grow in colonies. They are used in the same way you would a traditional tampon, except that you can reuse them.

- Compostables: If the reusable route just isn't for you, consider choosing organic, compostable pads, liners and tampons. There are established suppliers that make them free of fossil fuel–based plastics and without toxic chemicals like dioxins. They may be available with and without cardboard applicators, so try going without to cut back on waste.

Another consideration to keep in mind is the enormous amount of money you will save by opting for reusables. Yes, there is washing involved with reusable cloth pads, liners and tampons, but imagine not having to purchase any for years at a time! See Feminine Hygiene in the Resources section (page 176) for suggestions relating to these options.

Shaving and Hair Removal

There are several plastic-free shaving alternatives for both women and men that avoid plastic single-use razors and disposable razor cartridges:

- Safety razor: These are the old-style metal razors with a removable double-sided steel blade. They are now very easy to find online, both brand new trendy modern ones and vintage beauties. If you're taking one in a carry-on, you'll have to remove the blade and check it with luggage, or purchase new blades at your destination. As for recycling the blades, the best bet is to ask at your local recycling facility what is the best way to put them in the recycling stream. If it's mechanically processed you may be able to just add them in with the rest of your metals. You can extend blade life by ensuring it is dried after each use. Buying blades in bulk saves on packaging.

- Electric razor: Yes, it uses energy, but there's no disposable plastic or blade buying and changing involved, and it should last you forever if it's high quality.

- Straight razor: According to shaving experts, the closest shave imaginable comes with a straight razor. This is a completely plastic-free, long-term way to go. There is a learning curve involved here, and you'll need to be sharpening your straight razor regularly to get the best results. You want to be sure your straight razor does not get into the hands of children—it is a very sharp and dangerous personal care tool.

- Tweezers: Great for eyebrows and moustaches—and completely plastic-free— but this time-consuming and potentially painful approach might be a bit much for the whole leg or beard or underarm. A bonus for the pain is that, with time, this way will stop the hair from growing back.

- Some specifics for women:

  - Natural waxing and sugaring: Most commercial waxes are made of petroleum-derived paraffin, but there are some beeswax and tree resin-derived products out there so be sure to read the label and minimize packaging if you're looking for wax treatment. What's sugaring, you ask? It goes back to ancient Egypt as a natural technique for hair removal, and is something you can easily make on your own with just sugar, water and lemon juice.

  - Lasers and electrolysis: The idea here is to eliminate the hairs for good. If that attracts you and you have the funds to indulge—they are expensive procedures—this is one way to eliminate any plastic packaging you generate from waxing products.

WHAT ABOUT SHAVING CREAMS AND OILS?

It's now super easy to avoid the pressurized cans of synthetic shaving foam or gel, which are hugely wasteful from a packaging perspective and contain a raft of petroleum-derived ingredients as well as chemical fragrances (remember: "fragrance" on a label likely means phthalates are in there) and penetration enhancers, which help the cream get deeper into your skin.

Our preferred option is a simple, natural, organic shaving soap bar applied with a shaving brush or a sponge. Remember those old-style shaving brushes? They're still easily available and they work beautifully, for both women and men. The shaving soap bar can be kept in a little bowl. You wet the brush with warm water, rub it in a circular motion on the soap and lather up. We prefer boar bristle brushes over the common badger ones as they are more ethically harvested, and we do not know of any plastic-free vegan options.

We often think only of shaving creams, soaps and gels, but shaving oils work well, and can be an effective way to avoid razor burn and minimize nicks. Just make sure it's a natural oil; there are some out there with synthetic ingredients. You can use an organic vegetable oil: jojoba, olive, grapeseed or coconut will all work nicely.

Ideas for shaving-related products can be found under Shaving Equipment (page 176) in the Resources section at the end of the book.

Toothbrushes, Toothpaste and Floss

Brushing and flossing your teeth are among the most intimate and internal of bodily personal care rituals. The brush and the floss are right inside your mouth: the sensitive entryway to the rest of your body, including of course your bloodstream and organs. Not only that, you are subjecting the brush and floss to pressure and repeated friction against hard, sharp enamel teeth in that warm, acidic space. Do you really want to be using plastic in such a leaching-friendly environment?

TOOTHBRUSHES

In the non-plastic toothbrush realm, it's a question of balancing your values and what is most important to you. The pickings are currently slim. We know of only one completely non-plastic compostable toothbrush. The handle is made with sustainably harvested beechwood and the bristles are made of sterilized pig hair. It's a fine brush—and we don't say that because we sell it; we have been using them for years—but if you're looking for a vegan (non–animal product) toothbrush option, then this is not the brush for you, and for now you will have to accept some plastic in your bristles.

The best plant-based brush option in our opinion is made by Brush with Bamboo. Their brushes are made of a biodegradable organic bamboo handle, and the bio-based bristles are 62 percent U.S.-produced castor bean oil and 38 percent nylon. As well, all the packaging is completely biodegradable, and is compostable in commercial facilities.

The only way we know of currently to achieve completely plant-based dental care is to use a stick from a tree, but not just any tree. Certain woods, such as the neem tree, have exceptional anti-bacterial properties and can help prevent plaque on teeth.

Various types of wood are used around the globe for such "chewing sticks," with the oldest known ones dating back to 3500 B.C. Babylonia. In Africa, the Middle East and throughout Asia, "miswak" chew sticks come from the *Salvadora persica* tree. Options native to North America include the red osier dogwood (*Cornus sericea*), olive, sweet gum and walnut. This is what you do:

- Peel or carve back a bit of the bark at one end of the stick.
- Chew on the inner wood to break up and separate the wood pulp fibers— you're basically making a little brush.
- Gently rub these pulpy bristles on your teeth and along your gumline—no need for toothpaste!
- When you're done, cut off the frayed used portion, and it's ready for the next use.

Beware here of plastic packaging; such sticks may come packaged in plastic, so be sure to ask first how they are packaged if ordering online.

As for other store-bought "eco-friendly" toothbrushes, there are various options out there with pros and cons: other bamboo handled brushes with 100 percent nylon bristles, recycled plastic that can be recycled again (down-cycled into lesser products made of lower quality plastic), replaceable heads that decrease the plastic waste as you continue to use the same plastic handle. As well, they may be packaged in plastic.

We lay out a number of available options under Dental Care in the Resources section (page 177).

TOOTHPASTE

Plastic toothpaste tubes are generally not recyclable in your local recycling system. And the fact is, toothpaste is extremely easy to make yourself. Here's the easiest basic recipe we know of:

- 1 tablespoon (15 ml) baking soda
- 1 tablespoon (15 ml) coconut oil

Mix the baking soda and coconut oil together in a small glass jar. When you're ready to brush, take a bit on a spoon and add enough water to mix it into a paste; you can use your brush to mix and then just scoop it up on the brush once it's mixed.

That's it. After mixing the baking soda and coconut oil you might want to mix in a few drops of an essential oil you like (some suggestions: cinnamon, clove, lemon, mint, orange, peppermint, sage and vanilla). Instead of the essential oil, you could add in the actual sage or vanilla leaves, or lemon or orange rind, or ground cloves, cumin or fennel. Still too bitter and salty? Add in a bit of stevia or Xylitol to sweeten it up.

If you prefer a tooth powder over toothpaste, you can simply eliminate the coconut oil from the above technique (perhaps add in more stevia or Xylitol to minimize the saltiness of the baking soda). And you can still add in some ground-up "seasoning" to bring in added flavor and breath freshener.

Not into DIY toothpaste or toothpowder? There are excellent store-bought and small-scale options out there (always remember Etsy). At our local farmer's market and craft fairs, we regularly see completely natural handmade powders or pastes created with love. Lush offers a range of tooth powders and what it calls Toothy Tabs, which are little pill-sized tablets that you crunch between your teeth and then start brushing with your wet toothbrush. The packaging is recycled cardboard.

FLOSS

As you grind plastic thread between your teeth and watch it fray before your eyes you are witnessing the creation of nylon microplastics, some of which you may swallow, and others that will go down the drain when you rinse and spit. Furthermore, plastic floss is just plain dangerous in the waste stream. Being small and lightweight, it easily "leaks" out of waste management systems into the environment where its strength and length help it strangle and choke wildlife. It should never be flushed down the toilet as it can wreak havoc with plumbing systems or possibly end up making it through the system and out into waterways.

Most commercial dental flosses are made of nylon and come packaged in hard plastic containers. This packaging is enormously wasteful given that higher quality plastics (such as polypropylene) are used for these containers, but their standard linear life often leads them straight to a landfill after a few weeks of use.

Currently, the only plastic-free floss option is silk. There are natural silk flosses coated with beeswax or plant-based candelillia wax and packaged in metal or glass (they may have a small plastic sealing sticker that is removed when you first open it). Bea Johnson from Zero Waste Home suggests unraveling a piece of organic silk fabric and twisting together a couple threads to create your own home compostable floss. Various options are set out under Dental Care in the Resources section at the end of the book (page 177).

Reading Personal Care Product Labels

Label reading is especially important for personal care products because pieces of actual plastic could be lurking in a product you use on a daily basis.

Numerous synthetic and potentially toxic ingredients are used in many shampoos, conditioners, soaps, body scrubs and other personal care products. The Environmental Working Group (EWG) consumer guides are great resources to help you become aware of toxins in such products. For example, they have excellent guides on cosmetics, sunscreens and home cleaning products: www.ewg.org/consumerguides. As well, the EWG Skin Deep database provides a world of information and suggestions for safer personal care products (www.ewg.org/skindeep).

We are beginning to see more third party certifications for personal care products, and these can be of great assistance with your label analysis. The beauty of certifications is that they shift the burden of proof from the consumer to the manufacturer. Instead of the consumer having to carefully check the product ingredients for toxins, the producer is required to declare its product toxin-free, and prove it. The manufacturer may use the label on the product packaging only after their claims are verified by the certifying organization. See the sidebar below for personal care product logos to look for.

A FEW LOGOS TO LOOK FOR: THIRD PARTY CERTIFICATIONS OF SAFE, ECO-FRIENDLY PERSONAL CARE PRODUCTS

The Dutch-based Plastic Soup Foundation and North Sea Foundation have created the "Zero Plastic Inside" certification and label, which is the first certification specific to plastics. Manufacturers that declare and verify their products 100 percent plastic-free are allowed to use the Zero Plastic Inside logo on their packaging. (www.beatthemicrobead.org/en/look-for-the-zero)

™ Environmental Working Group (EWG) aims to make its "EWG Verified" program the gold standard in the health and wellness space. To use the logo, manufacturers must meet strict EWG standards for safe ingredients, good manufacturing processes and ensure their products are adequately preserved and free of contaminants. (www.ewg.org/ewgverified)

Ecocert is a French inspection and certification body specializing in creating standards and conducting certifications for natural and organic cosmetics, cleaning products, home perfumes and paintings and coatings of natural origin. For cosmetics, Ecocert requires that 95 percent of the total ingredients be of natural origin. Ecocert also considers the biodegradable and recyclable nature of the product packaging. (www.ecocert.com/en)

The Microbead Surprise: Brushing and Scrubbing with Plastic

In 2013, Texas-based blogger and dental hygienist Trish Walraven began seeing tiny blue pieces of what looked like plastic stuck in her patients' gums as she cleaned their teeth. She was baffled until she made the connection that these blue specks were coming from the toothpaste her patients were using, and she suspected they actually *were* plastic.

She was simultaneously excited and horrified to realize that she had some potentially plastic-infused toothpaste in her own home—toothpaste that was chosen and being used by her young daughter. Trish put on her "little scientist hat" to figure out exactly what these miniscule particles were. She did some experimenting to see if the blue bits would dissolve in nail polish remover (acetone) or isopropyl rubbing alcohol overnight.[6] They didn't. She was certain that they were plastic. In particular, she discovered, they were the common plastic known as polyethylene. She looked up polyethylene on the Crest website and found it described as "a safe, inactive ingredient used to provide color."

Trish wrote about her discoveries in a blog post that went viral entitled "Crest Toothpaste Embeds Plastic in our Gums." Procter & Gamble, the maker of Crest toothpastes, claims to have now removed plastics from its toothpastes, but Trish's post continues to generate disturbing testimonials from individuals and other dental professionals still witnessing the plastic bits in toothpaste and teeth. Thanks to her curiosity and tenacity—and outrage at her findings—Trish's efforts added considerable fire to a growing worldwide movement to ban plastics in personal care products.

These little microplastics are commonly known as plastic microbeads and they are one of the most pernicious, toxic and globally polluting examples of bad product design using plastic. The tiny pieces of synthetic plastic are generally made of either polyethylene or polypropylene plastic. They are added as color additives, scrubbing agents and abrasive exfoliants to a variety of personal care products: everything from toothpaste, facial scrubs and body washes to soaps and shaving foams. For example, a single tube of Johnson & Johnson's "Clean & Clear" facial scrub contains over 330,000 microbeads.[7] In some products—such as Trish's toothpaste—you can actually see the microbeads in the product with the naked eye.

You can also do a simple little experiment to highlight them. Squeeze a microbead-containing product into a glass of water, stir to disperse the product and then pour that water slowly through a white t-shirt. All the little colored particles you see are plastic microbeads. When conducting this experiment with a facial scrub use a black t-shirt because most of the microbeads in such scrubs tend to be clear or white and will show up as little white particles on the black t-shirt.

WHY ARE PLASTIC MICROBEADS A PROBLEM?

These minute beads of plastic are generally less than a millimeter in size—about the size of a grain of sand—and are designed by the product manufacturers to wash straight down your drain. That's a problem for several reasons, and taking a quick look at the life cycle of a typical batch of plastic microbeads explains why.

---

6   Trish Walraven, "Crest Toothpaste Embeds Plastic in Our Gums", 4 March 2014, Dental Buzz—A Jolt of Current: Trends, Innovations and Quirks of Dentistry. (accessed 4 March 2017: http://www.dentalbuzz.com/2014/03/04/crest-imbeds-plastic-in-our-gums/)

7   http://www.5gyres.org/microbeads/ (accessed 4 March 2017).

When you rinse the microbead-containing toothpaste out of your mouth—apart from the plastic bits stuck in your teeth and gums or swallowed!—it is flushed down the sink drain. Yes, drained away and out of sight. But of course, there is no "away." The microbead particles generally are too small to be caught by conventional municipal sewage treatment facilities, so they waltz through filtration systems and head straight out into our rivers, lakes and ultimately oceans. In New York State alone, nearly 19 tons (17 tonnes) of microbeads go down the drain every year.[8]

This is where the serious problems begin. Cutting-edge research has shown there are trillions of plastic microbeads present in freshwater systems like the Great Lakes and in all five major ocean systems in the world.[9] Yes, *trillions*.

The next problem is that plastic microbeads act like little sponges, soaking up harmful toxins that are already present in the water surrounding them. Such toxins could include petroleum products and radioactive waste, and all kinds of persistent organic pollutants such as pesticides, DDT, polychlorinated biphenyls (PCBs) and flame retardants. A further serious problem is that microbeads resemble tiny eggs or morsels of food and are gobbled up by fish, birds and other aquatic wildlife, infiltrating them up the food chain. Researchers estimate that a single microplastic particle in the ocean can be a million times more toxic than the water around it.[10] Eventually the microbeads arrive at the top of the food chain—us humans—at which point the level of toxins in both the microbeads and the animal's fat tissue is highly concentrated. And then we eat the fish, unaware we may be ingesting a toxic smorgasbord. Not good.

MICROBEAD BANS ARE HAPPENING!

Marine scientists and environmental groups like the 5 Gyres Institute have spent years collecting microbead pollution data in waterways and lobbying for bans on microbeads. In December 2015, the United States banned microbeads in personal care products by passing the *Microbead-Free Waters Act,* which will go into effect in 2018-2019. As well, Canada has added microbeads to the *Canadian Environmental Protection Act* Toxic Substances List, and has developed the *Microbeads in Toiletries Regulations* to restrict the use of microbeads in personal care products. The bans are phased in over a period of years to give companies time to change to non-microbead-containing products. Until such bans are fully in place, trillions of microbeads will continue to be flushed down drains and out into the environment. The upshot: There are trillions of reasons to avoid microbead-containing products now and always.

8   J. Nalbone (2015) "Unseen Threat: How Microbeads Harm New York Water, Wildlife, Health And Environment," New York: Office of New York State Attorney General Eric T. Schneiderman, p. 7 (accessed 4 March 2017: http://ag.ny.gov/pdfs/Microbeads_Report_5_14_14.pdf)

9   C. Rochman et al. (2015) "Scientific Evidence Supports a Ban on Microbeads," *Environmental Science & Technology*, 49:10759–10761.

10   Y. Mato (2001) "Plastic Resin Pellets as a Transport Medium for Toxic Chemicals in the Marine Environment," *Environmental Science & Technology*, 35(2):318–324.

ARE THERE ALTERNATIVES TO MICROBEADS?

There most definitely *are* alternatives. The irony of this story is that there are lots of non-toxic, readily available, naturally-derived and environmentally friendly alternatives to plastic microbeads. Furthermore, these natural alternatives tend to be even more effective at exfoliating and removing dirt and dead skin cells because they are coarser than the roundish plastic microbeads. A few of the numerous possible alternatives to microbeads include sea salt, ground coffee, coconut husks, apricot shells, walnut shells, crushed cocoa beans, seaweed and orange rind.

Plastic microbeads are essentially a cheap filler for personal care products. They are innately less effective abrasives than natural alternatives, which encourages daily or even more frequent use of the product (and thus more sales for the manufacturer). Before all the recent attention on microbead pollution and the resulting government action to remove them from consumer products, manufacturers had little incentive to use alternatives to plastic microbeads—even though they knew all along that microbeads would be washed down the drain.

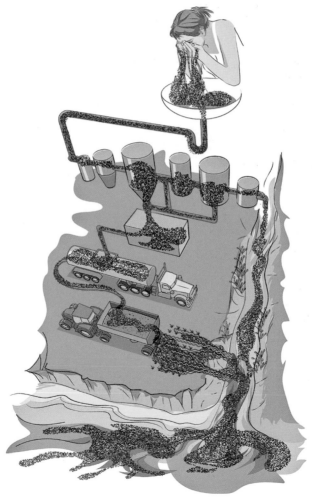

The toxic flow of plastic microbeads in personal care products from the bathroom sink into global waterways.

Many manufacturers have now pledged to remove plastic microbeads from their products. Nonetheless, because most of their phase-out plans extend over a period of years—and the legislative actions in Canada and United States won't likely come into force until 2018–2019—the more we can avoid microbead-containing products now, the better.

These are the plastics most often used to make the microbeads in personal care products:

- polyethylene
- poly(methyl methacrylate)
- polytetrafluoroethylene
- polypropylene
- nylon
- polyethylene terephthalate[11]

If you see any of these on the ingredients label, you can be sure the product contains plastic microbeads. The "Beat the Microbead" International Campaign Against Microbeads in Cosmetics has put together a comprehensive, regularly updated list and free downloadable app of microbead-containing and microbead-free products organized by country. The app is a handy resource to have loaded on your phone when shopping for personal care products.

- List: www.beatthemicrobead.org/en/product-lists
- App: get.beatthemicrobead.org

MAKE YOUR OWN SCRUB!

Of course, one of the best ways to avoid plastic packaging and ensure the personal care products you are using are safe for you, your family and the environment is to make them yourself using natural ingredients.

Here are a couple of super simple two-ingredient body scrubs courtesy of Lindsay Coulter, David Suzuki's "Queen of Green":[12]

SIMPLE FACIAL WASH

2 tsp (10 ml) sugar (fine)

1 tbsp (15 ml) olive oil

Stir the ingredients together. Apply to your face and wipe off with a warm cloth. Do not apply near sensitive skin around the mouth and eyes.

---

11   P. Sundt, P-E. Schulze and F. Syversen (2014) "Sources of Microplastic-Pollution to the Marine Environment," Norwegian Environment Agency (Miljødirektoratet), p.16 (accessed 4 March 2017: http://www.miljodirektoratet.no/Documents/publikasjoner/M321/M321.pdf).

12   Accessed 4 March 2017: http://www.davidsuzuki.org/publications/downloads/2010/two-ingredient_cosmetics.pdf

STRAWBERRY SCRUB

2 large, ripe, organic strawberries

2 tbsp (11 g) finely ground oats (use coffee grinder)

Mash the strawberries and work in the ground oats. Apply to your face and let sit 15 to 20 minutes. Wipe off with warm cloth. The strawberry seeds will do your exfoliating! Store in the fridge for one to two weeks.

Here is an invigorating coffee ground scrub served up by the 5 Gyres Institute:

COFFEE SCRUB

⅓ cup (79 ml) coconut oil (retains moisture & softens skin)

½ cup (45 g) ground coffee (anti-inflammatory & boosts circulation)

¼ cup (23 g) sugar (try coconut or turbinado sugar; it's naturally exfoliating and hydrating)

1 tsp vanilla extract (soothing and relaxing natural scent)

Melt the coconut oil on the stove in a small saucepot over medium heat. Once melted, remove from the heat. Meanwhile, use a coffee grinder to pulse fresh coffee beans into a medium to fine grind (or measure pre-ground grains). Combine the melted coconut oil, ground coffee, sugar and vanilla extract in a small glass container with a lid. Use it as you would any other body scrub: apply, gently scrub and rinse.

CLEANING

Plastics abound in cleaning supplies, whether it's the Swiffer sweeper, scrubbing sponges or the myriad of cleaning detergents and sprays in the typical home cupboard. A general rule to remember when it comes to cleaning detergents is that solids tend to be more easily available in plastic-free packaging than liquids. That's because liquids, unlike powdered solids, cannot be packaged in compostable materials like paper. One basic way of avoiding plastic in your cleaning supplies is to switch from liquids packaged in plastic to powder detergents packaged in cardboard. Of course, an even more basic way to deplastify your cleaning routine is to make your own cleaning products.

Make Your Own

We tend to seek out products with labels that describe exactly the cleaning chore we want to accomplish, such as "toilet bowl cleaner," "microwave cleaner spray" or "ceramic cooktop power cleaner." The reality is that a few basic simple ingredients can clean everything in your house from toilet to microwave. All you need is to keep a stock readily available of white vinegar, baking soda and borax (the last two items are easy to find in cardboard boxes) and perhaps some essential oils to add a fresh, pleasant smell to the mix. Here are some standard combinations that will allow you to clean pretty much everything in your house.

	WATER	WHITE VINEGAR	BAKING SODA	BORAX	INSTRUCTIONS
All purpose cleaner	1 cup (237 ml)	3 cups (710 ml)			Mix together and spray on surface, wipe clean
All purpose disinfectant	3 cups (710 ml) of hot water			3 tsp (13 g)	Mix together and spray on surface, wipe clean
Microwave cleaner	1 cup (237 ml)	¼ cup (60 ml)			Mix together and spray on surface, wipe clean
Mirror cleaner		1 cup (237 ml)			Spray undiluted on surface and wipe clean
Toilet cleaner		¼ cup (60 ml)	Sprinkle		Sprinkle baking soda and rinse with vinegar, brush clean
Fabric softener		1 cup (237 ml)			Add during rinse cycle
Rust remover		1 tbsp (15 ml)	1 tbsp (13 g)		Make paste, apply on rusty parts, let sit a few minutes, brush clean
Stovetop cleaner			1 tbsp (13 g)		Mix baking soda with lemon juice on stovetop, scrub clean
Shower cleaner		1 cup (237 ml)			Spray undiluted on surface
Dishwashing by hand	Hot water		4 tbsp (50 g)		Add baking soda to dish water
Dishwasher soap			1 cup (206 g)	1 cup (206 g)	Mix together with ½ cup (121 g) salt and add 1 tbsp (13 g) in soap compartment
Dishwasher rinse		1 tbsp (15 ml)			Add to rinse compartment in dishwasher

White vinegar is almost exclusively available in plastic jugs, so try and purchase it in the largest jugs you can, and then see if you can find a local store that sells vinegar in bulk and will refill your container. You might want to also consider soap nuts.

The Power of Nuts

Have you heard of soap nuts? They are extremely versatile and often packaged plastic-free in a box or cotton bag. Often marketed as a laundry cleaner, soap nuts can be used to clean pretty much anything in your house.

Soap nuts originate from Nepal and India and they are fruits, not nuts. They contain saponins in their shells which are the active ingredients with detergent properties. There are many ways soap nuts can be used to clean all over the house, potentially avoiding a whole slew of plastic packaged cleaning supplies.

A final note about laundry: you can avoid liquid fabric softener packaged in large plastic jugs by opting for funky wool dryer balls. Not only will they leave your laundry feeling soft, but they will help the clothes dry faster in the dryer because the balls get in and around the fabrics, allowing more hot air to circulate.

Cleaning Tools

For years, people have used discarded cotton clothing or cut-up old sheets as cleaning rags. It's only in recent years that large multinational companies introduced the plastic-based, cheap, disposable, synthetic cleaning cloths and marketed them as better than homemade rags. Being disposable, customers need to keep buying these synthetic cloths over and over again instead of washing them, thus generating eternal ongoing profits for the companies that make them. That's the deal with the Swiffers: you need to keep buying those synthetic refills. So the cotton rag stopped being used as primary cleaning cloth. Reclaim your cotton cleaning cloths! They work fabulously on all kinds of surfaces. For polishing jobs, try using a leather-based natural chamois.

To wash your floors, a mop with a head made of cotton strands or a cotton pad and a wooden handle will do the job. They still exist and can be found easily in hardware and home product stores. The same goes for metal buckets, which can outlast any plastic bucket and even be passed down to the next generation.

A Brush for Everything

For hard to access areas that really need a good cleaning, you can almost certainly find a natural brush to do the job. There are brush companies still making brushes the way they were made more than 80 years ago, before the advent of plastic. They use natural bristle materials ranging from ethically-sourced animal hair like horse, goat and pig to plant fibers that include tampico, arenga, cocoa and palmyra. Such brushes are made by hand using traditional techniques and have an old-world charm. (See the Resource section under Brushes on page 177 for a myriad of plastic-free options.)

Credit: Burstenhaus Redecker

Plastic-free brushes exist for pretty much any use you can imagine.

KITCHEN AND GROCERY SHOPPING

Ten years ago, in our local grocery store in Wakefield, Quebec, you would rarely see someone bring their own reusable bags. Now you rarely see someone NOT bringing reusable bags. It took some time, but the new habit has started to take hold and what was once perceived as normal behavior has completely reversed. The same applies to many other little habits you might want to start integrating into your daily routine. It's the example that you set for others that creates change in your community and beyond.

Choosing the Right Grocery Bags

Make sure you always have a bag with you when you go grocery shopping, whether it's in your handbag, your backpack, in the glove compartment or trunk of your car or attached to your key chain; even a secondhand plastic bag will do just fine. It's better than no bag at all, and you save a bag from going to the landfill. If, however, you want to go a step further and invest in the purchase of reusable bags, you might want to consider a few important factors.

MATERIALS

Ideally, you want to prioritize materials that close the loop of the bag's life cycle and go back to the Earth, and are not just recycled into a lower quality item (i.e., down-cycled). Cotton, jute and hemp are all natural materials that can be composted back into the Earth.

DURABILITY AND REPAIRABILITY

Not only will a reusable bag be a solid long-term investment, but its durability and repairability are also determining factors in how soon it will end up in a landfill. Can you repair a hole that forms at the bottom of the bag? If the bag is made of plastic, it will be harder to repair. A cotton canvas bag is easy to repair with a needle and thread or a sewing machine.

To ensure your bag is durable and solid, inspect the pressure areas. Seams are more likely to break at the top of the handles and at the bottom of the bag. Are these seams reinforced? Is the design flawed because of where the seams are positioned? Over time, seams located at high pressure points will weaken and may give out due to the pressure of constantly supporting the bag and its contents.

WASHABILITY

In a well-publicized 2011 study underwritten by the American Chemistry Council (a key lobby group for the plastic industry), researchers from the University of Arizona and Loma Linda University in California found that 51 percent of the reusable bags they tested as part of their research contained coliform bacteria.[13] The same study found that only 3 percent of reusable bag users washed their bags regularly, but that the simple fact of washing their bags would reduce the presence of bacteria by 99.9 percent. The plastic industry made sure to disseminate this study broadly in order to try and convince people that single-use plastic bags are more hygienic.

Don't let the plastic industry have the last word on this one. Get rid of that inevitable bacteria by washing your reusable bags regularly. When purchasing a reusable bag, it is important to choose a bag that is easy to wash, such as a cotton canvas bag. Bags should be washed about every second week, depending on their frequency of use.

---

13   C.P. Gerba, D. Williams and R.G. Sinclair (2011) "Assessment of the Potential for Cross Contamination of Food Products by Reusable Shopping Bags," *Food Protection Trends* 31(8):508–513.

The final factor to consider when purchasing reusable bags is whether the bag can be transported easily. Bags that can be folded back into a small compact pouch are more likely to be kept in a purse or a backpack or car glove compartment, and therefore will likely be reused more often.

PURCHASING A REUSABLE SHOPPING BAG					
	Disposable Plastic Bag	Reusable Plastic Bag	Compact Reusable Plastic Bag	Reusable Cotton Bag	Compact Reusable Cotton Bag
Reusable (many times)	x	✔	✔	✔	✔
Durable	x	✔	✔	✔	✔
Machine Washable	x	x	✔	✔	✔
Repairable	x	x	✔	✔	✔
Compostable/ Recyclable	x	x	x	✔	✔
Compact	✔	x	✔	x	✔

A final word about shopping bags: Although disposable plastic bags do not generally last very long and they do get dirty easily, it is possible to wash them under the tap and reuse them. In fact, there are wooden bag dryers that can be installed on a kitchen wall so you can easily hang up your bags to dry after washing. The smart design of such bag dryers keeps the bags open allowing them to dry quickly. See Bag & Bottle Dryer in the Resources section (page 178).

Bringing the Right Bags or Containers

When grocery shopping, there are typically six types of food items we purchase: 1) fresh fruit and vegetables; 2) cheeses and meats; 3) dairy products, juices, sauces and other liquid food; 4) basic dry ingredients such as flour, sugar and pasta; 5) frozen food; 6) processed and prepared food including breads.

FRESH FRUIT AND VEGETABLES

You are probably all too familiar with the flimsy plastic produce bag conveniently available on a roll in the produce section of your supermarket. These types of bags are rarely recyclable and they tend to be thrown out after a single use. Instead, keep several reusable cotton mesh bags with you when grocery shopping. These allow the cashier to see the item you are purchasing through the bag and they keep your produce fresh longer because they allow the items to breathe.

You can find many brands of cotton mesh bags that are completely washable and also double as great salad spinners. We use cotton mesh bags to spin our washed lettuce and other greens. You just step outside for a minute and rotate the bag a few times in order to get the centrifugal force going until all the water has been released. It actually works better than those large plastic salad spinners and takes up much less storage space in the kitchen.

For leafy greens, you might want to consider a greens bag that has a tighter weave than mesh bags and helps to keep greens fresh and crisp. When you get home, you should dampen the bag lightly and keep the greens stored in the greens bag in the fridge crisper drawer. If you purchased loose green leaves, clean and pat dry the leaves, dampen the greens bag and store them in the fridge crisper drawer.

Try to do as much of your food shopping as possible at a farmer's market. Farmers are generally much more laid back about packaging and will happily reuse packaging that is returned to them or fill up your own container. Ask them if they would take back your egg or vegetable cartons or plastic bags. Inquire about the existence of community supported agriculture (CSA) programs with local farmers in your area.[14] CSAs allow local residents, often city folks, to have direct access to high quality, fresh produce grown locally by regional farmers. Generally, when you become a member of a CSA, you're purchasing a "share" of vegetables from a local farmer and each week you'll receive a bin full of fresh seasonal produce.

CHEESES AND MEATS

Pre-packaged cheeses are almost always tightly wrapped in non-recyclable plastic. Fortunately, most grocery stores have a deli counter where you can buy cheese in bulk. Offer the deli clerk a stainless steel airtight container or a glass jar that has a sufficiently large opening. The clerk might readily accept your container and tare it (weigh it before inserting the cheese in it and then deducting the weight). If not, gently explain what to do. You must be willing to educate cashiers and other grocery store employees about new ways of doing things that help to reduce plastic waste. That's how things start to change. It may be painful at first, and you might receive puzzled looks or sighs of exasperation, but eventually it will become normal.

If you are a mega cheese fan and are willing to purchase a large piece of cheese that won't fit in any of your glass or stainless steel containers, you could use a large beeswax-coated reusable fabric wrap to package your cheese.

Try to avoid the pre-weighed meat placed on a styrofoam platter and shrink-wrapped in plastic. Ask for a fresh cut of meat and offer a stainless steel airtight container. Most meat counter employees will happily do it for you, and if they refer you back to the pre-packaged meat, let them know you are plastic-intolerant!

DAIRIES, JUICES, SAUCES AND OTHER LIQUID FOOD

Because plastic has the handy property of being waterproof, it is a material of choice for containing liquid products. As the prevalence of glass packaging has decreased markedly, shopping for liquids has become one of the trickiest parts of plastic-free grocery shopping. Glass is the best alternative to plastic for liquids, and only a few years ago, many wet products like ketchup and mayonnaise were still packaged in glass. Justifying their switch to plastic with arguments of cost reduction and customers preferring lighter plastic packaging that is less prone to breaking, manufacturers have progressively replaced more and more glass packaging. You can still find some brands that stick to glass for health and environmental reasons. They are rarer, but should be encouraged and congratulated. The natural food section of the grocery store is likely to contain more glass packaging.

LIFE WITHOUT PLASTIC

14   Visit localharvest.org and search the name of your town. You may be pleasantly surprised to find CSA programs you did not know existed.

Try to avoid purchasing acidic or oily products packaged in plastic containers or metal cans with a BPA lining because of the increased risk of toxins leaching into the food. You may be able to find metal cans with BPA replacements, but as we have described in Chapter 3 (page 40), many of the BPA-free linings are no better than BPA and may present similar hormone-disrupting health risks.[15] From a recycling point of view, however, cans are preferable to plastic containers. When plastic packaging is the only option, make sure you select a plastic container made with a resin that is highly recyclable, such as polyethylene terephthalate (PET, recycling code #1), high density polyethylene (HDPE, recycling code #2) or polypropylene (PP, recycling code #5) and try to purchase in large bulk quantities.

Milk may be available in your community in glass bottles on a consignment deposit program. These programs are fantastic because they reuse glass instead of recycling it. The glass bottle is washed and refilled.

If you have a bulk store nearby that accepts outside containers, bring your own glass jars or stainless steel containers and a funnel to fill them up. The selection of wet products is often limited but make sure you always bring your own containers just in case.

The very best plastic-free way to deal with this liquid category of food is to purchase a good blender or food processor. Many liquid products can be created quickly and easily by purchasing the raw ingredient in its dry form in bulk and transforming it with a blender. For example, a cup (237 ml) of almonds can be transformed into almond butter or almond milk with the addition of water.

BASIC DRY INGREDIENTS SUCH AS FLOUR, SUGAR AND PASTA

Bring some bulk bags, glass jars and stainless steel food containers. If you run out of reusable bags or containers, instead of plastic bags, use paper bags available in other sections of the store such as the bakery. It's handy to carry a marker with you to write on the container and identify what you are buying (most markers can be washed off stainless steel containers and glass). Another option is a non-toxic grease pencil (also known as wax pencils or peel-off china markers). They work well on all sorts of non-porous surfaces, such as glass jars and metal canning lids. The markings are moisture-resistant in the fridge or freezer, but can be easily rubbed off with a towel.

It's a wise idea to plan ahead of time and make a list of everything you are planning to buy at the bulk store. You will need a bag or a container for every item. If you are planning to buy some spices, bring small spice containers. If you are planning to get some honey, bring a mason jar. You can purchase more than 75 percent of your grocery needs in a bulk store, so the better prepared you are, the more plastic packaging you will avoid. Consider marking some of your storage containers and bags "permanently" with the name of a particular dry product you purchase regularly, and then filling up that container or bag with the same item every time you go shopping. That way, even if you don't have time to clean the container or bag in between trips to the bulk store, you can use these pre-identified ones and avoid cross contaminating your food with other types of food.

---

15   For an overview of which brands of canned food offer BPA-free linings, see: http://www.ewg.org/research/bpa-canned-food (accessed 26 February 2017).

FROZEN FOOD

It is nearly impossible to purchase frozen food without plastic packaging. Plastic packaging will prevent frozen food from leaking during transportation from the grocery store to your freezer on a hot summer day. Plastic packaging also prevents freezer burn, which happens when moisture in the outer layers of the food evaporates into the freezer air, thus drying out the surface of the food. A freezer is an extremely dry environment, so food needs to be stored airtight to be protected. While you may see some cardboard boxes in the frozen section of your grocery store, if you look inside you will find either an inner plastic bag to protect the food or you will notice that the inside of the box is sealed and lined with plastic inside.

Even if you decide to give up pre-packaged frozen food as you adopt a plastic-free lifestyle, it doesn't mean you no longer need to make use of your freezer. On the contrary, the freezer is your plastic-free friend! There are many types of food that you can buy fresh in large quantities—such as nourishing, succulent fruits and veggies at harvest time—and freeze in large, clearly identified airtight containers.[16] Freezing food can help you avoid oodles of plastic packaging.

PROCESSED AND PREPARED FOOD, INCLUDING BREADS

Grocery stores have aisles and aisles of processed food with long lists of chemical-ridden ingredients. Soups, sauces, cereals, macaroni and cheese, brownie mix, spaghetti sauce and salsa. All of these items can be created from scratch using the base ingredients purchased in bulk or in glass containers. Often it is the time savings and convenience that makes processed foods so appealing. You don't necessarily have to give up the convenience of prepared foods to have a plastic-free life; you just need to be cautious and diligent. Here are a few rules to follow when buying processed or prepared foods:

- Seek out the natural and organic section of your supermarket, which may have exactly what you're looking for in a glass container.
- Beware of the cardboard box; it may contain a plastic pouch.
- Avoid frozen processed food.
- Look for cake or brownie mix in a paper bag.
- Potato chips are hard to find not packaged in plastic. If you can't do without them, buy the biggest bag possible and reuse it as a garbage bag (see the Kitchen Tools section on page 105 for more details).

Other prepared foods made directly on site at the grocery store can be purchased without plastic. Bread is a good example. Bring your own bread bag or ask for a paper bag.

Storing Your Food

Food storage is one of the first aspects of plastic-free living we focused on when we started Life Without Plastic. At the time, we were storing all our leftover food in plastic food containers and re-heating them directly in the microwave. We now cringe at the idea, but we didn't even think twice at the time until we started reading about the leaching of plastic additives from plastic into food, especially when it's heated and the food is oily and/or acidic.

---

16   See the section on Canning, Freezing and Dehydrating (page 112) for suggestions on how best to freeze your own garden food or culinary creations.

Various considerations come into play when deciding what container to use for food storage. For example, is it a leftover that you may want to reheat later? Is it something you want to freeze? Is it dry food that may go rancid over time if not properly stored?

There are now plastic-free options to choose from that can suit practically any need. Beware of marketing that tries to convince you that silicone is a "great plastic-free" alternative. It's not. It is non-plastic in name only. It has favorable characteristics of being stable and resistant to temperature extremes, but it is not a naturally-occurring product and it is not easily recyclable.[17]

Because each of the options we highlight has its pros and cons, we've put together the illustrated table below to help you navigate possibilities based on your specific needs.

STORING YOUR FOOD WITHOUT PLASTIC

Type of Food	Best Option	Image
Leftovers to be re-heated in the microwave	Glass container with bamboo, stainless steel or glass lid	
Leftovers to be reheated on the stove or in the oven	Stainless steel airtight container	
Leftover salad in salad bowl	Beeswax wrap cover	Credit: Abeego
Cold food	Stainless steel container (airtight or not, depending on nature of food)	Credit: Lunchbots
Wet food	Glass jar or stainless steel airtight container	
Warm food	Stainless steel insulated thermal container	Credit: Lunchbots

17   See the section on Silicone in Chapter 3 (page 51) for more detail.

STORING YOUR FOOD WITHOUT PLASTIC

Type of Food	Best Option	Image
Muffins or potatoes	Glass, ceramic or stainless steel bowl with a fabric bowl cover	
Food to be frozen	Stainless steel airtight container or glass jars with at least an inch for expansion	
Small portions of food to be frozen (baby food, concentrated broth, herbs)	Stainless steel ice cube tray	
Bread	Depending on how crunchy you like it, a bread bag might suffice or a beeswax wrap or stainless steel airtight container	
Flour, grains or pasta purchased in bulk	Glass, ceramic or stainless steel airtight container	
Cookies, loose leaf tea, spices	Tins, large or small	

GLASS

There exist a number of plastic-free options for storing your food, but glass is the most common and the cheapest. Not only are mason jars inexpensive, but you can obtain glass jars for free just from purchasing products packaged in them at the supermarket. Food such as spaghetti sauce is often packaged in a glass jar that you can clean and reuse. Virtually all lids that come with a glass container are made of plastic or coated with a plastic lining that may contain BPA; make sure you never fill up your jars to the point that food is in contact with the lid.

Glass jars are great for storing all kinds of food: dry goods, wet food, liquids and slices of cheese . . . You can also use them safely in the freezer as long as you leave about 20 percent of extra space to allow for expansion.

Glass is especially handy for storing leftovers because you can actually see the food inside of the container. If you store leftovers in a glass container, you can reheat them directly in your microwave or toaster oven after removing the lid, but to prevent the glass from cracking if you are taking it directly from the fridge or freezer, be sure to give the container time to warm to room temperature.

STAINLESS STEEL

Stainless steel has emerged in recent years in North America as a superb alternative to plastic for food storage. Asian populations have known this forever. Stainless steel containers are durable, practically unbreakable, repairable, safe and with the addition of some silicone in the grooves of their lids, they can be made airtight. And a surprising advantage of stainless steel is that it has a positive recycling value. This means that you can be paid to return stainless steel to a scrap dealer.

When storing leftovers in a stainless steel container, it's a good idea to identify the contents directly on the container with a Sharpie marker or a grease pencil. Markers, even the non-erasable ones, wash off easily with baking soda and a little elbow grease.

Stainless steel containers work well in the freezer, especially with an airtight lid. The frozen food is protected against freezer burn and dehydration, and the food can be defrosted directly in the container on the stove at low heat. We use our large rectangular airtight containers that have a capacity of over 4 gallons (15 L) to store frozen tomatoes freshly picked up in the summer months. Jay then plops them whole into the spicy Indian dal he makes often in the winter.

As well, we use a large rectangular airtight container to store our bread and pastries. The bread doesn't dry out, and the pastries stay fresh for several days. Airtight stainless steel food containers work very well for storing certain types of produce in the refrigerator. For example, with lettuce, kale and beet greens, just add a little bit of moisture at the bottom of the container or wrap the greens in a damp cotton towel or greens bag.

Make sure you purchase high quality, food grade 304 stainless steel of 18-8 or 18-10 quality. You may find less expensive stainless steel containers of grade 200 quality. This is a lower quality grade of stainless steel that generally does not contain any nickel, which means it is more prone to rust. When we first started our business, we offered some dishes and containers on our site that were made with 202 stainless steel. We were soon getting complaints from customers that patches of rust were visible after dishwashing. We quickly stopped offering these products. Even though rust is not in itself dangerous to human health, it's not a desirable thing for a product being used for food or beverages and it may alter the taste of the food or drink.

TINS

Tins are relatively popular as ornamental gift packaging. You often see tin boxes filled with cookies around Christmas time and you might wonder how you can reuse them at home. The problem with tin containers is that they rust very easily. They should only be used for very dry food. Even cookies that are too moist can cause some rusting in the container over time.

Use tin containers to store dry goods that you plan on consuming in the coming month or so. Tin containers are rarely airtight and the contact with air will make your flour or grains go rancid more quickly. They can work nicely for spices and loose leaf tea. Tins are also great for storing powdered cleaning products such as baking soda and borax.

FABRIC

Fabric provides some level of insulation without being airtight. For baked goods such as cookies or muffins, an airtight container may keep them too moist and sticky on the surface when the desired texture is a bit crunchy. A cotton bowl cover on top of a ceramic bowl works perfectly. Similarly, for a baguette, a bread bag is ideal. Keep the baked goods in the fabric bag for a few days and then transfer them to an airtight container to keep them from drying out too much—there is a limit to that desired crunchiness.

You can also use fabric bags to conserve some dry goods you've purchased in bulk for a short period of time (less than one month). Sugar, salt and dried beans are good candidates, as long as the pantry where they are stored is very dry.

BEESWAX WRAPS

For almost ten years now, beeswax wraps have been on the market as an eco-friendly and natural alternative to plastic cling wrap. Typically, they are made of cotton or hemp dipped in a blend of beeswax and natural oils. They smell like honey and they can be molded to the shape of a bowl with just the heat of your fingers. They are truly magical and entirely natural. Keep a few handy to cover leftover bowls, salads, a half-cut melon or a piece of cheese. They also work well with bread. Just make sure you do not wash them in hot water or the beeswax will melt and wash away in your sink drain. Simply wipe them clean with a damp soapy cloth or wash them in cold water with soap. Keep a few sizes handy and replace them about once a year, depending on the level of use.

	GLASS	STAINLESS STEEL	TINS	FABRIC (BAG OR COVER)	BEESWAX WRAP
Food to freeze	✓	✓			
Dry goods	✓	✓	✓	✓	
Wet goods	✓	✓			
Liquids	✓				
Leftovers	✓	✓			✓
Cheese	✓	✓			✓
Meat & deli	✓	✓			
Spices	✓		✓		
Bread, pastries		✓	✓	✓	✓
Water	✓	✓			
Greens		✓		✓	

STICKY PLASTIC

One last thing to say about food containers. You may think that unless your plastic containers are cracked, you can still use them for storing your food. The reality is that plastic containers continue to leach their many chemical additives all through their existence. Additives give plastic products special properties. They may include flame retardants, plasticizers, stabilizers, color pigments and lubricants. Because they are not chemically bound to the plastic resin, they will leach into whatever food or beverage you put in the plastic container. Plastic will even leach faster when the container is old and scratched, frequently washed in the dishwasher or washed with harsh detergents. Have you ever wondered why some plastic containers are sticky on the surface and no matter how hard you try, that stickiness just won't wash away? That is the chemical additives that progressively leach and eventually appear on the surface of the plastic. If that's the case, those are containers you want to recycle, or discard if they cannot be recycled.

Kitchen Tools

The art of cooking without plastic is a matter of getting your kitchen equipped with the right tools. Knowledge of what materials are solid replacements for plastics is essential. Plastic kitchen tools have taken over most of the aisles of kitchen stores. Everything seems to be either in plastic or silicone, from colanders to blenders to salad tongs and oven mitts. Fortunately, plastic-free alternatives do exist.

CUTTING BOARDS

Let's start with one of the most basic kitchen items: the cutting board. We use two beautifully handcrafted wooden cutting boards for our daily cooking chores. They get dirty and we clean them with soapy water and a cloth, but you've got to wonder if it's enough. Don't bacteria build up in the pores of the wood? Aren't plastic cutting boards safer?

A 1993 study concluded that hardwood cutting boards are much more sanitary than their plastic counterparts.[18] In this study, researchers inoculated cutting boards with a broth containing bacteria such as *E. coli* and *Salmonella* and found that bacteria would multiply over time in the plastic (polypropylene) cutting boards but get absorbed and disappear in the wood cutting boards. More proof that nature knows best how to protect us.

COOKWARE (NON-STICK COATING IS PLASTIC)

Teflon (Polytetrafluoroethylene or PTFE) is a plastic, or more precisely a thermoplastic polymer. When you cook anything in a pan coated with PTFE, you're basically cooking it in direct contact with plastic. As we describe in Chapter 3 (page 43), there have been serious toxicity issues with PTFE, so we consider anything with Teflon better avoided. A safer, more precautionary route is to opt for a cast iron pan or all stainless steel pan with a metal handle so that you can place it in the oven if you need to broil the top of your frittata or bake your golden cornbread.

KITCHEN UTENSILS

Pretty much all cooking utensils needed in a fully functional kitchen can be found in non-plastic versions. They are easily available in wood, bamboo, or stainless steel—salad tongs, stirring spoons and spatulas. Scrapers, the type of spatulas used for folding ingredients into batters and cleanly scraping out mixing bowls, are more challenging

18   N.O. Ak, D.O. Cliver and C.W. Kaspar (1994) "Cutting Boards of Plastic and Wood Contaminated Experimentally with Bacteria," *Journal of Food Protection* 57(1):16–22 (accessed 5 March 2017: http://www.treenshop.com/Treenshop/ArticlesPages/SafetyOfCuttingBoards_Article/CliverArticle.pdf).

to find in non-plastic versions. They used to be made with a wooden handle and a removable rubber head. They've largely been replaced with either plastic or silicone, but there are places that still have rubber versions. For some existing options we have found, see Kitchen Tools in the Resources section on page 178.

Colanders are relatively easy to find in stainless steel versions at a good kitchen store. As for salad spinners, even the ones that look like they're made of metal actually hide a plastic interior. Our preferred salad drying method is to use centrifugal force and a cotton mesh produce bag. Fill the bag with your cleaned lettuce pieces, go outside and spin the bag around. Water will just fly off the bag. It is fast and efficient.

Beware of silicone everything . . . in recent years, silicone has invaded the kitchen. It is being labeled as a healthy plastic-free alternative, but this is misleading. Just like traditional plastics, silicone also contains chemical dyes and additives that could leach out. Moreover, silicone does not degrade easily and can't be recycled, so it is not gentler on the planet. We prefer to avoid silicone unless it is absolutely necessary, such as to create a seal for the lid of an appliance or container.

MICROWAVE VERSUS TOASTER OVEN

After ten years of aspiring to a plastic-free lifestyle, we've discovered that the toaster oven is one of our best friends. We use it all the time; just as often as we used a microwave oven in our previous plastic-full life. With a toaster oven, you can reheat your leftovers directly in the plastic-free storage container. There aren't any foods that cannot be reheated in a toaster oven. Even frozen burritos. If you don't want the food to dry out on the surface while warming up, just add a stainless steel lid or an upside down stainless steel plate to the container.

FILTER AND STORE YOUR OWN WATER

Every time we see people loading up cases of 24 plastic water bottles in their shopping carts, we can't help but cringe at all that plastic consumption—really, is it necessary? Some of the leading brands of water that you buy actually comes directly from a filtration plant. It's just filtered tap water. Perhaps the problem is that tap water does not have a communications and marketing team dedicated to convincing consumers that it is generally just as good for one's health as bottled water.

Regardless, it may still be a good idea to filter your water to remove traces of chlorine or other contaminants such as lead that could be present in the pipes that deliver your water. One of the best ways we've found to filter our water in a plastic-free natural way is to drop a Japanese binchotan charcoal stick in it. Charcoal has innate detoxification properties and an extremely porous surface to which the ions of contaminants become attracted. It is effective at removing chlorine from water, and also removes lead, mercury, cadmium and copper. It is also said to impart calcium, magnesium and potassium back to the water. Moreover, you can revitalize your charcoal once a month by boiling it in water. You should replace the stick after four months, but the used one can then serve as a fridge deodorizer.

To store water, there are glass or ceramic water dispensers available, but chances are the spigot will be made of plastic. Another option is a stainless steel water dispenser that has been specially treated for water storage. Some people use Italian stainless steel olive oil dispensers to store water but they don't realize that oil actually prevents rusting whereas water causes it. Rust is a chemical reaction involving iron, water and oxygen. When they mix, the result is hydrated iron oxide, or rust. Water is the catalyst that causes the oxidation process, so in order to prevent rust, you need to keep water away. As oil and water naturally separate and do not mix, oil is

Making the Most of Your Binchotan Charcoal

1) Drop the charcoal stick in a container and add water.

2) Once a month, boil your stick in water for 10 minutes.

3b) Alternatively, you can use your stick at the bottom of a plant to improve drainage.

3a) After 3-4 months, retire your stick to the refrigerator where it will absorb odors.

effective at preventing rust on metal. With its nickel and chromium composition, stainless steel does not normally rust, but some parts of the dispenser may be more vulnerable to oxidation such as the seams or the spigot in contact with water. This is why the treatment process is essential as it basically super cleans the surface to remove any potentially rust-causing impurities. When purchasing a stainless steel dispenser for water storage, make sure it is specifically designed to hold water. (See Water Dispensers in the Resources section on page 178.)

If you are a soda drinker, just get a soda maker to avoid purchasing carbonated drinks in plastic bottles or aluminum cans. Soda Stream uses a system of returnable and refillable canisters to add CO_2 to your water.

What About Garbage?

If you're serious about leading a plastic-free lifestyle, then you need to address how you deal with the garbage you generate. Before proposing an optimal way to deal with trash, it is important to understand the typical composition of our trash. According to the U.S. Environmental Protection Agency, in 2014:

- 40 percent of pre-recycling trash in the United States was composed of paper, glass and metals—all of which are recyclable in most municipal recycling programs;

How to Deal with Your Garbage

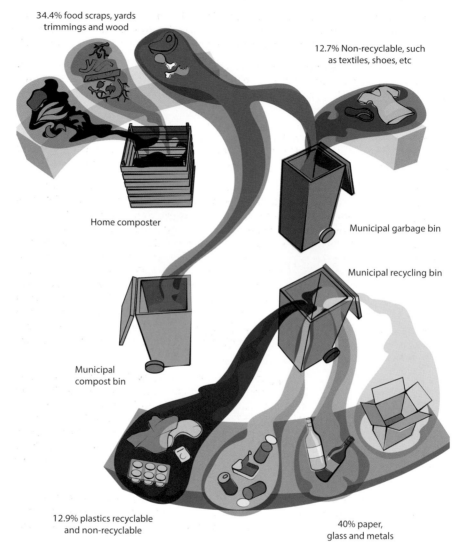

34.4% food scraps, yards trimmings and wood

12.7% Non-recyclable, such as textiles, shoes, etc

Home composter

Municipal garbage bin

Municipal recycling bin

Municipal compost bin

12.9% plastics recyclable and non-recyclable

40% paper, glass and metals

- 12.9 percent was composed of plastics—some or most of which can be recycled depending on the restrictions of your municipal program;

- 34.4 percent was composed of biological waste including food scraps, yard trimmings and wood; and

- 12.7 percent was composed of other types of waste including non-recyclables such as rubber gloves and textiles.[19]

Here are general suggestions on how to deal with each of these types of trash items (these may vary based on the recycling program in your area). First, all paper, glass, metal and recyclable plastics should go in your blue recycling bin. This will deal with about 45 percent of your trash. Your food and yard waste should be composted at

19   U.S. Environmental Protection Agency (2015) Municipal Solid Waste in the U.S.: 2013 Facts & Figures (accessed 5 March 2017: http://www.eia.gov/energyexplained/images/charts/total_msw_generation_by_material-large.gif).

home or as part of your municipal composting program. You don't want to send compostable items to the landfill as they may generate methane gas.

Composting at home is relatively easy, even if you live in a downtown high rise. For small downtown apartments, there exist a number of indoor composting systems you can consider. (See Indoor Composting in the Resources section on page 178.)

If you have a yard, there are even more options and even fewer reasons not to do it. Just type "composting 101" in Google and you'll find dozens of websites with detailed tips. When composting at home, make sure you do not add meat scraps, dairy products, fats, oils and grease, and pet feces to your composter. We recommend wrapping these items in newspaper or paper towels and storing them in a well identified box, bag or area of your freezer (except perhaps the pet feces, which are likely best flushed down the toilet). When garbage day comes, just add the frozen items to your garbage bag. They won't smell or attract animals.

The remainder of your trash that cannot be recycled or repurposed in some way will need to go in the regular garbage and will likely end up in a landfill. This garbage should normally be all dry and fit in a small bag, or if possible in your area, directly in a trash bin with no bag at all. You may think that a compostable garbage bag would be the best way to dispose of this rubbish, but the best is really not to use a bag at all if possible. The reason is that landfills are not meant to encourage decomposition. They are dry and anaerobic spaces that essentially "mummify" anything contained in them, including plastic. Until it is full and closed, any decomposition that does occur in a landfill creates undesirable methane, a heat-trapping greenhouse gas that is roughly thirty times stronger than carbon dioxide.[20] The release of methane from open landfills contributes to global warming, and thus climate change. Of course, the best is to minimize your waste so you are not sending anything to landfills.

If your municipality requires your garbage to be in a bag, avoid getting new plastic garbage bags from the grocery store. Instead, use a plastic food packaging bag such as a large bag of potato chips that previously fulfilled another function besides being used for garbage. Potato chips are rarely available in non-plastic packaging, so if you do indulge in them, then you'll have bags at hand and will be giving them another use. We're not saying you should be eating chips or anything else that comes in plastic packaging just so you have some bags to use for your garbage, but if you do, then this is a way to use those bags.

Finally, keep in mind that when your garbage is mostly dry, there is no need for a bag in each garbage bin of your house. Just put a little bit of newspaper at the bottom and empty the bins either directly in your municipal garbage bin or in the repurposed plastic bag discussed above.

Coffee and Tea Without Plastic

Ahhhh, coffee . . . That powerful potion and guilt-free addiction embraced by folks around the world at the beginning of each day. Chantal cherishes her morning coffee, and her daily ritual involves grinding the beans freshly then using a pour-over ceramic dripper. Jay is mostly a tea guy. He finds that coffee, even decaf, wires him pretty strongly, but he does love a frothy latte once in awhile; it's a bit of a delicacy for him, so when he does indulge, he wants it to be high quality and well-brewed coffee.

---

20   Princeton University, "A More Potent Greenhouse Gas than Carbon Dioxide, Methane Emissions Will Leap as Earth Warms," ScienceDaily, 27 March 2014 (accessed 7 May 2017: https://www.sciencedaily.com/releases/2014/03/140327111724.htm).

Teas and coffees are hot beverages, so we definitely want to do our best to avoid them coming into contact with plastic. That goes for any beverage in our books, but the potential for toxic chemicals leaching from plastics is substantially increased when boiling water is involved.

Did you know that most tea bags contain plastic? This is something we discovered not too long ago. That was a sad day, because we love tea, and tea bags are super convenient. Note that we're not talking only about those pyramid-shaped mesh tea bags that actually look and feel like they are plastic. Those definitely are plastic— usually nylon or polyethylene terephthalate (PET, recycling symbol #1)—and should be avoided because they leach phthalates right into your tea.[21] No, we're talking about the regular-looking tea bags enrobed in a soft paper pouch. The ones that we've always thrown in the compost bin with all our other organic waste. It appears to be an industry-wide practice to include a small amount of polypropylene plastic (PP, recycling symbol #5) in these standard tissue tea bags, which are in fact only about 70 to 80% biodegradable.[22] You can be pretty confident this is the case with the big name mainstream brands like Lipton, Twinings and Tetley. The tea manufacturers seem to think that customers don't notice and likely don't care about the polypropylene addition. Well, we've now noticed and we certainly care!

It's worth checking with the manufacturer to see if there is plastic in their teabags, as some apparently do not contain plastic, or use a corn-based bioplastic. Of course, one way to be sure you are going plastic-free with tea is to opt for loose-leaf. You can brew it up the traditional way in a teapot, or get yourself a little stainless steel tea ball or a one-cup filter if you're making tea for one.

We have a variety of plastic-free coffee creation mechanisms and accessories that we use depending on the type of coffee we want and the time we have available to make it. (See Coffee and Tea Tools in the Resources section on page 178.)

How about the standard-issue drip coffee makers that are a staple in so many homes? Not recommended, in our opinion. You're boiling up water in a plastic tank, just like a plastic kettle. It's not uncommon to hear stories of a strong plastic taste in the first few batches of coffee made with a brand-new drip coffee maker.[23] Practically all of them have lots of plastic parts, and most importantly, a plastic water storage and heating tank: perfect for chemicals to leach from the plastic into the boiling water. We have come across only one electric drip coffee maker that does not have any plastic parts at all. The Ratio Eight is made of borosilicate glass, aluminum and black walnut wood, and it's stunningly beautiful. We are not fans of aluminum, and this is one pricey machine (about $600), but if you absolutely want to have an electric drip coffee maker and are willing to trade one toxin for another (plastic chemicals vs aluminum), it may be for you.

The same caution applies when considering an electric espresso machine: you need to check carefully to ensure that the water holding tank is not lined with plastic, and there are no plastic parts in the other workings. Or just opt for a stainless steel stovetop espresso maker, which can be found in pretty much any kitchen store.

21   T. Orci (2013) "Are Tea Bags Turning Us Into Plastic?" Theatlantic.com (accessed 4 March 2017: https://www. theatlantic.com/health/archive/2013/04/are-tea-bags-turning-us-into-plastic/274482).

22   R. Smithers (2010) "Most UK Teabags Not Fully Biodegradeable, Research Reveals," Theguardian.com (accessed 4 March 2017: https://www.theguardian.com/environment/2010/jul/02/teabags-biodegradeable). See also L. Miles (2014) "The Scandalous Plastic in Tea Bags—Who Knew?" Treadingmyownpath.com (accessed 4 March 2017: http:// treadingmyownpath.com/2014/07/11/the-scandalous-plastic-in-tea-bags-who-knew).

23   Nick Usborne, "The Plastic Taste in New Coffee Makers—Just a Bad Taste, or Toxic Too?" coffeedetective.com (accessed 4 March 2017: http://www.coffeedetective.com/plastic-taste-coffee-makers.html).

Coffee percolators used to be as common as Starbucks. Jay's parents had a stovetop one made of aluminum and glass that he remembers from growing up. He loved to watch the coffee bubbling up into the glass perk top of the cap as it made a funny gurgling noise. You can find electric and stovetop percolators these days with only stainless steel touching the water and coffee at all times.

Pour-over drippers are a superb plastic-free coffee-making alternative. There are several elegant glass or ceramic pour-over dripper options for making coffee—even one-cuppers that fit snugly on the cup. Pair one of these up with a reusable filter made of organic cotton or hemp, and you have a sustainable, plastic-free system. If a fabric filter just doesn't work for you, most manufacturers of glass and ceramic systems also offer disposable filters made of unbleached FSC-certified paper (these can be composted in a home composter). Or avoid the removable filter completely by going with a stainless steel stovetop Italian espresso coffeemaker or a French press (also great for loose teas). You could also delve into the realm of artisanal coffee-making and go for an elegant manual espresso maker.

For kettles, it's pretty easy to find a decent stainless steel stovetop one in the kitchen section of any store or at a kitchen products store. The challenge is more with finding a plastic-free electric kettle. It's well worth investing in a plastic-free kettle because the kettle is going to be making the boiling water for your tea or java every single day, maybe even multiple times a day. If your kettle has plastic parts that are in direct contact with the boiling water, it is essentially guaranteed that there is going to be leaching of chemicals from the plastic over time. The stress on the plastic from repeated long term exposure to boiling water is enormous. The challenge is often to find a steel electric kettle with an exclusively stainless steel interior and without a transparent plastic window to indicate the water level (often they are located in the handle of the kettle as well). If the body is stainless steel, but one of these plastic water level windows is present, you are still going to have the boiling water constantly in contact with plastic.

WHAT ABOUT THOSE COFFEE POD MACHINES?

So here it is straight up: the ubiquitous disposable plastic coffee pods—such as the K-Cup—are a plastic scourge. The amount of them used annually when placed end-to-end is estimated to be enough to circle the globe 10.5 times.[24] About 10 billion K-Cups were sold in 2014 alone and sales have increased since. And most end up in landfills. But also, do you really want to be drinking your morning espresso—or tea for that matter—that was brewed at boiling temperatures in a tiny, inevitably leaching plastic cup? While some recyclable and reusable options are appearing, most are still made of a plastic and aluminum mix, which can't be effectively recycled. To recycle them, the hot coffee grounds, the filter, the lids and the plastic in every pod would have to be separated every time. That just doesn't happen, so they go straight to landfills.

There has been a fair bit of backlash against these systems. The city of Hamburg, Germany has banned plastic coffee pods.[25] The anti-K-Cup movement has been spurred on by a video called "Kill the K-Cup," which went viral and spawned the popular hashtag #killthekcup.[26] Despite the backlash, coffee pod systems are as popular as ever because of the convenience they offer.

24   J. Hamblin (2015) "A Brewing Problem: What's the Healthiest Way to Keep Everyone Caffeinated?" theatlantic. com (accessed 4 March 2017: http://www.theatlantic.com/technology/archive/2015/03/the-abominable-k-cup-coffee-pod-environment-problem/386501). The Keurig company purposely blocks competitors from being able to offer competing pods that are recyclable or compostable by inserting a digital code in the pods to create incompatibility.

25   Lloyd Alter (2016) "Trouble Brewing for Coffee Pods as German City Bans Them to Reduce Waste" Treehugger. com (accessed 4 March 2017: http://www.treehugger.com/sustainable-product-design/trouble-brewing-coffee-pods-german-city-bans-them-reduce-waste.html).

26   See: http://www.killthekcup.org (accessed 4 March 2017).

If you do have one of these machines and are feeling guilty after reading the above, don't despair, there are now options for reusable coffee pods. The best is reusable stainless steel, but if you feel you have to go disposable, there are now compostable single-use coffee pods that are compatible with the standard machines. See Reusable Pods and Compostable Pods in the Resources section (page 179) for some suggestions.

STORING AND TRANSPORTING YOUR COFFEE AND TEA WITHOUT PLASTIC

Storing your coffee and tea to keep them fresh is as important as brewing them well. Our friend Anne Winship, owner of fair-trade coffee purveyor Bean Fair Coffee, recommends storing coffee beans in a non-plastic airtight container and leaving them on your counter—not in the fridge—to maintain maximum freshness and aroma. Same goes for tea leaves. Airtight glass or stainless steel containers work beautifully for this purpose . . . hello mason jar!

And of course, if you're taking your cuppa joe or a floral tisane on the go, there are plenty of stainless steel, glass or ceramic mugs around. We've listed several under Coffee and Tea Mugs in the Resources section (page 181). We tend to prefer glass mugs for use in the car, but for longer use throughout the day we opt for a stainless steel thermos that can be handily turned into a mug by simply changing the cap. Such high quality insulated thermoses can keep beverages steaming hot for a good six to eight hours.

FOOD PRESERVATION: CANNING, FREEZING & DEHYDRATING

An excellent way to decrease the flow of single-use, disposable plastics into your home is to preserve your own food. Not only does it eliminate the plastic packaging from the foods you would normally buy from a store—especially during winter months when farmer's markets and fresh produce may be harder to come by—but you are also reaping the profound health benefits of food that was preserved when fresh and nutrient-rich.

Canning

Years ago, when Jay was a boy, he thought canning meant just that: storing food in cans. He wondered how people would seal the cans. Did everyone have some sort of can-sealing apparatus? It seemed complicated. He soon learned that while canning did originate in the eighteenth century as a practice of preserving food in tin containers, the term now refers to the common practice of preserving food in an airtight container to prevent spoilage.

Canning is a popular food preservation, plastic-packaging reduction activity that anyone can jump into, regardless of where or how you live. We are canning novices, and we're not here to show you how to do it. There are lots of great expert resources out there for that.[27] But we are here to help you do it with less or no plastic.

The big one is the jars and their lids. You'll know by now that we absolutely love glass mason jars, but we do not love the fact that the lids, while metal (usually tin-plated steel), have a bisphenol A (BPA) or BPA-free plastic (still plastic) interior coating that is in direct contact with the food or liquid in the jar. This is why, if you are using

---

27   This handy guide by Mother Earth News is a great start: http://www.motherearthnews.com/real-food/canning/home-canning (accessed 4 March 2017).

a mason jar in a way where the food will be in contact with the lid, we suggest switching to a stainless steel lid—but unfortunately, these stainless steel mason jar lid replacements are not intended for the rigors of canning.

The major mason jar manufacturers—such as Ball, Bernardin and Kerr—now offer BPA-free lids for canning, but they will not say exactly what the new plastic coating is, claiming it is proprietary information. Jarden Home Brands, which makes Ball and Kerr jars, will only say that it is a "BPA-free modified vinyl and the varnish is a modified epoxy."[28] What does that even mean—a "modified vinyl" and "modified epoxy"? Our experience with vinyls in general is not good given that the vinyl family includes the most toxic consumer plastic still in use: carcinogenic, endocrine-disrupting polyvinyl chloride (aka PVC; see the description of PVC on page 33 in the Common Plastics section). Similarly, BPA is used in a lot of epoxies, such as the lining of most canned foods; so if it is a "modified epoxy" then perhaps it contains a BPA-like chemical. Who knows? Here is another instance to put the precautionary principle into practice and simply avoid such lids.

As far as we can tell, the only way to be sure your canning is plastic-free is to use glass lids with natural rubber seals. We have found two options for obtaining glass mason jar lids.

The first is to scour the local markets and thrift stores or head online to eBay to look for vintage traditional glass lids and rubber seals. They are out there, often in full sets and with rubber seals. You'll just want to ensure that the size of the lids will work with your mason jars or wide mouth mason jars by getting precise measurements from the seller—or purchase complete sets, jar included.

The second option is to consider newly made glass canning jars and lids. We know of only two brands that offer glass lids: Le Parfait from France and Weck from Germany. The varied sizes of jars have an old-world style and work with natural

28   Diary of a Tomato (2013) "Mastering Food Preservation: More on Identifying Ball's BPA-Free Lids," (accessed 4 March 2017: https://diaryofatomato.com/2013/07/19/mastering-food-preservation-more-on-identifying-balls-bpa-free-lids).

rubber sealing rings. Neither types use standard screw-on lids. The Le Parfait ones have hinged glass lids with pull-down clamps on one side of the lid. With the Weck system, the glass lids are held on tight with at least two clip-on stainless steel spring clamps. The sealing mechanism is rather ingenious: when the seal on the jar is intact and airtight, the tab on the rubber sealing ring will face downwards. Once the jar has sealed, the clamps can then be removed, and the jars stored in your pantry until you're ready to crack them open. With both jar types, to release the vacuum created by the seal, you simply pull on the rubber seal tab until you hear a whizzing or hissing sound of air moving quickly. The lid can then be removed easily. Nifty.

If you're not willing or able to make the switch to glass mason jar lids—there is extra cost involved—and you have a ton of traditional mason jars all ready to go (who doesn't?), then you might want to consider using the boiling water bath (BWB) method of canning, rather than pressure canning. This at least minimizes plastic lid contact with the food. With the BWB method, you can leave sufficient space at the top of the jar between the food and the lid and be careful when moving the jars to avoid the food coming into contact with the lid. From a plastic-free perspective, it's still not ideal because you will have condensation from the hot food dripping down from the lid into the food, but it is still much better than the food being in direct contact with the plastic-coated lid.

If none of those options work for you, then you might be interested in other food preservation methods, such as freezing and dehydrating.

Freezing

As he was growing up, Jay's mom always had a garden. Tomatoes were a key part of that garden. Her freezing technique was easy. She would simply wash and core the tomatoes, then lay them out on a flat metal cookie sheet and put them in the freezer. Once frozen, she would put them in Ziploc plastic bags.

Jay uses this same method to this day, substituting the plastic bag for a stainless steel container. The beauty of this method is that you can use it for practically any fruit or vegetable. You can do it for apple or orange wedges, strawberries or blueberries, or fresh hardy greens such as kale or chard.[29] With the greens, if you only want to take out a single portion, simply break off as much as you want. A key tip is to make sure that after you have washed the fruit or vegetables, you have dried them as much as possible (excess moisture can lead to freezer burn and cause the food to stick together in clumps). With the cookie sheet, it's also easy to do this with pre-cooked veggies. Once cooked and drained, just put them in little mounds on the sheet as though you were making cookies. Again, once frozen as individual clumps, put them in a non-plastic container for storage in the freezer and just take out as much as you need each time.

---

29   The freezing experts out there strongly suggest blanching vegetables before freezing them to retain the maximum freshness. This involves "flash boiling" the vegetables and then cooling them immediately in ice water to arrest the cooking process. The blanching process is said to slow the loss of nutrients and stop enzyme action in the veggies, which can lead to loss of flavor, color and texture. See S. Chen (2015) "How to Freeze Vegetables for Maximum Freshness," Lifehacker.com (accessed 3 March 2017: http://skillet.lifehacker.com/how-to-freeze-vegetables-for-maximum-freshness-1693677697).

Anne-Marie Bonneau, aka the Zero Waste Chef, is someone else who uses the cookie sheet freezing technique (as well as the glass jar technique described below), and in describing her plastic-free freezing experiences, she provides an idea of the wide range of foods that freeze well using these techniques—everything from grapes and lemon zest to cookies and bread, and she also offers up some enticing recipes linked to her favorite foods to freeze.[30] Note that for freezing bread, she uses her own homemade cloth bags.

GLASS AND STAINLESS STEEL CONTAINERS

Regarding containers, freezing without plastic is straightforward: glass or stainless steel both work beautifully. Glass jars are so easy to come by in whatever size you might need. We traditionally might think of freezing as only for cooked foods such as carrot ginger soup or Cajun chili, but freezing keeps most foods fresher. We use mid-sized glass jars for nuts and berries, and larger jars for grains, flours, granola and muesli. We use round and rectangular stainless steel airtight containers (with silicone seals) in the same way and label them with non-permanent marker so we know what's inside without having to open up the container. Make sure you label the container on the side facing out so you can see the label right away without having to rearrange the whole freezer to figure out the contents of a container.

If you're freezing a liquid, or a solid food that has a lot of liquid in it, be sure to leave some space at the top of the jar for expansion. The amount will depend on the size of the container, but generally an inch or two is plenty to avoid the container cracking or deforming from the food expanding as it freezes. As well, you have to be careful with temperature extremes when using glass jars, as they could crack on you. Jars in which you have just put hot food should be allowed to cool to room temperature before putting them in the freezer. And similarly, you don't want to immediately heat up frozen jars of food just removed from the freezer.

We recommend glass or stainless steel for meats. Standard butcher paper is coated with petroleum-based paraffin wax. Some might suggest aluminum foils, but we don't recommend them given the potential toxicity of aluminum.

POPSICLES AND ICE CUBES

Both popsicle and ice cube molds are most commonly found in multi-colored hard plastic versions. Fortunately, there are now plastic-free, stainless steel options for both!

---

30   A.M. Bonneau (2016) "How to Freeze Food Without Using Plastic," Zerowastechef.com (accessed 3 March 2017: https://zerowastechef.com/2016/01/06/how-to-freeze-food-without-using-plastic).

Stainless Steel Ice Cube Tray   *Stainless Steel Ice Pop Mold*

Jumping back to Jay's formative years, his mom also had an aluminum ice cube tray with a lever you pull up to break the cubes. You can still find these vintage beauties on eBay, but again, the aluminum is not ideal. Based on this model, back in 2009 we created the first stainless steel version of an ice cube tray, and it works very nicely indeed. Now there are other fine stainless steel ice cube tray options on the market as well. Apart from making ice cubes, this is a great way to freeze small portions of baby food, or liquid stock for cooking. Looking for larger single portions than what an ice cube tray allows? Use a muffin tin.

Similarly, stainless steel popsicle molds—available with bamboo sticks and silicone gaskets—are a hardy, elegant alternative to the plastic ones that have kids licking plastic from all angles.

Wraps

If you're looking for a short-term freezing method (about a month maximum), consider using a reusable beeswax-coated cotton food wrap. This might be handy for something hard like a block of cheese, especially if you are looking to save space in a full freezer and want to avoid a space-intensive container completely.

Dehydrating

Dehydrating is another food preservation technique that maintains the nutritional power of food and can significantly reduce the flow of disposable plastic packaging into your home.

The three ways we know of to do home dehydration are: using the sun, your oven or an electric food dehydrator. All three can be done with zero plastic.

Regardless of the technique, there are some prep and storage steps that are applicable across the board:

- Wash well and cut up the fruit or vegetable you wish to dry out, halving or quartering juicy fruits and slicing vegetables thinly. Being low in acid, vegetables will spoil more readily if not in smallish pieces. You want the pieces to be of a similar size so they dry at an equal rate.

- Blanching first is an option to arrest the enzymes that cause deterioration in storage. We prefer to skip this step and just get on with the pure dehydration, but some swear by it.

- Once the food is dry—when it gets wrinkled up like a leathery raisin, but is still pliable—store it without plastic in a glass jar or a stainless steel container (no refrigeration necessary).

SUN DEHYDRATION

Sun dehydration is still an option if you have the time and patience. Whether done indoors or outside on your deck, you'll need several sunny days of direct sun and a low humidity environment (so if you're doing it outside, a dry hot climate is most realistic for this technique). It will likely require some experimentation depending on what you're dehydrating and your conditions, but here's a simple way to give it a go:

- Lay the fruit or vegetables uniformly on a flat baking sheet.

- Leave them in a sunny spot in your home or outside, covered with a mesh material (such as cheesecloth) if insects getting at them is a concern.

- Check and turn them once a day. If outside, bring them in at night to avoid dew and animals.

The low humidity and constant sun are pretty key, otherwise the food may spoil before it dries out sufficiently. This method can work well for things like apples, pears, apricots and tomatoes, with the sun concentrating the natural sugars to bring out a deeper level of sweetness. Fresh herbs couldn't be easier to dry in the sun. Just place them or hang them in a bundle in a sunny spot. That's it.

OVEN DEHYDRATING

No direct sunshine needed for this technique. Because you are using an oven there will be an energy cost with the oven being on for several hours. If the oven has a fan (such as a convection oven) that's helpful for air circulation, but isn't absolutely necessary. A toaster oven can work just fine for smaller amounts of food.

Here are few basic tips to get you started—but don't be afraid to experiment with your particular setup:

- Set the oven to the lowest possible setting. For many ovens, this might be around the 145 to 150°F (62 to 65°C) range. If your oven has a "warm" setting, use that.

- Lay the fruit or vegetables uniformly on a flat baking sheet. Or you could lay them on a wire rack on a cookie sheet to increase air circulation. If the fruit or veggie pieces are large enough, you can lay them directly on one of the oven racks.

- You can keep the oven door closed, though this will increase the heat and humidity in the oven, and decrease air circulation if there is no fan. If your oven doesn't have a fan, you could increase air circulation by keeping the door open a few inches and placing a small fan in front blowing into the oven.

- The amount of time required will depend on the food, but could be anywhere from about 6 to 20 hours.

- This technique is so variable that you might want to try it out with a small amount of food and see how it goes.

USING AN ELECTRIC DEHYDRATOR

This is our preferred technique, especially given our climate and low direct sun context (we live in a forest). It consumes significantly less energy than the oven technique. A dehydrator is a long-term investment and comes with an up-front cost that will likely be in the hundreds of dollars for a decent one. If cost is prohibitive, you could consider purchasing a dehydrator with a group of like-minded friends and sharing it around on a rotating schedule.

Many dehydrators on the market have plastic trays for holding the food, and some even have plastic interiors. These interiors might be made with plastics like polypropylene or acrylics, which are relatively stable, but we still prefer to avoid them for food use whenever possible. Some are even made with polycarbonate plastic, which is composed of toxic, hormone-disrupting bisphenol A (BPA)—definitely to be avoided in our opinion. Apart from being inherently toxic, plastics like polycarbonate will leach more readily when subjected to heat and when in direct contact with food, especially oily and acidic foods. Some dehydrator trays are made of BPA-free plastic, but as we explain in the Common Plastics section (page 40), this does not necessarily mean they are any less toxic than BPA; they may even exhibit more pronounced hormone-disrupting behavior. See the Resources section (page 179) for suggestions of dehydrators with an all–stainless steel interior and metal trays.

Apart from dehydrating fruits, veggies and meats, there are other neat things you can do with your dehydrator, including making granola and yogurt. It's a versatile addition to the kitchen.

Now for a little background on parchment paper, including a "lemon-marinated banana parchment paper replacement experiment" Jay did that went slightly awry. Parchment paper is designed to be grease- and moisture-resistant and somewhat heat-resistant. Thus, it is a useful tool when dehydrating moist items or cut-up foods that are too small to be placed directly on the metal racks. Using a flat metal baking sheet in a dehydrator is not ideal as it impedes the air circulation and it might be hard to find metal trays that will fit in your dehydrator. Parchment papers come in bleached or unbleached versions, and in our opinion the bleached are best avoided because the chlorine bleaching process may leave residues of carcinogenic dioxins. Unbleached parchment paper is the best choice.

The problem is, all parchment papers we have found are impregnated with silicone, which we have mixed feelings about. We consider silicone relatively safe, depending on the use—and you can read more about our take on silicone in the Common Plastics section on page 51—but it is not completely inert and non-leaching.

For one of our first batches of dehydrated lemon-marinated bananas Jay thought maybe that silicone coating isn't necessary because you're drying the food out anyway, right? He tried using regular, unbleached uncoated kraft paper. The temperatures in the dehydrator are so low, there is no fire hazard.

Well, that silicone is necessary. As one might expect, the kraft paper soaks up the juices of the food very effectively. The result was that Jay's lemon-marinated bananas were more or less glued to the paper! They had to be carefully peeled-scraped-chiseled off the paper, but they still tasted great. Live and learn!

If you are going to be using parchment paper regularly, and exposing yourself to silicone at any rate, you may be better to opt for a reusable silicone baking mat, which can be used over and over.

THE BATHROOM

All members of our family, including our son—or should we say *especially* our fourteen-year-old son—really enjoy a hot bath several times a week. The bathroom transforms into a sanctuary of repose. We dim the lamps or light up candles and enjoy the moment, away from all stresses of life.

If your bathroom contains only the essential plastic-free items, it will feel even more like a sanctuary where the air is pure and chemicals are off-limits. Three types of products make up most of the plastic waste generated in a bathroom: toothbrushes, razors and personal care products. Please refer to our Personal Care Product section (page 79) where we discuss the best way to replace these items with safe plastic-free alternatives.

Shower Curtains

Cheap shower curtains made of polyvinyl chloride (PVC) are notorious for off-gassing hormone-disrupting phthalates and other noxious chemicals for weeks after their installation.[31] PVC-laden shower curtains are made of flexible plastic, sometimes transparent, that has the look and feel of a thick plastic food wrap—plastic food wraps are also often made of PVC. And you can also recognize PVC from its recycling code #3, which may be on the shower curtain label.

The best plastic-free shower curtain alternative we have found is hemp. Although more expensive than its plastic counterpart, a hemp shower curtain is naturally mildew and mold resistant up to a point. You must ensure your bathroom is well ventilated to allow the curtain to dry completely, and you should wash your curtain with vinegar if you do see any mold developing.

Toilet Brushes

Plastic toilet brushes need to be disinfected frequently due to the disgusting pink scum that accumulates on the bristles of the brush after a few weeks of regular use. This pinkish substance is actually a bacterium called *Serratia marcescens* that is fortunately harmless. Because plastic is porous, the pink color does not seem to go away easily. As a result, you may feel the need to replace your toilet brush once a year. Plastic toilet brushes often come with a plastic base holder. So when replacing the plastic brush, you must also replace the plastic holder which adds to the plastic load going to the landfill.

Opt for a wooden toilet brush made with natural bristles. You can find stylish base holders made of wood with a ceramic plate to hold the dripping liquid. Such a set is more expensive than a plastic one, but you can replace only the brush instead of the entire set. At the end of its usable life, the brush can be used as kindling for a campfire.

---

31   Up to 108 VOCs can be emitted from a PVC shower curtain: David Suzuki Foundation (2014) "What's the Eco-Friendliest Shower Curtain?" (accessed 4 March 2017: http://www.davidsuzuki.org/what-you-can-do/queen-of-green/faqs/toxics/whats-the-eco-friendliest-shower-curtain).

Towels and Bath Mats

Look for 100 percent cotton towels and bath mats. Polyester is often blended with cotton and makes the towel feel softer to the touch. Resist the temptation and instead use wool balls in your dryer to make your towels feel soft.

THE LIVING SPACE

Shelter is one of the most fundamental human needs. It protects us. It keeps us alive. So why not treat your home like a living organism that supports your life? In doing so, you ensure that it is made of healthy materials that won't make you sick. Unfortunately, plastics have invaded our homes and they can make us sick.

Floors

There are many options: laminate, carpets, ceramic and wood. Here's the lowdown on each option.

In the past few years, laminate flooring has become popular because of its low price and amazing resemblance to wood floors. The technology has evolved to the point where you can hardly tell if it's a real wood floor. Retailers might even make you believe it is actual wood by using terms such as "floating wood tiles." Laminate flooring is actually synthetic floor layers, usually made of melamine resin and fiber board material, fused together with large volumes of glue that may contain formaldehyde and other harmful materials. The top layer contains a photographic appliqué layer made to look like real wood. Depending on the quality of the product, you can expect some off-gassing of toxic chemicals. The off-gassing is always worse in the first few years after installation, so if the floor has been there for a while, there is probably minimal release of toxins.

If you're planning on having a carpet, ensure it is made of 100 percent natural fibers. Synthetic carpets are made of nylon or polyester fibers that wear off into the ambient air constantly. The air you breathe becomes filled with microscopic plastic particles that disperse in your entire house and beyond. The consequence of breathing such particles is still unknown. Moreover, wall-to-wall carpeting usually involves very strong glues that can off-gas toxic chemicals for a long time after its installation. Wool and cotton are much better options.

Ceramic floors are a wonderful plastic-free alternative as long as they are made of real ceramic; that is, clay hardened by heat. Some manufacturers offer fake laminate ceramic that looks just like the real thing, so make sure you are getting authentic ceramic. Glazed ceramic will be easier to clean. Be aware that the more porous the ceramic, the more chances it will stain.

Wood floors are beautiful. They add warmth to a space with the colors and textures of the various wood essences. Unfortunately, the great majority of them are coated in plastic. In order to make them easier to clean and maintain, most manufacturers now add a coat of polyurethane, a plastic-based coating. Even if these types of wood floors are more durable and easier to clean, they wear off over time, which means that microscopic particles of plastic will progressively invade the air you breathe. Instead, look for oiled wooden floors. Although they require more maintenance because you need to re-apply oil when the floors start to fade, they are healthier and offers a matte natural look that shiny polyurethane can't match. We've had oiled larch wood flooring installed in our home and we don't regret it. The extra maintenance is really not that bad.

Furniture

Most upholstered furniture created before 2013 is practically certain to contain flame retardants, thanks to a California law that encouraged the use of them in upholstered furniture (both in the fabric and the polyurethane foam). As of 2015, California law requires new upholstered furniture to have a label indicating whether or not it contains flame retardants, but there is no requirement to specify which chemicals may have been used. So the upshot is that you should ask the manufacturer to be sure. For example, IKEA sells certain furniture that has wool wadding and no flame retardants at all.

As well, the fabric on your furniture may contain a plastic coating for stain prevention. Something else to ask about before making your purchase. Because of its natural flame resistance, wool is a good option and it is also a great moisture barrier. For a cushion without plastic, look for down, natural organic rubber or cotton instead of polyurethane foam.

Window Coverings

It is important to choose natural fibers when choosing to install curtains on your windows as synthetic fabrics such as polyester and nylons tend to be photodegradable with daily exposure to light, thus dispersing plastic microparticules into the air. Natural fabrics such as cotton can be transformed into thick canvas or elegant velours that can block the light very efficiently. Hemp and linen are other fine options.

As for blinds, look for natural Asian paper or blinds made from natural woven wood or bamboo. So many natural stylish options exist that plastic blinds can be easily avoided. Moreover, vinyl blinds may be made of lead-laden PVC.

THE BEDROOM

For seven years following the birth of our son, there was only one bed in our home, the family bed. Because three people, and especially a small child, depended on its safety and comfort, we did not hesitate to invest in the best possible quality for our bed. We had the unbelievable chance to be friends with the owner of one of the most eco-friendly mattress manufacturers in North America, Obasan. Jean Corriveau, president and owner, recommended a natural organic rubber mattress with an organic cotton and wool outer covering to protect the mattress. We spent a lot on our mattress but never regretted it. It was comfortable from day one, and we knew that because it was all natural and organic, it did not emit any VOCs or contain any toxic flame retardants that we would be breathing at night. When you spend a significant part of your day sleeping and in close contact with a surface, it makes sense to ensure it does not slowly make you sick.

The Various Components of a Bed

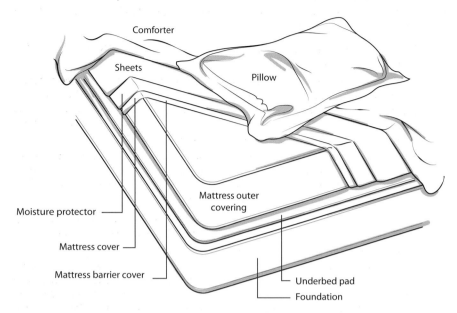

Mattresses can be particularly dangerous as a direct result of the application of U.S. Federal Regulation 16 CFR Part 1633, administered by the U.S. Consumer Product Safety Commission. This federal "Standard for the flammability (open flame) of mattress sets" requires manufacturers to ensure that their mattresses won't burst into flames too quickly.[32] But why would a mattress ignite quickly in the first place? They would if they are made of plastic, which the great majority of mattresses are. Yes, plastic, in the form of highly flammable polyurethane foam. It is so flammable that it is even referred to as "solid gasoline." As a result, manufacturers offering polyurethane mattresses in the United States are required to douse them in significant amounts of flame retardant chemicals to ensure they meet the regulations.

A mattress made of natural rubber and covered with wool is naturally non-flammable and meets the U.S. federal regulation without the addition of chemicals. Manufacturers such as Obasan have conducted their own flammability tests to prove that their mattresses comply with the law and will not combust quickly in the event of a fire. In looking for a natural mattress that is not drenched with chemicals, at least two options exist: natural rubber mattresses or spring mattresses. As far as we know, no memory foam mattresses are completely natural, contrary to misleading information circulating on the web. Read closely between the lines. The natural part might be just the core latex part of the mattress, not the top layer containing the memory foam. Memory foam was originally developed by the U.S National Aeronautics and Space Administration (NASA) and is essentially made of polyurethane. It is the added chemicals that make it comfortable. There is nothing natural about memory foam.

---

32   Although the purpose of the regulation is to prevent ignition with a lit cigarette, the requirement was updated in 2007 from a smoldering ignition source (lit cigarette) to a substantial propane flame directed on the surface of the mattress for at least 70 seconds. This change required mattress manufacturers to add even more flame retardants to their mattresses.

The Various Components of a Bed

A comfortable safe bed requires more than just a natural healthy mattress. There are many layers to a mattress.

- Choose natural materials for the structure holding your mattress, whether it is a box spring, a foundation or a platform.

- An underbed pad prevents premature wear and tear caused by the mattress rubbing against wood bed slats or a rougher type of foundation. It also prevents the undersides of the mattress from being exposed to dust. Wool is the perfect material for an underbed pad because it creates a natural friction that prevents the mattress from easily moving on its base.

- The mattress outer covering is the fabric envelope sewn onto the mattress to protect it. Its composition is indicated on the tag attached to the mattress when it is purchased. Make sure it is made of natural materials. Our mattress outer covering is made of a blend of organic cotton and wool.

- The mattress barrier cover helps prevent dust mites from migrating all the way from the mattress to the sleeper. Opt for tightly woven organic cotton and make sure it fits snugly on your mattress.

- The moisture protector is important to prevent the mattress from absorbing the humidity your body releases during sleep. It also will stop body fluids from entering your mattress so that it remains clean. Cleaning a mattress is difficult, so it is best to prevent any source of moisture from getting to it. Wool is ideal as a naturally antibacterial moisture protection barrier.

- The purpose of the mattress cover is to protect the mattress from spills and stains and to offer extra padding for comfort. Look for cotton flannel for softness, and ensure it is machine washable.

- When choosing sheets, make sure you read the labels very carefully. Most sheets offered in large retail stores are made of a blend of cotton and polyester. Look for 100 percent cotton or even bamboo for softness. If you can afford the luxury, silk is another natural option.

- To stay cozy in bed, opt for a simple wool blanket or choose a comforter that will keep you warm in the winter and cool in summer. There are many plastic-free options for the insulative filler: feathers, down, wool, cotton batting, silk and kapok, even milkweed. Make sure the shell is 100 percent natural whether it is made of cotton or silk. A high thread count will ensure the filling does not come out easily.

- If you can't afford an all-natural high quality mattress, then make sure your pillow is healthy. Your head is in direct contact with your pillow for many hours each day and microscopic particles from your pillow may make their way inside of your lungs when you inhale. Most pillows have synthetic filler made from foam or synthetic plastic fibers. The most common plastic-free options are feathers and down. They are more expensive, but totally worth it. You can also find cotton, silk, wool and even buckwheat as natural fillers. Make sure the cover of your pillow is made of 100 percent natural cotton or silk. Once again, it is so important to read all the labels.

The Baby's Bed

You might think that the regulations on flammability would not apply to baby mattresses. They do, and because children have growing bodies and brains, they are even more vulnerable to the harsh effects of the flame retardant chemicals off-gassing from their mattresses. A May 2013 article published in *Scientific American* described the link between PBDE (polybrominated diphenyl ether) flame retardants and lower IQs in children.[33] Fortunately, these flame retardants have largely been phased out of manufacturing since 2004, but we don't want to wait for conclusive research on the effects of the replacements for PBDE before adopting a precautionary approach.

Plastic-free crib mattresses made of wool, springs and organic coconut coir are available at specialized stores. Once again, beware of "natural" memory foam mattresses that may not be as natural as they seem.

CLOTHING

Unless you're a nudist living year round in a warm climate, clothes likely spend a lot of time right next to your porous skin, the largest organ in your body. And you may not even realize that a lot of the clothes you are wearing are made of plastic. Yes, it may seem strange to think of clothing being made of plastic when we typically envision plastics as hard or filmy materials used to make dishes, bottles, bags and toys. But there are all kinds of plastic fabrics used to make clothes, and these synthetic textiles can be chock full of toxic chemicals, which can penetrate your skin and contribute to serious health issues—an estimated 8,000-plus chemicals are used in the manufacture of clothing.[34]

The most egregious toxins lurking in some common plastic fabrics include endocrine-disrupting phthalates in vinyl, carcinogenic perfluorinated compounds (PFCs) in Gore-Tex[35] (also Scotchguard and Teflon), skin-irritating isocyanates in Spandex and Lycra and carcinogenic thioureas in neoprene.

Going beyond pure plastic fabrics to include semi-synthetics like rayon, and even natural fabrics like cotton, there is a whole slew of other toxic chemicals to be aware of:

- Carcinogenic formaldehyde in fabrics claiming to be wrinkle-resistant or wrinkle-free, stain-resistant, shrink-resistant, anti-static, anti-cling, waterproof, perspiration-proof, moth-proof and mildew resistant.

- Endocrine-disrupting polybrominated diphenyl ethers (PBDEs) used as flame retardants bonded into the fabric and intended to persist for 50+ washings.

- Hormone-disrupting triclosan used as an anti-bacterial agent.

---

33   D.F. Maron (2013) "Flame Retardants Linked to Lower IQs, Hyperactivity in Children", *Scientific American*, 6 May 2013 (accessed 4 March 2017: https://www.scientificamerican.com/article/flame-retardants-linked-lower-iq-hyperactivitiy-children).

34   Anna Maria Clement and Brian Clement, *Killer Clothes: How Seemingly Innocent Clothing Choices Endanger Your Health... And How to Protect Yourself!*, West Palm Beach: Hippocrates Publications, 2011; G. Luonga (2015) "Toxins Remain in Your Clothes," *ScienceDaily* (accessed 4 March 2017: www.sciencedaily.com/releases/2015/10/151023084508.htm).

35   Note that Gore Fabrics has pledged to remove "PFCs of environmental concern" from all their consumer clothing by 2023 (http://www.gore-tex.com/en-us/experience/responsibility/environmental/fluorochemicals) (accessed 4 March 2017). It will be important for them to ensure that the replacement is a sufficiently safe alternative.

- Miniscule silver nanoparticles in some anti-odor, stain-resistant and wrinkle-resistant clothing—the full consequences of these ultra microscopic particles are yet unknown, but they are so tiny they can easily traverse the skin and go straight into your bloodstream to be transported around the body. Note that anything that does go through your skin will initially bypass your liver—the key toxin-removing organ in the body.

Oh wait, we're not done . . . there are also carcinogenic dyes, insecticides, pesticides and fungicides. And you will recall the serious environmental problem we discussed above of microplastic particles from synthetic clothing, such as polyester fleeces, washing down the drain when laundered: they have become a massive global pollutant of our waterways. Besides being inherently toxic plastics, they adsorb toxins in the water and concentrate them up the food chain through aquatic wildlife and right into the bodies of humans who consume fish.

If you have health issues that you are unable to get to the bottom of—things like skin irritation and rashes, itching, chronic fatigue, headaches, breathing difficulty—you may want to take a close look at your clothing (and perhaps bedsheets and towels too) and test out if using natural fibers in place of synthetics makes a difference with your symptoms. It's worth keeping in mind that the synergistic and cumulative effects of a mix of chemicals, such as are found in clothing, may be making you sick.

If, after reading all that, you feel compelled to do a frantic purge of your synthetic clothing, consider keeping things in perspective and going bit by bit—unless of course you are chemically sensitive and you suspect your clothes are clearly worsening your condition. Then drastic action might be worth it. Having experienced chemical sensitivity, we know how debilitating and difficult to diagnose it can be.

All this brings up a few points we want to share, along with a variety of tips to consider when trying to avoid synthetic plastic and other chemically-infused clothing. Note that the Resources section at the end of the book on page 180 provides some suggestions of companies offering healthier, plastic-free clothing.

Use natural fibers as much as possible.

- Cotton: Cotton is soft, breathable and absorbent, and won't retain odors the way synthetics do. As well, you can't blame cotton for static cling because it won't hold a charge. Ideally, you want organic cotton.[36]

- Wool: It's a fabulous insulator, even when wet (it's naturally absorbent), and breathes well, making it comfortable in warm and cold temperatures. And there is no need for added chemicals to give it special properties; it's naturally durable, mold and mildew resistant, wrinkle resistant, non-allergenic and has built-in flame retardant properties. Organic, local or ethically sourced is best.[37]

- Hemp: Similar to cotton, it breathes well and is soft on the skin. Being naturally insect- and mold-resistant, it grows with minimal if any need for fungicides and pesticides. It's still a good idea to try and go for organic hemp—if it is available; it's not that common yet—but even with non-organic, any chemical load likely will be vastly less than synthetics or conventional cotton.

---

36 Conventional cotton crops soak up about 16% of the world's insecticides, more than any other single crop, and many of these highly toxic insect-killing mixtures are confirmed carcinogens and linked to the deaths of cotton workers around the world. See Environmental Justice Foundation & Pesticide Action Network-UK (2007) "The Deadly Chemicals in Cotton," Environmental Justice Foundation (accessed 4 March 2017: http://ejfoundation.org/report/deadly-chemicals-cotton).

37 Pesticide use is high in conventional wool production (applied to sheep to kill parasites such as lice) and cruelty to sheep is a possibility in the harvesting of conventional wool.

- Bamboo: The texture, softness and breathability of bamboo fiber is similar to that of cotton and hemp, but you have to be careful here because not all bamboo clothing is created alike. Similar to hemp, the beauty of bamboo is that it can be grown quickly without the use of pesticides, herbicides or fertilizers. But a lot of bamboo clothing falls more into the fiber category of rayon, which is a semi-synthetic polymer made from practically any plant cellulose using harsh toxic chemicals to break down the cellulose pulp and make it into a fabric. You'll want to be sure the clothing has a Lyocell or Tencel label, which indicates it was made using a much less chemical-intensive, closed-loop process in which the chemical solvents used are recovered.

- Leather: Leather is tough, timeless and trendy. If you are looking to buy a new leather product, then make it a high quality, ethically-sourced one that you can see yourself using for the rest of your life. Or, go used—there is no shortage of amazing leather products in secondhand thrift and vintage stores. Be careful of pleather or faux leather (aka Naugahyde). It may well be toxic PVC; but there are less toxic faux leathers out there for vegans—just be sure to ask what it is made of and to assess its toxicity. Ethically sourced or used are best as leather production can come with some heavy issues attached to it.[38]

- Silk: Silk is a staple in the making of Indian saris and Japanese kimonos. It is soft, smooth and, well, "silky," in its luster and drape. It has powerful properties that make it comfortable to wear when active and in both warm and cold weather: it absorbs moisture well and has low conductivity, which keeps warm air near the skin. The naturally tight weave prevents mosquitoes and flies from biting through it. There is an increasingly popular alternative form of silk, known as "peace silk" that is made in India from the cocoons of moths and does not require killing them. The cocoons are collected once the moth has emerged and flown away.

- Some other possibilities: alpaca, angora, cashmere, jute, linen, merino and mohair.

Note on vegan options: Our purpose with this book is to focus on the issue of plastic toxicity and pollution and offer up safer, less-polluting alternatives, but we do not condone or support cruelty to animals, and we realize that some of you may be seeking strictly vegan clothing alternatives that have no direct impact on animals or any living beings. If that is the case, buying used clothing is an excellent option. You also may wish to take a look at the list of vegan clothing companies compiled by People for the Ethical Treatment of Animals, which suggests vegan alternatives to materials like wool, silk and leather.[39] Just be aware that many of the alternatives are made with plastics (though possibly upcycled for creative reuse, and thus diverted from ending up in a landfill) so you need to do your due diligence to assess the toxicity of vegan alternatives.

MORE PLASTIC-FREE CLOTHING TIPS:

- Do some research. Have a good idea of what you need or want. Look around online for brands that offer plastic-free and ethical alternatives to something you might traditionally find in plastic or with plastic parts. For example, instead of opting for a vinyl raincoat, look into something different you may not have considered, such as wool or leather or waxed cotton oilskin.

---

38   The leather industry, most of which is situated in developing countries, is notoriously polluting and chemical intensive (especially the toxic tanning processes which can be dangerous to workers) and involves using the skin of animals, mostly cows. While the use of the skins can be considered a byproduct of the beef industry (the skins would otherwise go to waste), a growing demand for leather products indicates that 30% more cows will need to be slaughtered by 2025 to meet the demand. See K. Martinko (2016) "Why It's Time to Say Goodbye to Leather," Treehugger.com (accessed 4 March 2017: http://www.treehugger.com/culture/why-its-time-say-goodbye-leather.html).

39   See: http://www.peta.org/living/fashion/cruelty-free-clothing-guide/ (accessed 4 March 2017).

- Start with what touches your skin. Choose natural organic fiber fabrics for the clothing closest to your skin to reduce your potential chemical exposure: underwear, socks, pajamas, tights, camisoles and t-shirts. Many bras tend to have extra foam padding, so seek out ones that are foam-free.

- Embrace your personal style. Find a few high quality items that represent your style. If you don't know what "your" style is, just focus on clothing that makes you feel good when you wear it, and then look at how you can source that type of clothing in plastic-free, non-synthetic ways.

- Go for multi-use, simplicity, versatility, high quality and great fit. Choose beautiful, well-made items that can easily be mixed and matched with other clothes, as opposed to things you might wear a couple of times a year. Quality over quantity. Durable top quality items will last longer and can be more easily repaired (leather, metal belts and buckles). Much better to spend the same amount on a few quality items that will last decades or longer, over a multitude of cheap, toxic threads that don't stand up to wear and that you'll be getting rid of in a year or two. Make sure what you buy fits you to a tee.

- Support causes that sell clothing. You can even hone in on ones that will use the revenue to address plastic toxicity and pollution issues such as Plastic Pollution Coalition, the 5 Gyres Institute and Plastic Ocean.

- Secondhand and vintage clothing (thrift stores, consignment shops, flea markets, Freecycle, Craigslist, Etsy, eBay "pre-owned"). Does this idea make you cringe? Let's debunk a couple of myths straightaway:

  - They're dirty. This is practically never the case in our experience. If the clothes do happen to be dirty, then wash them. And at any rate, any store-bought clothes should be washed, new or secondhand. Brand new clothing may be even dirtier than pre-cleaned used clothing, having been tried on by various folks, or even purchased-worn-never washed-then returned.

  - They're in bad shape. Again, not our experience at all. Most used clothing stores pick and choose only the best to display. You rarely see things with holes or tears (unless it's part of the look). And if they are in bad shape, don't buy them.

Now let's hone in on the compelling advantages of second hand clothes:

  - They are vastly less expensive than new clothes.

  - They may come from estate sales or family donations, so you can find timeless, high quality gems and exclusive designer labels.

  - If you're buying synthetics, used clothing has a huge advantage over new: the clothes will have largely gassed off, thus exposing you to far fewer chemicals.

  - The obvious environmental advantages: you are reusing; no new resources (or chemicals!) are implicated; no transport and energy inputs required.

- Make your own clothes using natural fibers. Just be sure to do your diligence on the fabric you buy, ensuring it is certified organic and from a trusted source.

- Give away clothes you no longer wear. Friends, family, co-workers, people in need in your community, Goodwill. Organize a regular clothing swap with your friends.

- Repurpose or recycle clothing that is worn out. Don't throw it in the garbage. At the very least, use it as a rag. Patagonia has excellent DIY repair guides for its clothing and even goes on tours to university campuses with its funky "Worn Wear" mobile repair truck offering free clothing repair lessons and services.[40]

---

40 See: https://www.patagonia.com/worn-wear-repairs (accessed 4 March 2017).

If it's synthetic and you just want to get rid of it, contact the manufacturer to ask how best to recycle or dispose of it with the least environmental impact. Maybe they can recycle it. As we consistently preach, recycling should be a last resort, just ahead of disposing of something in the trash. For recycling, Goodwill provides large recycling bins for both natural and synthetic clothing. And of course, there is always the The Freecycle Network, the largest reuse and recycling web hub in the world, where you can find a local group to help you reuse and recycle.[41]

- What about shoes? Not much different from clothes. The same issues and characteristics apply, in some ways even more so. They are often a plastic-heavy, synthetic chemical dump we carry around on our feet, especially sports shoes. It's pretty impossible from what we can tell to avoid sports shoes with plastic, so the best bet is to buy a high-quality pair that fit you well, and use them for as long as you possibly can, then recycle them (see the Sports Shoe section in Chapter 5, page 151).

- Bring your bags. If you are going out clothes shopping, whether for new or used apparel, don't forget to bring your own reusable bags for carrying home your wares. If you forget your bags, you can simply use some of the clothing you purchase to create a bundle.

BABIES AND KIDS

It is often when having children that we start being concerned about toxins in our environment. This wee person becomes more important than even our own selves and we want the best for her or him. That's what happened to us. It is really when our son was born that we started being worried about all the plastic products he was in contact with and wondering how safe they were. From toys to sippy cups, everything seemed to be made of plastic.

Cloth Diapering

One decision we made early on was to use cloth diapers, not only because we wanted to avoid contact with the numerous chemicals contained in popular brands of disposable diapers that could cause rashes or irritation on our baby's soft skin, but we also wanted to limit the amount of disposable plastics we generated. In 2014, 3.6 million tons (3.3 million tonnes) of disposable diapers were generated in the United States, according to the Environmental Protection Agency.[42] That's a lot of very gross, toxic, smelly plastic!

Cloth diapering has evolved in the past 30 years and it is actually much easier than many might think to switch to cloth. There are a lot of cloth diapering systems to choose from, and figuring out what's the best for you and your baby may appear overwhelming. Here is a brief overview of the main systems.

There are two types of cloth diaper systems: 1-step and 2-step. The traditional one is the 2-step cloth diaper system. It involves the use of an absorbent layer protected with a waterproof diaper cover. Unsurprisingly, the great majority of diaper covers are made of plastic, generally nylon or even, incredibly, toxic polyvinyl chloride (PVC). As far as we know, wool is the only natural, plastic-free waterproof material

41   See: https://www.freecycle.org (accessed 4 March 2017).

42   U.S. Environmental Protection Agency, "Advancing Sustainable Materials Management: 2014 Tables and Figures," December 2016, p. 25.

The 2-Step Cloth Diaper System

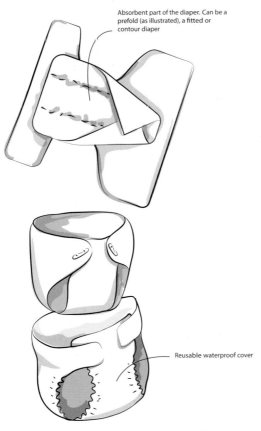

Absorbent part of the diaper. Can be a prefold (as illustrated), a fitted or contour diaper

Reusable waterproof cover

that works well as a diaper cover. We recommend wool covers with snap buttons instead of the slip-on ones that are difficult to put on and a bit uncomfortable for the baby.

The 1-step resembles the disposable diaper because it combines the absorbent layer and the waterproof layer in one diaper. As of the time of writing, we still have not found any 1-step diaper systems without plastic. Avoid the popular pocket system which often uses microfleece for the pocket part and is notorious for generating hundreds of microscopic plastic particles every time they are washed.

For plastic-free shopping options, see Cloth Diapers in the Resources section (page 180).

Toys

On November 10th, 2010, we posted a YouTube video on our blog showing a very cute little nine-month-old baby, interacting with his toys in a playroom.[43] It's a time lapse video taped over a four-hour period. The baby puts a plastic toy in his mouth about 300 times over the span of the video. And that's only four hours in the life of this baby. Because babies are curious and enjoy discovering the world through their mouths, it is extremely important to ensure they are not chewing on plastics.

Many options are now available thanks to the power of the Internet, but you may not be able to find them at large toy store chains. The mainstream stores are palaces of cheap plastic toys. Rows and rows of plastic junk that will end up in a landfill in the next year or so, because plastic toys are often such low quality that they break easily and don't necessarily get passed down to the next sibling. Look for wooden trucks, silk fairy dresses, wool felt fake fruits and vegetables. Some online stores specialize in natural toys, and the selection is impressive.

Because children love to imitate their parents, another toy theme to consider is mini versions of adult tools such as mini baking kits, mini gardening kits and mini tool kits . . . all made of natural materials such as wood, metal and natural fibers. These items can continue to be used by the parents even after the child has grown into other types of games.

---

43   See the video here: https://youtu.be/8vNxjwt2AqY (accessed 4 March 2017).

Dishes

If you're cautious about not exposing your children to plastic toys, you'll likely also want to ensure they are not eating their food and drinking out of plastic cups, plates and bowls. Stainless steel dishes are the best plastic-free option for many reasons. There is the obvious avoidance of leaching chemicals. But another key one is that, contrary to glass or ceramic, they won't break if they fall on the floor. They are extremely durable and can be passed on to the next generation. They can be repurposed as camping dishes. They have a positive recycling value, meaning you can get money for taking stainless steel items to an industrial recycler. And very importantly, they can be completely sterilized at high temperature in a dishwasher.

Unfortunately, most childcare centers don't use stainless steel, and must instead use chemical sanitizing solutions to sterilize dishes between meals. Melamine[44] dishes are often the dishes of choice for such centers because each dish piece is so inexpensive. However, this is a short-term saving because melamine dishes wear out quickly and discolor over time. A child care center director who supervises four child care centers told us he needs to replace parts of his dish inventory every six months. Consider recommending stainless steel dishes to your daycare center or request that your child be allowed to use her own stainless steel dishes.

Clothing

When it comes to children's clothing, it is especially important to choose sleepwear made of natural fabrics because of a flammability regulation in force in the United States. This law requires children's sleepwear sized above nine months and up to size fourteen to pass certain flammability tests or be sufficiently tight fitting.[45] Various chemicals are added to pajama fabrics to meet these standards, including chlorinated and brominated flame retardants. These particular flame retardants tend to accumulate in the body and they do not wash out of clothes easily because the regulations require the chemicals to be able to sustain at least 50 washes. All pajamas made of synthetic fabrics contain flame retardants.

The best way to avoid them is to avoid synthetic fabrics such as polyester and nylon. Instead, purchase a snug-fitting natural fiber pajama, such as organic cotton. Snug-fitting sleepwear meets the flammability standard because it is sufficiently close to the body that no loose fabric can catch fire easily. Non-organic cotton pajamas will likely still contain flame retardants. Another good textile for pajamas is wool because it is naturally flame retardant.

THE HOME OFFICE

As owners of an online business, we spend a lot of time working from our home. We strive for plastic-free office spaces, but we haven't been able to find non-plastic alternatives for some of the most important elements of a home office; for example, our printers.

Printers

We own more than one printer and we have gone through a few over the years. They just aren't built to last. In fact, the business model of the home printer industry is based on waste. You can easily find an inexpensive printer, but you must buy the expensive

---

44   See the section in Chapter 3 on the dangers of melamine plastics.

45   See Code of Federal Regulations at 16 CFR Part 1615 for children's sleepwear sized above 9 months and up to 6X, and at 16 CFR Part 1616 for children's sleepwear sized 7 through 14 (accessed 4 March 2017: https://www.law.cornell.edu/cfr/text/16/part-1615).

plastic cartridges for the rest of the life cycle of the printer. This is how printer makers generate ongoing profits. The plastic cartridges are very pricey, sometimes up to a 1,000 percent markup. A cheap piece of plastic containing a little bit of ink goes for $20 to 25 apiece but probably costs less than two dollars to make. Recently, companies such as Epson have introduced to the market printers with large ink tanks that only need to be refilled once a year or less. When refilling the tanks, you must purchase a bottle of ink. Although the ink refill is packaged in a plastic bottle, this system allows you to save several disposable plastic ink cartridges.

Another option is to get your cartridges refilled by a specialized shop. Retail chain Costco offers this service. Supported brands include HP, Canon, Epson and Brother printers. Finally, if you are a DIY kind of person, you can purchase a refill kit where you can inject ink into an empty cartridge using a syringe-type of device. We've tried it a few times and it can be messy, but it works. The kits are widely available at major retail chains and online.

Stationery

Millions of plastic ballpoint pens are sold every year and thrown away. Because of its multiple components, the plastic pen is hard to recycle. Instead, consider a fountain pen with a refillable cartridge and a bottle of ink. Discover the joy of handwriting again! If you like to use various colors of ink, a glass pen might be just for you. They retain the ink in thin grooves along the glass nib and you can easily change the color after a quick rinse of the pen.

Glue is simple to make with equal parts flour and sugar and then just add water to get it to a pasty consistency. Or you could go for the Italian-made Coccoina almond paste all-natural glue in a metal tin.

PETS

Let's start with the messy stuff. Pet waste is a tricky one to deal with. You don't want to put it in your own home composter as it could contaminate the future compost soil. Chances are your municipal composting program won't accept it because of bacteria and disease contamination issues. You don't want to use a compostable bag and send it to the landfill because of the potential generation of undesired methane. And as well, some municipalities prohibit disposing of pet waste through the municipal garbage system. So assuming there is nowhere for your pet to run wild and do their thing au naturel, then from our perspective you have a few options, depending on what's available where you live: (1) use a composting pet waste toilet (yes, they do exist); (2) discard it in your home toilet; (3) use a pet waste collection service (yes, they do exist in big cities); or (4) take it to a central pet waste composting depot (yes, they do exist—there's an impressive one called EnviroWagg in Denver, Colorado).

As for transporting the pet waste, compostable baggies or paper bags are great if you're going to be composting it. If not, you could consider designating a little bucket or a container with a lid and a carrying handle as the poop container you take with you on walks to collect the poop. Once back home, just flush it in the bathroom toilet. This will require regular washing after each walk, but completely eliminates the need for bags.

Regarding food, try to purchase in bulk and in compostable paper packaging if possible. Serving it up can be done in stainless steel or ceramic bowls, both for the food and water. A multi-layer (at least two) tiffin is a very handy pet travel kit. It has a built-in carrying handle, and can include a container for a dry food, or wet food and once you've arrived at your destination, or en route, you can set up a portable water station with another layer of the container. Airtight stainless steel containers can also be handy for transporting more liquidy wet foods.

Try to steer clear of pet toys made of plastics and synthetic fibers, for exactly the same reasons they are not recommended for children. They go straight in the mouth and will be chewed and likely torn and ripped over time. Go for natural toy materials like organic cotton, hemp, rope, wood and wool.

Grooming brushes are available made of wood and natural bristles. For example, a wooden dog grooming brush may have one side with hard wooden bristles to get out knots and tangles, and the other side light plant fiber bristles to smooth Rover's coat to a sheen. As for cats, most love to be groomed, if they feel like it and are in the mood, and don't have something better to do like lounging or sleeping, or ignoring tedious humans. A wooden brush with soft plant fiber bristles avoids the standard plastic fare.

THE GARDEN

Growing your own food is an excellent way to decrease the single-use plastic packaging you bring into your home—not to mention the phenomenal health benefits of fresh, local and organic produce, combined with the deep satisfaction of working the soil with your own hands to feed yourself and your family. Given the complex mix of toxic chemicals in plastics that can leach into the soil and contaminate your lovingly nurtured fruits and veggies, it makes sense to use as little plastic as possible when you garden.

Plastic-free living experts Beth Terry and Lindsay Miles have wonderful posts on their blogs about their experiences with plastic-free gardening, and we highly suggest checking them out, especially if you are starting from scratch in creating your own garden and want to use as little plastic as possible.[46] Based on some of their tips as well as others we have picked up from friends and our own experience and research, we've compiled a basic list of ways to garden with less plastic:

- Garden tools: Wooden and metal tools—trowels, shovels, hoes, pitchforks, pails and wheelbarrows—are quite easy to find in a standard garden or hardware store, or purchase secondhand (Kijiji, Craigslist). Better yet, borrow from a friend, neighbor or a local tool lending library.

- Soil beds: If you don't already have garden beds with fertile organic soil to start with, you'll need to create them. This is quite easy to do using either pots or planters or building a simple raised bed with wooden planks that have not been treated with any chemicals—remember that whatever touches the soil can end up in the plants.

- The soil: If you're buying a small amount of soil it's pretty hard to avoid it being packaged in plastic bags. And if you don't have your own compost, you may need to purchase compost or manure to provide needed nutrients for your soil, again usually packaged in plastic. One way around this is to buy in bulk together with neighbors. If you do go the route of buying soil in bags, then try and recycle the bags if they are recyclable in your area (you'll need to clean them first). As the weight of soil is substantial, these plastic bags are pretty heavy-duty thick polyethylene plastic, so it is such a waste when they are simply thrown in the garbage. Lindsay Miles came across an interesting

---

46   Beth Terry, My Plastic Free Life: Gardening Without Plastic, Parts 1-3 (accessed 4 March 2017: https://myplasticfreelife.com/2011/05/gardening-without-plastic-part-1; https://myplasticfreelife.com/2011/07/gardening-without-plastic-part-2-planting-and-replanting; https://myplasticfreelife.com/2011/07/gardening-without-plastic-part-3-mulching-and-watering; https://myplasticfreelife.com/2012/04/3-cool-tips-for-plastic-free-gardening). Lindsay Miles, Treading My Own Path: Zero Waste (+ Plastic Free) Gardening (accessed 4 March 2017: http://treadingmyownpath.com/2016/06/09/zero-waste-plastic-free-gardening).

compromise that significantly decreases the plastic waste: coconut coir, which is a waste product from coconut harvesting. A foot-square block of the stuff will expand into a wheelbarrow full of potting filler that can be mixed with soil, compost, manure or fertilizers for added nutrients.

- Pots and planters: Over the years we have accumulated quite a collection of pots and planters, some plastic and some terracotta clay. We definitely prefer the clay ones, but still use some of the plastic ones for flowers. Most such plastic pots and planters are made of either polypropylene (PP, #5) or high density polyethylene (HDPE, #2), both of which are higher quality plastics that are recyclable. If you are buying plants in planters and have no use for the plastic containers (say you are transplanting them to other pots you already have), return them for reuse to the store or nursery where you purchased the plants. There are bioplastic planters made from renewable grain fibers such as rice husks; they can last several years and are compostable in a municipal composting facility. As well, you can find molded fiber pots and planters made from recycled waste paper, which are designed to last about a season, and can be planted directly in the soil.

- Seeds: It is easy to find seeds packaged in paper envelopes. Any garden store will have an array of choices, or a quick Internet search for organic seeds will reveal lots of options for high quality, non–genetically modified seeds. Better yet, buy quality seeds in bulk and trade them with friends and neighbors. Once your garden is rolling you can save seeds from your harvest to use the following year—store them in glass jars.

Use a metal soil blocker to create plastic-free seedlings. No need for a plastic tray.

- Seedling containers: Seedlings are notorious for being grown in thin cheap polystyrene (PS) or expanded polystyrene (styrofoam) plastic molds. Both are plastic recycling symbol #6, and are best avoided whenever possible because they leach styrene. Not only is the plastic toxic, but it is so thin in this application that the containers easily tear, and crumble, making them useless for reuse (not that you would want to anyway for food plants, given the toxicity). Plus, polystyrene plastics are minimally recycled. There are, fortunately, several DIY plastic-free options:

  - Soil blocker: This is the cookie cutter of gardening and it totally eliminates the need for any type of plastic tray or container. You use the soil blocker device to create little cubes of soil with a hole in the middle where you insert your seeds. Then add a final layer of soil and let them sprout away, or just plant them directly in the final soil if you don't need to wait for a sprout.

  - Paper egg carton or toilet paper rolls: The little compartments in egg cartons are the perfect size for starting seedlings, and once they've sprouted you can just cut or tear them apart and plant them directly in the soil. Or you can make little pots from cardboard toilet paper rolls by making four even cuts with scissors about a quarter of the way up one side of the tube and then folding them up to create the bottom of the your seed pot. In both cases, the carton biodegrades naturally in the soil

  - Paper seedling containers: You can make your own little seedling containers by rolling a long strip of newspaper or kraft paper (about 4 to 5 inches [10 to 13 cm] wide) around the bottom of a concave-bottomed wine bottle and then fold and scrunch up the bottom to make a little pot. If you just Google "newspaper seedling pots" various sites come up with images and videos of how to do this. The only issue here is the ink on the newspaper. If you don't like the idea of that ink going into the soil, then best to use some repurposed kraft packing paper. Definitely avoid colored newspaper as the colored ink contains more additives, which may include heavy metals.

- Plant label sticks: When you buy seedlings or plants from a garden store or nursery they generally come with little plastic stick labels identifying the plant. These are usually made of polystyrene plastic. There have been times when we've ended up with oodles of them and relegated them to the recycling bin, knowing that they will likely end up in a landfill. A better solution would be to try and take them back to the nursery where you bought the plants so they can reuse them. If you're growing all your own plants from seed or seedlings, once they are in the ground you can identify them using hand-labeled popsicle sticks, or a twig with an empty seed pouch stuck on it.

- Mulch: What's mulch, you ask? It's something you put on top of the soil all around your plants to prevent weeds from coming up, while keeping the soil moist. Some common forms of mulch include organic straw, untreated grass clippings and leaves. But black plastic sheeting is also commonly used, especially on long rows of plants, because it not only keeps weeds down, but also warms the soil and keeps it moist. The problem is that the sun constantly beating down on the plastic increases potential leaching of chemicals into the soil. There are now some bioplastic mulches out there that claim to be 100 percent biodegradable, but as we indicated in the Bioplastics section (page 53) you have to be very careful about biodegradability and compostability claims in the bioplastics realm. It could be a bioplastic that is really just plastic that breaks down faster, or it could be a plant-based bioplastic that is chock full of additives, just like petroleum-based plastics. Best to go with natural mulch if you can, as it's guaranteed to biodegrade and feed the soil with rich nutrients.

- Watering: We love our galvanized steel watering can, and that is definitely our watering tool of choice through the summer months. That said, when you have a lot of plants spread all around your property, you may prefer a hose. We actually also have two hoses. A polyurethane one and a rubber one, both of which we purchased years ago. First we got the polyurethane one thinking it was a good choice because it wasn't highly toxic polyvinyl chloride (PVC), which is definitely to be avoided—PVC hoses leach lead and endocrine-disrupting phthalates. We needed a second hose to be able to reach right around our house, so we got the rubber one thinking it was a better choice than polyurethane. Then we read Beth Terry's blog post on plastic-free gardening where she explains that most rubber hoses are not made of natural rubber, but rather of petroleum-derived, synthetic ethylene propylene diene monomer (EPDM) rubber. Should have done our research better. And then there are the hose fittings, possibly made of brass, which may contain leachable lead. You also want to avoid hoses that might have an antimicrobial or antifungal treatment such as Microban or Microshield, which likely contains hormone-disrupting triclosan. And there's the possibility of bisphenol A as well. It's just one thing after another with garden hoses! As we have not yet come across a natural rubber hose, the upshot seems to be that the best hose choice is currently a lead-free, BPA-free, phthalate-free, FDA drinking water safe-approved, polyurethane hose. Yes, it's plastic, but it appears to be the lesser of all evils at the moment. You can find some possibilities under Garden in the Resources section (page 181).

- Compost, compost, compost! If you can find a way to compost your organic waste, do it, whether it's a full compost bin in your backyard or a vermiculture red wiggler worm composting bin in your apartment. You will be amazed how much composting decreases your waste in general. If you have the space, it's easy to set up a composter.[47] You can find lots of home composters out there made of plastic, but you can also easily build your own. It's basically just a box that can breathe and be opened at the top and bottom. We built our own out of four old wooden pallets and some plywood, and it's still standing, surviving and thriving after ten years.

Composting with your own home composter or through a municipal system goes hand-in-hand with plastic-free living and overall waste reduction.

---

47 The U.S. Composting Council and the Compost Council of Canada both provide a world of composting resources on their respective sites: http://compostingcouncil.org/resources; http://www.compost.org (accessed 4 March 2017).

CHAPTER 5

PLASTIC-FREE LIVING
ON THE GO

PACKING A LUNCH

Convenient and processed, pre-packaged foods have taken over the lunch boxes of many children and adults these past few decades, and this has become an enormous source of disposable plastics.

Sandwich

Let's start with the sandwich. So many options now exist for packing a sandwich without plastic. The first question to ask is if it's a "juicy" sandwich. If not, then a fabric bag is a good option. There are cotton and hemp options, but recently we've discovered juco as an excellent material to pack a sandwich. Juco is a blend of jute and cotton. It's less absorbent than cotton and thus preferable for reusing the bag several times between washings. It's stiff like jute, but still very flexible. These natural fabric bags can be washed in the washing machine and reused over and over. Look for closures made with a metal snap button, metal zipper, cotton string, wooden button or other plastic-free material. Plastic velcro, snap buttons and zippers do not biodegrade, so try to make sure the entire bag is plastic-free. Glass or stainless steel containers also work well for sandwiches, but if it's juicy sandwich, airtight is best. Not only will it prevent a spill, but it will retain the integrity of the sandwich.

Juice

The individual juice box with a little plastic straw packaged in a little plastic sleeve stuck to the box with a glue dot is a significant source of lunch box plastic waste. Despite claims from the Tetra Pak company that their containers are recyclable, few municipal programs accept them. It's very easy to just pour some juice in a stainless steel drinking bottle and throw a reusable straw in the lunch bag. Choose a drinking bottle with a lid that has a stainless steel interior.

Snacks

So many store-bought lunch snacks are wrapped individually—in plastic. Think of yogurt, cookies, trail mix, fruit leathers and pretzels. You can even find crackers and cheese in side-by-side plastic compartments and a mini plastic stick to apply the cheese to the crackers. Crazy!

Homemade snacks simply take a little planning, and it's now easy to find a wide assortment of stainless steel containers to carry all shapes and sizes of snacks. There are divided square boxes, airtight round boxes, small containers for dip or hummus, and even airtight containers with dividers or an inner plate to separate various types of food.

Warm Food

When we first started our business, all stainless steel thermoses had plastic inside the lid, which was problematic because warmth triggers more leaching from the plastic into the food. Warm food steam condenses on the lid and that condensation drips back into the food. There are now several brands of thermoses with stainless steel on the interior of the lid. So before you buy a thermos, be sure to check what the interior of the lid is made of.

Keep it Cool

Ice packs are generally encased in plastic and contain soft gels made of a mix of water, hydroxyethyl cellulose and sodium polyacrylate and their only purpose for existing is to be an ice pack. When they tear or are broken, they can't be recycled and go straight into a landfill.

A few years ago, we suggested in one of our blog posts to freeze some applesauce in a small airtight stainless steel container overnight and then use the frozen container as an ice pack and a healthy treat for your kids. This method works really well, but if you find that a food container takes too much room in the lunch bag, we have another suggestion. Use a stainless steel flask—yes, the same ones known for harboring liquor and slipping innocuously into a hip or coat pocket. Fill it with plain drinkable water up to about 80 percent capacity and freeze it overnight. If you are sending the flask in your child's lunch, it may be a good idea to write your child's name on the flask with a marker (even permanent marker ink can be washed away on stainless steel) and perhaps the words "100% WATER CONTENT" or something like that . . . just in case the teacher wonders . . .

Lunch Bags

When searching for an eco-friendly lunch bag that is good for the Earth and your health, you may come across "neoprene" lunch bags. They have beautiful fashionable shapes and patterns and they claim to be eco-friendly, but this is debatable, apart from their reusability. Neoprene is a petroleum-based product that is not biodegradable. Even worse, when it degrades, it tends to break down into dust-like particles that float in the air and can end up in your lungs. As far as we know, neoprene is not recyclable. It appears the "eco-friendliness" of neoprene lunchbags comes from what they are not, rather that what they are. They do not contain lead or polyvinyl chloride (PVC). That's it. In our books, this is green-washing. We prefer products whose claim to eco-friendliness is about what they are—durable, natural, recyclable, biodegradable and healthy—rather than what they are not.

Apart from neoprene bags, the great majority of lunch bags or boxes are insulated with a layer of aluminum foil fused with expanded polyethylene foam material. The casing is often made of polyester. Be especially mindful that some cheap lunch boxes—generally from China—may have a polyvinyl chloride (PVC) exterior, which may contain lead. None of these materials are really recyclable, and they are not easily repairable. Chances are, after a year or so of use, you may want to replace it and it will end up in a landfill.

LUNCH ACCESSORIES

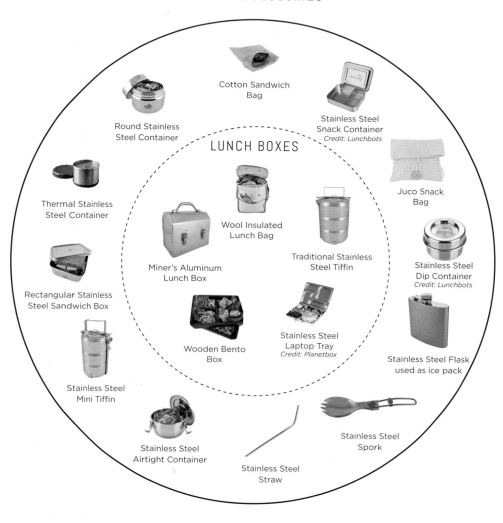

LUNCH BOXES

Cotton Sandwich Bag

Round Stainless Steel Container

Stainless Steel Snack Container
Credit: Lunchbots

Thermal Stainless Steel Container

Juco Snack Bag

Wool Insulated Lunch Bag

Traditional Stainless Steel Tiffin

Stainless Steel Dip Container
Credit: Lunchbots

Miner's Aluminum Lunch Box

Rectangular Stainless Steel Sandwich Box

Wooden Bento Box

Stainless Steel Laptop Tray
Credit: Planetbox

Stainless Steel Flask used as ice pack

Stainless Steel Mini Tiffin

Stainless Steel Airtight Container

Stainless Steel Straw

Stainless Steel Spork

The key is to use a durable lunch bag made of natural materials that is easily repairable and washable. A good option is a wool-insulated cotton lunch bag with metal zippers.

Other excellent plastic-free options include metal lunch boxes, such as the traditional aluminum miner's lunch box. Then there is the stainless steel laptop lunch box, which opens like a laptop. It tends to be a favorite with children and adults alike.

Finally, there are elegant wooden Japanese bento boxes that are works of art. They generally come in two parts with small compartments to separate various types of food. You may find them finished with traditional *urushi*, which is a natural lacquer. When it hardens, it seals and waterproofs the wood, just like a chemical-based varnish. They are hand-crafted, and generally quite expensive.

Return of the Tiffin

Dabbawallas, which literally means "box carriers" in Hindi, have been part of the Mumbai landscape for well over a century. Warm homemade meals are transported to Indian workers every day. Traditionally, the wife would prepare the meal for her husband and have it hand delivered by the dabbawallas in a metal layered tiffin. The dabbawallas are still active today in the streets of Mumbai, with meals generally prepared by catering businesses or restaurants.

We have a wholesale client located in Paris who contacted us about five years ago with the idea of launching a food delivery service using our airtight stainless steel containers. The name of his business is *Les Marmites Volantes*, which literally means "the flying cooking pots."[1] They deliver the food containers filled with delicious meals and customers return the containers when a new delivery arrives. Since then, similar initiatives[2] have appeared in North America using anything from mason jars[2] to traditional Indian stainless steel layered tiffins.[3]

We use stainless steel tiffins of various sizes when creating our daily lunches. We often use a small two-layer one that we fill, for example, with fresh cut vegetables in one compartment and hummus in the other.

Utensils and Straws

Don't forget to include stainless steel utensils in the lunch bag if the type of food included requires them. Metal utensils from home work just fine, as does a compact stainless steel "spork"—a spoon and fork in one. A glass or stainless steel straw may be a good idea as well to prevent the temptation of getting a disposable plastic one at the cafeteria. Glass ones are much tougher than you may think, and generally come with lifetime replacement warranties. You can find stainless steel ones that come in a pouch with a handy brush for immediate cleaning.

RESTAURANTS AND TAKEOUT

In November 2016, four non-profit conservation organizations launched "The Plastics BAN (Better Alternatives Now) List," which identifies the most harmful plastic products used in California, both in terms of toxicity and pollution.[4] Practically all of the products highlighted are "to-go" items such as takeout containers, beverage bottles, caps and lids, straws and food wrapping. Another core finding of this study was that many of these products are plastics manufactured with toxic chemicals. This was a California snapshot, but the findings are equally applicable to the rest of the world, including the fact that safer, more sustainable alternatives are currently widely available for virtually all products on the list.

So how to go about tackling the ubiquitous plastic offenders on the BAN List while out and about eating and drinking?

1   See http://www.marmitesvolantes.com/marmites (accessed 4 March 2017).

2   See http://Ancolie.co located in Greenwich Village, New York City (accessed 4 March 2017).

3   See http://currymobile.ca located in Ottawa, Canada (accessed 4 March 2017).

4   The Plastics Ban (Better Alternatives Now) List was researched and drafted by The 5 Gyres Institute, Clean Production Action, Surfrider Foundation and UPSTREAM, and is available here: http://5gyres.org/s/PlasticsBANList2016-11-4.pdf (accessed 4 March 2017).

All it takes is a little planning. Basically, you just need to pass your intended destinations through a plastic-free filter before you head out. Whether you're going to a restaurant or takeout place, think about the single-use disposable plastics you may come in contact with: plastic cups, plastic stir sticks, styrofoam food containers, plastic water bottles, plastic utensils and straws. Then consider what you need to bring with you to avoid using or coming home with any disposable plastic. There are alternatives. You just need to adopt them and carry them with you. We'll go through the most common and worst offenders.

Water Bottles and Coffee & Tea Mugs

For years before we became "plastic-aware" we would reuse single-use disposable water bottles over and over, washing them religiously and using them until they were cracked and practically crumbling. Our instinct was good: fill a "reusable" beverage container with tap water rather than continually purchase bottled water. But the execution required some adjustment.

Here are a few reasons to opt for tap water over bottled water:

- The obvious: Exposure to plastic chemicals. Most single-use bottles are made from polyethylene terephthalate (recycling symbol #1), which may leach the possible carcinogen antimony trioxide.

- Even though the recycling rates for plastic single-use water bottles are relatively high, they are still a significant source of plastic waste in the environment.

- Tap water is more regulated than bottled water, with regular monitoring and testing done by municipalities. The $170 billion global bottled water industry is largely self-policing, with water quality monitoring and testing being essentially voluntary.[5]

- Tap water in North America is generally safe, but you should check your local source. If you are concerned about your home tap water, consider having it tested, and if necessary, get a water filter.[6]

- Tap water is extremely inexpensive. Bottled water comes at a significant cost to the consumer, even though the bottled water company may have paid little or nothing for the water it has bottled.

- Bottled water may just be tap water that has been refiltered, as is the case with Dasani and Aquafina.[7]

Water refilling stations are becoming more and more common at public venues like airports and universities. Concerts and festivals ranging from Bonnaroo Music & Arts Festival to The Winnipeg Folk Festival have gone bottled water–free, encouraging festival goers to fill up their own reusable bottles or mugs at water filling stations throughout the festival site.

So what are the best plastic-free options for water bottles and coffee or tea mugs? (For specific product brand ideas see Bottles and Mugs in the Resources section, page 181.)

---

5   K. Stastna (2014) "Bottle vs. Tap: 7 Things to Know About Drinking Water," CBC News (accessed 3 March 2017: http://www.cbc.ca/news/health/bottle-vs-tap-7-things-to-know-about-drinking-water-1.2774182).

6   The Environmental Working Group has created a handy Water Filter Buying Guide (but note that many of the options are plastic): http://www.ewg.org/research/ewgs-water-filter-buying-guide (accessed 3 March 2017).

7   V. Tong (2007) "Aquafina Source Is Same as for Tap" Washingtonpost.com (http://www.washingtonpost.com/wp-dyn/content/article/2007/07/27/AR2007072701962.html).

- Glass: The main pros of glass bottles and mugs are: they are completely inert so they do not leach any toxins (as long as the glass is lead-free, which is likely the case unless perhaps you're drinking from a leaded crystal vase); they don't impart any flavors; and you can see what you're drinking through the glass. The major cons are fragility and weight (glass can be heavy, especially thick-walled bottles). Mason jars are wonderful and can be both a water bottle and mug (and food container!).

- Ceramic: Ceramic has the same pros and cons as glass, with the additional con of some extra weight and the additional pro of potential for unique artistic flair. They are often functional works of art, shaped and glazed by hand. You'll want to be sure the glazes used are lead-free.

- Stainless Steel: For water bottles, stainless steel is our go-to choice hands down. And for many it's the go-to choice for both water bottle and to-go mug. It's light, tough and safe.

Regarding travel mugs, most have plastic parts, be it the handle or casing or lid, or all of the above. We have not yet found a stainless steel travel mug with no plastic. A plastic-free lid with an adjustable sip hole would be fantastic so that the liquid has no contact with plastic. Most lids are currently made of polypropylene (recycling #5), which is a more stable plastic, but still not ideal, especially as it is in direct sustained contact with boiling hot liquids.

Be aware that there are a lot of aluminum bottles on the market that may look like stainless steel, though feel a little lighter. Because aluminum readily reacts with food and drink, aluminum bottles and the ubiquitous aluminum food and drink cans have a thin interior lining that is generally made of a BPA-based plastic epoxy. Some such linings have been changed to BPA-free plastics, but that is no guarantee that these new plastics are safe given that many BPA-free plastics exhibit endocrine-disrupting activity as well. We consider aluminum to be a potent toxin as it has been linked to various central nervous system disorders.[8] So we take a precautionary approach and prefer to simply avoid it.

Once you've got your bottle and mug, the key is to remember to bring them with you wherever you go. A carabiner can be a handy memory-relieving tool to attach your bottle or mug, or both, to a bag or backpack so they are always there, pre-attached as you head out the door.

Some coffee shops will give a discount when you provide your own mug. We prefer to support small, local, independent coffee shops—and in our experience there is never an issue with bringing your own mug to such cozy havens—but it's worth noting that some of the larger chains are starting to encourage the bring-your-own-mug movement as well. Starbucks offers $0.10 off and Tim Horton's in Canada gives a 10 percent discount for mug-toting customers.

Food Containers

In Quebec, Canada, there is a unique and popular fast food dish called "poutine," which consists of French fries with a layer of lumpy cheese curds on them, smothered in gravy. It's a staple at little takeout restaurants and stands, and is commonly served up in plastic styrofoam single-use disposable takeout containers. Seeing this always makes us cringe. Not only because of the single-use waste, but also because of the toxic soup it creates with the hot oily poutine being contained

8   C.A. Shaw et al. (2014) "Aluminum-Induced Entropy in Biological Systems: Implications for Neurological Disease," *Journal of Toxicology* 2014:491316; C.A. Shaw and L. Tomljenovic (2013) "Aluminum in the Central Nervous System (CNS): Toxicity in Humans and Animals, Vaccine Adjuvants, and Autoimmunity," *Immunologic Research* 56(2-3):304-316.

The ultra-versatile mason jar: cool lemonade, salad to go and hot java.

in polystyrene. The heat of the fries mixed with oily cheese and scalding hot gravy are help to make that grease-laden poutine much more unhealthy than it already is as chemicals leach out of the styrofoam. It's a perfect example of the importance of bringing your own takeout container to reduce your disposable plastics footprint *and* to safeguard your health!

Here are a few tools to help make your takeout or restaurant experience plastic-free:

- Mason jars: Have mason jar, will travel. Hello takeout and leftovers. Enough said. You know by now how we feel about the versatile, uber-accessible and low-cost mason jar.

- Airtight glass and stainless steel containers: When you're on the go, there can be nothing handier than an airtight, watertight container to confidently contain the saucy juices of your lasagna or balsamic and goat cheese salad. Whether round, square, rectangular or oval, they have a silicone seal and the lid either snugly screws on or clamps down tightly. There are glass options with stainless steel lids and you can easily find glass Pyrex containers with plastic clip-on lids (usually the relatively stable polypropylene #5). While the plastic lids are not ideal, these accessible containers can be a perfectly suitable option to eliminate plastic waste in transporting takeout and leftovers from restaurant to home. Just try and avoid the food touching the plastic lid.

- Insulated stainless steel containers: Can't finish your lunch chowder or chili, but you want to keep it warm for a late afternoon snack? The best insulated stainless steel containers—which are double-walled and have a silicone seal for airtightness—keep foods and liquids (coffee perhaps?) surprisingly warm, or cold, for several hours.

- Tiffins: As highlighted in the Lunch section (page 136), the Asian tiffin culture is legendary. These multi-layered stainless steel or ceramic tiffin containers have a built-in carrying handle making them an all-in-one food carrying case—no need for a bag. Plus, the separate compartments keep multiple items intact. A tiffin is a great option when you're going to pick up takeout and want to be sure your dumplings won't get too friendly with your egg rolls.

- Bento boxes: Another cultural wonder tool, this time from Japan. These stainless steel or wooden or enamel boxes, with dividers to separate portions or items, work magnificently for things like sushi, tapas and fruits and vegetables transported in the same little container without mixing.

- Reusable non-plastic wraps and pouches: These are a relatively new and wondrous phenomenon that make a splendid replacement for lots of takeout and leftover packaging materials: sinister PVC plastic wrap, aluminum foil, wax paper, paper napkins, paper or plastic bags. They are made of a blend of hemp and organic cotton cloth that is infused with beeswax, tree resin and jojoba oil to allow the food to breathe while also being water resistant. They are easy to handle, soft and pliable, and smell fabulous. The uses are endless, but in the takeout and leftover realm, picture a half-eaten burger, burrito or sandwich being wrapped up and snugly tucked in your purse. Just like plastic wraps, they are self-adhesive, with the wrap sticking to itself so you can create little sealed packages and pouches.

Figuring out a few containers to bring along with you is the easy part. The hard part is going to be having the gumption to habitually ask to use your own container, and training the restaurants and takeout places you frequent to accept this as the new norm. The more people that make this request, the faster it *will* become the norm.

Here are a few basic tips for eating out and taking out:

- Plan for leftovers. When going to have a sit-down meal at a restaurant, assume you will have leftovers and automatically get in the habit of bringing a container with you, or leave one in the car or your bag all the time.

- Of course, one way to avoid a plastic leftover container if you forgot to bring your own is to avoid leftovers. Don't over order. Order according to your hunger. Some restaurants are very open to serving a half portion if asked. Consider sharing a meal with someone else if you think it's going to be too much for each of you to order a full meal.

- When ordering in advance for takeout, let them know on the phone that you will be bringing your own to-go container and ask them when you need to arrive to have your container filled.

- Be open minded about your takeout choices. You may have a specific idea of what you want, but then realize that the restaurant simply isn't open to serving it without packaging. Choose something else on the menu that doesn't come with single-use packaging waste. Or go to a different restaurant.

- If you see something you like, but that has plastic wrap or other packaging, ask if they can make it fresh for you and put it in your own container.

- Refuse any condiments, utensils, straws, napkins, ketchup and vinegar pouches you don't need. If you're going to be eating your order right away, do you really need a napkin and paper bag? Just eat it carefully so you don't need a napkin, or carry a reusable one with you.

- Bring your own reusable carrying bag so you don't have to take a bag from the restaurant or takeout place. This is especially important for something like sushi, Chinese or Thai food, which may have multiple containers (or bring a couple of tiffins with you to avoid all those containers).

- If you have no container of your own and have to accept a container from the restaurant, ask them for a compostable one. If they don't have compostable takeout containers, ask them why not, and send them to the Biodegradable Products Institute to find some: www.bpiworld.org.

- Find out which takeout places near you offer paper or compostable packaging and are open to accommodating people looking to reduce their waste.

- A zero-waste meet-up group in your community could be a great source of resources, as well as a way to meet like-minded folks with the lowdown on the most waste-free food establishments in your community.

- Consider eating less takeout and cooking and eating at home more—this could save you money, improve your health and give you more quality time with your family.

Ever heard of the Takeout Without movement (takeoutwithout.org)? It's cool. It's a website hub where you can find restaurants that make special efforts to minimize their waste and encourage clients to bring their own reusable containers. Many offer incentives if you bring your own reusables. Restaurants can apply to join, and you can also suggest your favorite restaurants; if approved they will be listed (for free). As well, they offer downloadable wallet cards and posters to spread the word and encourage restaurants to significantly reduce their waste. One of the suggestions: "Reduce the amount of packaging to what is only absolutely necessary."

Utensils

Remember that poutine (page 141)? Well, it's also usually served up with a polystyrene plastic fork. Same problematic toxic formula: single-use plastic waste + hot oily toxic plastic mix (in this case, going into your mouth and direct contact with warm acidic saliva, which will further increase chemical leaching) = not good.

We keep stainless steel sporks everywhere. Glove compartment of the car, backpacks, lunch bags, office desks, Chantal's leather purse, Jay's black hemp side bag, our son's lunch bag and even carry-on baggage. (We have never had one confiscated by airport security in ten years of travelling with them! But we get lots of comments on how cool they are.)

There are also handy bamboo spork and utensil and chopstick to-go options that are lightweight and elegant and can come in handy carrying cases. If you want to go high end, you can even find gorgeous hand-carved wooden utensils crafted from Canadian maple. (See Utensils in the Resources section on page 181.)

Or, simply keep some standard stainless steel utensils from home in these same places—desk, car, bags and pockets. The best option is always to use what you already have.

A foldable stainless steel spork, ideal for all needs.

Straws

Now let's do a bit of a deeper dive into straws, one of the absolute worst single-use disposable offenders, and an ubiquitous restaurant and takeout staple.

From their first appearance going back to ancient Mesopotamia where Sumerians sucked in beer with straws made of gold and lapis lazuli, to today's decidedly less glamorous and durable single-use straws, the plastic straw has become another symbol of our painfully destructive, throwaway culture.[9] It is a scourge on the environment and treacherous hazard to innocent wildlife, as you will witness shortly in this section. Knowing what we now know about plastics leaching synthetic chemicals, sucking liquids directly into your body through a cheaply made plastic tube cannot be good for anyone's health.

The first question to ask when at a restaurant is: Do I really need a straw? Do you just sort of stir the ice cubes around in your glass with it once in awhile? Or do you take it out as soon as you receive your drink and leave it on the table completely unused? Pure plastic waste. Some folks really do prefer to use a straw, and that's totally understandable. Using a straw can decrease the shock of the drink on your teeth, thus reducing teeth staining and erosion issues. Or, like our son with his smoothies, maybe you just plain enjoy drinking through a straw. They can be great fun for playing with your drink and, *ahem*, food fights. If the straw is that important to you, consider investing in a reusable one and carrying it with you all the time as you might a pen.

Providing a plastic straw with a drink is automatic in many restaurants and bars. For those straws that are actually used, it's likely just for minutes. Then most are thrown directly in the garbage (a very small portion are recycled). They end up in a landfill, or worse, as waste that "leaks" out into the broader environment of urban and rural landscapes and waterways.

It's estimated that 500 million plastic straws are used and discarded each day in the United States alone. That amounts to 175 billion each year just in the United States! For a little more perspective on this craziness, consider the following:

- 500 million straws could fill over 127 school buses each day, or more than 46,400 school buses every year. End to end, straws used daily in the United States could circle the planet more than two-and-a-half times a day. And in just over three days we could reach the moon in straws.

- 500 million straws per day is an average of 1.6 straws per person per day. Based on this national average, each person in the U.S. will use approximately 38,000 or more straws between the ages of 5 and 65.

Note that these estimates do not include all the straws attached to juice and milk cartons handed out in school lunchrooms and included in lunch boxes every day.[10]

---

9   D. Thompson (2011) "The Amazing History and the Strange Invention of the Bendy Straw," TheAtlantic.com (accessed 3 March 2017: https://www.theatlantic.com/business/archive/2011/11/the-amazing-history-and-the-strange-invention-of-the-bendy-straw/248923).

10   Eco-Cycle (2011) "Be Straw Free Campaign: Frequently Asked Questions," Be Straw Free Campaign (accessed 3 March 2017: http://ecocycle.org/bestrawfree/faqs); World Centric, "Do You Really Need That Drinking Straw?" (accessed 3 March 2017: http://worldcentric.org/do-you-really-need-that-drinking-straw).

Most straws are made of polypropylene plastic (recycling symbol #5), which, as we know, is a petroleum-derived plastic that does not break down easily. The Worldwatch Institute describes plastic straw production as follows:

> Colorants, plasticizers (which make the plastic more flexible), antioxidants (which reduce the interactions between oxygen and the plastic) and ultraviolet light filters (which shield the plastic from solar radiation) are added. Straws are then individually wrapped in sleeves or bulk-packed in plastic or cardboard containers.[11]

These plastic straws do not biodegrade, they photodegrade, breaking down into smaller and smaller pieces that are easily eaten by wildlife. Because it is a tougher plastic, when polypropylene goes into the marine environment it adsorbs toxins for a long time. These toxin-heavy plastics are then often ingested by wildlife, slowly poisoning them.[12]

In 2015, a research team from Texas A&M University temporarily caught a mating Olive Ridley turtle for a genetic study, and noticed that there was something white and hard in one of its nostrils. A barnacle? A worm? No, a plastic straw! They were able to safely remove the complete straw, and a video they made of what happened went viral almost immediately.[13] While graphic and disturbing, it serves as a powerful wake-up call to take action against single-use disposable plastic waste.

So now that you are more aware of the pernicious implications of the plastic straw, what are the reusable straw options? (See Straws in the Resources section on page 182 for specific product suggestions.)

- Glass: Available in short, tall, straight, bent, smoothie size and child size, green dots (seriously). They come in a wide array of sizes and colors. They are generally handmade from borosilicate glass and often even come with a lifetime automatic replacement guarantee. That doesn't mean they are not going to break if you hurl them at a brick wall, but they are surprisingly tough. To make it a complete to-go kit, you can include a cleaning brush and store them both in a carrying pouch.

- Stainless steel: Another tough, take-anywhere option for every use and occasion. You might be thinking, hmmm, those would be great for camping. Yes, they are, but so much more as well: lunches, elegant cocktails, takeout, pool-side, surf-side and patios. Throw one in the purse, backpack or glove compartment so it's always available.

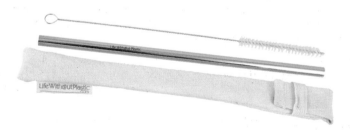

11   G. Gourmelon (2015) "Plastic Straws: A Life Cycle," Worldwatch Institute Blog (accessed 3 March 2017: http://blogs.worldwatch.org/plastic-straws-a-life-cycle).

12   C. Rochman, E. Hoh, B. Hentschel and S. Kaye (2012) "Long-Term Field Measurement of Sorption of Organic Contaminants to Five Types of Plastic Pellets: Implications for Plastic Marine Debris," *Environmental Science and Technology* 47(3):1646–1654; K. Kerlin (2013) "Plastics and Chemicals They Absorb Pose Double Threat to Marine Life," UCDavis.edu (accessed 3 March 2017: https://www.ucdavis.edu/news/plastics-and-chemicals-they-absorb-pose-double-threat-marine-life).

13   Video: "The Story of the Sea Turtle with the Straw—No to Single Use Plastics," 1 November 2015 (accessed 4 March 2017: https://youtu.be/4MPHbpmP6_I).

- **Bamboo:** Bamboo provides a completely natural alternative to single-use disposable straws. They are made from whole bamboo stalks and are washable and reusable. If cleaned and dried after each use, they can last for years.

- **Biodegradable and compostable disposables:** This an option we mention hesitantly, because they are disposables, but there may be times that you need a disposable straw, so it's best if it is biodegradable and compostable. There are options made of chlorine-free paper using safe dyes for a wide range of colorful options. There are also hand-harvested and cut straws made from actual straw—from organically-grown winter rye crops in particular.

Remember to say these words the next time you are getting takeout or ordering drinks at restaurant or bar: "No plastic straw, please."

Jackie Nunez took it several steps further. She created a movement called The Last Plastic Straw (thelastplasticstraw.org), which encourages bars and restaurants to eliminate straws completely, or to at least simply state on their menus: "Straws available upon request." As a way of promoting businesses willing to make the change, the site includes a map of participating restaurants that have eliminated plastic straws from their establishments. She also teamed up with the Plastic Pollution Coalition to encourage individuals to be personally accountable in avoiding plastic straws by taking the "No Plastic Straw Pledge" and leaving little informational cards in their local restaurants asking them to serve straws only upon request.[14] Hop on board, if you feel like joining the movement!

TRAVELING

Depending on how you travel, your preparations for a plastic-free voyage are going to be different. If you travel often, it might be a good idea to have a little travel bag always ready with all your essential plastic-free items ready to go.

Traveling by Plane

If you are traveling by plane, there are at least two constraints to consider when going through airport security: (1) you are not allowed to bring a filled water bottle with a capacity of more than 3.4 ounces (100 ml) of liquid, and (2) your toiletries (creams, lotions, shampoo) must fit in 3.4 ounce (100 ml) or less containers. When these restrictions came into force in the years following the 9/11 tragedy, the plastic bottled water industry benefitted greatly. Many people began purchasing water bottles on the other side of the security checkpoint. Unsurprisingly, the sale of miniature containers of toiletries such as shampoo bottles, toothpaste, sunscreens and contact lens solution exploded.

When leading a plastic-free lifestyle, the second restriction doesn't really matter because one tries to bring dry items that can be hydrated with water. Liquids are to be avoided as much as possible because they are often packaged in a plastic bottle.

---

14   The pledge and downloadable informational cards are available here: http://www.plasticpollutioncoalition.org/no-straw-please (accessed 3 March 2017).

To address the first restriction, here are two important items you might want to bring in your carry-on bag:

- A reusable stainless steel water bottle. It might be a good idea to bring a double-walled insulated water bottle so you can use it for coffee in the plane and refuse the styrofoam cup. You might also want to consider a collapsible stainless steel tumbler or a double wall tumbler if you want to travel light.

- A binchotan charcoal. As explained previously in the Kitchen Tools section (page 105), a stick of Japanese charcoal can remove chlorine and other toxins from your water. Bring a charcoal stick and an empty water bottle. Once you've passed security, go to a water fountain (or a bathroom if there's no fountain available), insert the stick in the bottle and fill it up with tap water.

If you are traveling by bus or train, you can bring a water bottle full of water, but having the charcoal stick is still a very good idea.

The following is a list of plastic-free ideas for your next trip, regardless of your mode of transportation.

- A spork or reusable utensils. Get a foldable stainless steel spork, a bamboo spork or a set of portable bamboo utensils.[15]

- A reusable straw. Get a stainless steel or a glass straw with a little brush so you can clean it right after use. This is especially important when traveling because sticky sodas or juices can soil your straw and you won't be able to use it again until you find a decent kitchen to clean it.

- Baking soda in a small tin. You can mix it with a little bit of water to wash your dishes, your clothes or almost anything else, including your teeth.

- Earphones. Some airlines just throw out the ones they give away on the plane right after the plane has landed.

- An airtight stainless steel container that you can fill up with food at a restaurant while waiting to board your plane.

- Sunscreen in a cardboard tub or small tin container.

- A fabric hanky that doubles as a napkin.

- One or two compact shopping bags.

- A plastic-free wooden toothbrush.

- A compact stainless steel safety travel razor.

- A multi-purpose soap bar that you can use as body cleanser and shampoo.

- Some solid paste deodorant in a glass container.

- A cotton shower cap.

- A cotton eye mask for sleeping.

- Rubber ear plugs.

- A hemp, cotton or linen breathing mask, especially if you travel to places such as Beijing or Mexico City, which are notorious for air pollution.

- A pair of cotton slippers.

- A buckwheat neck pillow encased in a cotton sleeve.

---

15   See the Resources section under Utensils (page 181).

If you are a woman, you might want to add these extra items:

- A menstrual cup and a couple of reusable sanitary napkins.
- Some reusable cotton makeup removers or a face cloth.

You may not be able to find a dry replacement for an essential item on your list such as contact lens solution or a liquid supplement you absolutely cannot get in another form. In such cases, for increased versatility, try to fill compact travel glass bottles that are under 3.4 ounces (100 ml) with these liquids.

Road Trips

Road trips are a great way to slowly discover the beautiful planet we live on. Going plastic-free on a road trip requires just a little bit of planning, especially regarding the food and water you bring.

When we go on road trips, we like to bring a medium-sized 2.6 gallon (10 L) stainless steel water dispenser that we keep in the trunk of our car. When we take a pit stop, we make sure to refill our individual water bottles directly from the dispenser. Bring a large charcoal stick with you in case you need to refill the dispenser in a public bathroom.

In order to avoid the waste associated with takeout and drive-in food, make sure you have several reusable coffee cups handy and keep several reusable sporks and straws easily available in your car. Keep a cotton napkin handy and have a few reusable containers. Prepare snacks ahead of time and store them in large reusable containers. Bring many reusable bags; you probably don't realize how many you will need, as they always come in handy.

Hotel Stays

If you are planning to stay at a hotel, make sure you have your own version of the small plastic convenience products that are typically offered for free in every hotel room. If you have your own, you will not be tempted to use the hotel's plastic offerings. Here's a list:

- Water bottle with binchotan stick filter
- Reusable coffee mug
- Powdered milk or cream in a little glass container
- Shampoo bar
- Soap bar
- Safety razor
- Bath salts
- Toothbrush and toothpaste
- Cotton shower hat
- Cotton slippers

SPORTS AT THE GYM AND IN THE GREAT OUTDOORS

The improvement of performance in sports is directly connected to advancement of plastic technologies. Our teenage son loves snowboarding and he is great at it. When he needs a new board, there is no way we'll ever be able to convince him that his board should be all wood to minimize his plastic footprint. Modern snowboards have a wood core, but are laminated with resins and plastic components such as fiberglass. His boots are made of nylon and insulated with plastic foam. His snowsuit is almost entirely made of polyester.

Does adopting a plastic-free lifestyle mean you must give up on high-performance sports? Of course not. Life would suddenly become less exciting. What we need is the collaboration of the industry to develop new types of plastic that have less impact on the planet and for customers to try them out even if they may be a bit more expensive. In the snowboarding world, leading companies such as Burton are integrating sustainable materials in the fabrication of some of their boards. Patagonia is very aware of the compelling need for more eco-friendly sportswear. Look for these components and let the company know that it made a difference in your product selection.

Sports Clothing

While plastic clothing has been traditionally associated with performance, some companies are rediscovering the virtues of natural fibers and developing technologies to improve their characteristics. Merino wool is a good example of this trend. In recent years, it has evolved as a much thinner layer that is easily washable and will not shrink easily. It offers great advantages especially as a base layer for winter sports because it stays warm even when it gets wet through perspiration.

Silk is another fiber that is making headway in the world of sports. It is a strong fiber that is breathable and can keep you fresh through the hardest workouts. Other natural fibers that are increasingly popular in the world of sports include organic cotton, hemp and linen.

In recent years, bamboo has emerged in the market as an eco-friendly fabric that was marketed as having a smaller footprint because of the fast growing rate of its bamboo fibers. What manufacturers did not say was that large doses of harsh chemicals such as sodium hydroxide, carbon disulfide and sulfuric acid are needed to process the tough cellulose bamboo plants into a soft material. In 2010, the Canadian Competition Bureau ordered manufacturers to remove from the labeling of textiles made from bamboo cellulose the "eco-friendly" claim, which was considered misleading to consumers. The fibers must now say that it is "bamboo viscose" or "bamboo rayon" which implies a chemical process. If the bamboo clothing has a Lyocell or Tencel label, this indicates it was made using a much less chemical-intensive, closed loop process that recovers the chemical solvents used. All this to say that when shopping for sports clothes you should look at textile labels carefully and choose natural fibers as much as possible.

Sports Shoes

If you want to find all-natural sports shoes nowadays, you'll have to look at the vintage section of eBay to find old Adidas made entirely of leather. Sports shoes fabricated without any plastic components simply don't exist anymore. If you can't get a pair of natural shoes, at least make sure to dispose of them properly. There are two ways:

- If your shoes are still wearable and could make someone less fortunate happy, there are a few organizations you can contact who will happily take your shoes and redistribute them. In the United States, contact Soles 4 Souls (www. soles4souls.org) to find a drop-off location. In Canada, check out the Shoe Bank (www.shoebankcanada.com). Elsewhere in the world, contact a shoe retailer chain and ask about their shoe re-use program. Most large chains will be able to refer you.

- If your shoes are at the end of their sporting life, then you need to recycle or repurpose them. Contact the MORE foundation (www.morefoundationgroup. org) or visit the Nike Grind program (www.nikegrind.com), which accepts any type of shoes, not just Nikes, preventing them from heading to the landfill and down-cycling them into sports court surfaces.

Yoga

Unsurprisingly, given the type of clientele who tend to practice yoga, this industry is making important efforts to bring sustainability to the practice of the sport. Most yoga mats are made of polyvinyl chloride (PVC), which is not the best type of plastic as indicated throughout this book, but you can now find them in a variety of natural materials from organic cotton and hemp to natural rubber and jute.

A few companies offer natural rubber yoga mats that are great options as long as you are not allergic to latex. Otherwise, you may find 100 percent hemp yoga mats that can be used alone or as a topper on a natural rubber mat.

Camping

As plastic-free enthusiasts, we enjoy exploring our natural environment and basking in the beauty of it. Nothing beats the feeling of an evening spent sitting around a fire pit with good friends out in the woods. But plastic-free camping gear is hard to come by.

You could consider sleeping in a tipi. Keep in mind that they take some effort and skill to set up, so you'll likely want to be staying in the same location for several days once you have it up. Another option is the cotton canvas tent. They are available in various sizes and the spacious ones can be quite luxurious. And then there are magnificent Siberian yurts, the ultimate home away from home.

Natural sleeping bags are available, with an outside liner made of cotton and an inside one made of either cotton or merino wool. No more nylon stuffed with synthetic fill!

For plastic-free shopping options, see Sports at the Gym and in the Great Outoors in the Resources section (page 182).

THE OFFICE AND SCHOOL ENVIRONMENT

Whether you are a student or full-time worker, you don't always get to choose the elements that create the working space where you spend a great deal of your time. Unless you are a partner at a law firm or can choose the desk you occupy by virtue of hierarchy or special status, chances are you will sit in a chair covered with plastic fabric at a manufactured wood desk.

Furniture

There is a substantial price difference between manufactured and solid wood desks. So much so that few corporations can afford solid wood desks for all their employees. Manufactured wood sometimes looks very much like the real thing because of its layer of plastic veneer on the surface that contains an appliqué mimicking the look of wood. This veneer layer is typically made of formaldehyde-based melamine. Under this top layer is pressed board, which is made of wood composite compressed using copious amounts of glue.

Your chair is probably made of synthetic foam and polyester fabric with plastic arms. Your computer and screens probably contain a lot of plastic. There might be cubical dividers made of polyester fabric boards. The floor is probably covered with a plastic carpet. And if there is a window, there may be vinyl casing and blinds or synthetic curtains on it. Paints and adhesives around you probably release some VOCs, including benzene. In fact, the air that surrounds you probably contains a lot of benzene and other chemicals according to a warning by the World Health Organization published in 2010.[16]

Although there is not much you can do about the choice of furniture in your office space, you can certainly try to inform your boss about your intolerance to VOCs, plastics and other chemicals (isn't every human being intolerant to chemicals that can make them sick?). Maybe even offer to bring your own desk and chair. But doing that will only solve part of the problem because the air you breathe still receives plastic microparticles and chemicals from other workstations.

Atmosphere

One solution to at least improve the air you are breathing is to bring some hearty air-purifying plants. Tall office buildings rarely have windows that can be opened. Instead they rely on an air circulation system that brings in only about 10 to 20 percent new air and recycles the rest. The National Aeronautics and Space Administration (NASA) published a study of the best plants for air purification in 1989.[17] The illustration on page 153 lists the most common plants that have proven effective at removing benzene, formaldehyde and other unwanted chemicals from the ambient air.[18]

---

16   World Health Organization, "Exposure to Benzene: A Major Public Health Concern" (accessed 5 March 2017: http://www.who.int/ipcs/features/benzene.pdf).

17   B.C. Wolverton, W.L. Douglas and K. Bounds (1989) "A Study of Interior Landscape Plants for Indoor Air Pollution Abatement" NASA, NASA-TM-108061 (accessed 5 March 2017: https://archive.org/details/nasa_techdoc_19930072988).

18   See a more complete list of air purifying plants here: https://en.wikipedia.org/wiki/NASA_Clean_Air_Study (accessed 5 March 2017).

AIR-PURIFYING PLANTS			
Plant	Image	Chemicals It Removes	Toxic to Domestic Animals
English Ivy (*Hedera helix*)		Benzene, Formaldehyde, Trichloroethylene, Xylene, Toluene	Yes
Spider Plant (*Chlorophytum comosum*)		Formaldehyde, Xylene, Toluene	No
Peace Lily (*Spathiphyllum cochlearispathum*)		Benzene, Formaldehyde, Trichloroethylene, Xylene, Toluene, Ammonia	Yes
Snake Plant (*Sanseieria trifasciata*) also known as mother-in-law's tongue		Benzene, Formaldehyde, Trichloroethylene, Xylene, Toluene	Yes
Aloe Vera (*Aloe vera*)		Benzene, Formaldehyde	Yes

The Microwave

Most office kitchens and school cafeterias in North America have a microwave available for employees and students to use during their lunch breaks. While it is a very fast and convenient way to warm food up, remember that plastics and microwaves do not get along at all. The action of the microwaves tends to encourage the transfer of plastic additives from the plastic container to the food itself during the heating process,[19] especially if the food is oily or acidic.

19   "An analysis of 455 common plastic products (. . .) found that 70% tested positive for estrogenic activity; that number went up to 95% when the plastics were microwaved." From O.B. Waxman (2016) "That Plastic Container You Microwave in Could Be Super-Toxic," *Time* Magazine, 4 May 2016 (accessed 5 March 2017: http://time.com/4229503/plastic-in-microwave-is-it-safe).

In order to reduce the risk of your food becoming laced with plastic chemicals, follow these two tips:

- Use glass or ceramic containers instead of plastic to heat your food in the microwave oven;

- Do not cover your food with plastic wrap; use a paper towel instead.

Alternatively, you could bring a warm lunch to school or work in a thermal container, or you could try and convince your employer to acquire a toaster oven. Toaster ovens are great for re-heating a lunch stored in a stainless steel container. There is no need to transfer the food to another container. Just re-heat it directly, and bon appétit!

CHAPTER 6

RADIATING THE PLASTIC-FREE LIFESTYLE

AND SHARING IT WITH YOUR FAMILY, FRIENDS AND CO-WORKERS

It's easy to see how positive influences encourage the adoption of positive behavior just from watching the children of admirable people. These children have spent their entire lives watching their parents work for a cause and became inspired to pursue the same mission. Just look at Severn Cullis-Suzuki, daughter of Tara Cullis and David Suzuki, two well-known Canadian environmentalists, who has been an active and visible figure of the environmental movement since age nine. Just as we can influence our own children, we can also influence our siblings, our parents, our nieces and nephews—one person at a time.

While you are progressing on your plastic-free journey, remember that it is a very personal one. The "aha" moment comes to different people at different times, and being judgmental or argumentative is rarely going to help someone come to a realization. Instead, they may cling to their position more firmly in order not to lose face.

One great way to share your point of view with your friends, family and co-workers without pushing the issue strongly is to organize a plastic awareness event and ask them for help. For example, a beach clean-up or a film screening is a good place to start. By helping you, they will personally get involved in the issue and may have a plastic epiphany. If not, at least you know that you have made them more aware. It is all about small steps.

Above all, it's important to remain kind and compassionate, and not be too hardcore drastic—especially with friends and family—if you sense serious conflict arising. For example, you don't want to refuse a gift because it is made of plastic or it is packaged in plastic. It is rude, hurtful and it could create a long-lasting grudge with someone who had really good intentions.

Dinner with Friends

When inviting friends over for dinner, try not to create an opportunity for them to bring something plastic. Most people want to contribute something to the dinner out of courtesy and they will often ask "what can I bring?" Suggest something you are pretty sure is available without plastic such as a bottle of wine (cross your fingers that the one they choose has a real cork) or a bottle of sparkling water or apple cider. You could also perhaps ask for a homemade salad or a fresh bread. If you ask for chips or nachos, you're stuck with a plastic bag.

Gift Giving

Telling friends and family that you do not want to receive any plastic gifts, whether the gift itself is made of plastic or is wrapped in plastic, is a very delicate subject. After all, a gift is something that people offer from their heart and they don't want to be told what it should be; otherwise, it is not really a gift. It's just like someone placing an order. The beauty of the gesture is lost.

Here are a few suggestions that may help you let important people in your life know that it is very important to you not to receive any plastics at your special event, without hurting feelings:

WRITE IT DOWN

If you are uncomfortable saying it with your own words during a phone conversation or at a family dinner, how about announcing it in an email or on Facebook to many people at once, so no one feels more targeted than anyone else? You could announce that this is a new commitment you have made to yourself and you need everyone's collaboration.

ENCOURAGING DONATIONS TO ORGANIZATIONS THAT FIGHT PLASTIC POLLUTION

You could let your loved ones and colleagues know that you are now engaged in the global fight against plastic pollution and that if they find it impossible to offer a plastic-free gift, they can always make a donation on your behalf to an organization engaged in the fight against plastic pollution.[1]

CREATING A WISH LIST OR GIFT REGISTRY WITH A STORE WHERE PLASTIC-FREE GIFTS CAN BE FOUND

Find your favorite eco store and create a wish list of all the plastic-free gifts you would like to receive, and send the link to family and friends. If it is an online shop, just inquire ahead of time to ensure they will pack your online order without the usual plastic fillers, such as styrofoam peanuts and bubble wrap, and that they will not use plastic tape.

ASKING FOR A GIFT CERTIFICATE

A gift certificate will allow you to choose a plastic-free item from a store's entire offering. A real advantage of a gift certificate is that it allows you to ask for an experience instead of a thing. You may receive a certificate for a night out at a restaurant or a day at a Scandinavian spa (Chantal's personal favorite), which can be entirely without plastic.

---

1   See the Resources section at the end of the book for a list of possible organizations to donate to.

At Events

Due to the need for convenience, disposable plastics seem to invade every aspect of event organization, from decorations to dishes to name tags and door prizes. Fortunately, many plastic-free options exist for the most wasteful aspects of a large-scale event, if you are willing to stretch your budget. And if you've gotten this far through our book, then you know it's worth it! Three basic categories of products need to be purchased or otherwise provided for big gatherings:

- Drinks
- Food
- Decorations and name tags

DRINKS

Drinks are one of the most challenging aspects of plastic-free party planning because liquids tend to quickly deteriorate any readily compostable material. As well, for safety purposes, some venues may require that plastic cups be used. We've already discussed bioplastics and explained that they are actually not necessarily a solid alternative to plastic products, at least not yet. They don't necessarily biodegrade easily or quickly, they may only compost under certain conditions, they may contain chemical additives and they are not recyclable.

Unfortunately, paper cups pretty much all contain a plastic liner. Although some municipal composting programs will accept them, tiny fragments of plastic from the liner will remain as tiny microplastic fragments in the soil produced through the composting process. The fragments can ultimately get washed out with the rain and end up in rivers, lakes and oceans, where they can have a negative impact on marine ecosystems.

Only use cups made with compostable bioplastics if you are certain that they can be disposed of safely in an industrial composting facility; assuming there is such an industrial composting program in the town where the event takes place. Otherwise, your next best option is to use stainless steel reusable cups, which is a good option for most types of drinks. If you are planning to offer wine, you should consider a dish catering service that provides actual glass wine glasses they will collect back, wash and reuse.

FOOD

While few options exist for drinkware, many truly compostable and toxic-free options exist for foodware. They are made of leaves, bamboo veneer, paper pulp, sugar cane and so on. The list on page 158 presents various options currently available.

As for utensils, many companies offer wooden utensils. Ecoware offers birch cutlery sets that are 100 percent natural and compostable in recycled paper packaging. Bamboo options also exist. One Indian company, Bakey's, recently made the viral rounds on social media after publishing a video of its edible cutlery. It's an ingenious idea and hopefully it will be available in North America soon. The cutlery is made from a blend of rice and wheat and is available in plain, sweet and savory flavors.

Plastic-Free Compostable Dinnerware

DESCRIPTION AND BRAND	HIGHLIGHTS	PRICE RANGE
Verterra: Compostable dinnerware made from fallen palm tree leaves (made in India).	100% compostable or they can be washed and reused. Microwave-safe. Can hold liquids.	5 x 5-inch (13 x 13-cm) bowls $15/ 25 pcs ($0.60/pc)
Bambu: Compostable dinnerware made from 100% certified organic bamboo (made in China).	100% compostable. Certified organic. Not microwave-safe. Can hold liquids.	5 x 5-inch (13 x 13-cm) plates $66/100 pcs ($0.66/pc)
Leaf Republic: Plates made with two leaves with a layer of paper in between stitched together with fibers from palm leaves (made in Germany).	100% compostable. Not microwave safe. Can hold liquids. Look really cool!	7-inch (18-cm) diameter €46.41/100 pcs ($0.50/pc)
DoEat: Edible foodware made from potato starch (made in Belgium).	100% compostable. Edible—last 6 to 12 months. Organic and gluten-free. You have to put them together yourself with a sponge and water.	9 x 2.8-inch (23 x 7-cm) containers €9.95 ($11.75)/ 25 pcs ($0.42/pc)
Natural Value: Plates made from paper (not polycoated) (made in USA).	100% compostable if pre-shredded. Microwave-safe. Can hold liquids.	9-inch (23-cm) diameter $5.21/40 pcs ($0.13/pc)

DECORATIONS AND NAME TAGS

Skip the balloons and glitzy plastic banners. Just opt for paper. Paper confetti, paper banners, paper garlands, paper pom-poms . . . There is no shortage of ideas. Just hop on Pinterest and discover hundreds of suggestions of beautiful paper decorations. Specialized green party stores also have a lot of options.[2]

As for plastic nametags, they are extremely wasteful. Often used only once, they can't be recycled and go straight to the landfill. Once again, it is easy to use plastic-free options such as DIY rigid cardboard or wood and attach the tag with a cotton ribbon.

---

2   For example, http://ecopartytime.com.

Spreading the Awareness

So you've begun to make substantive changes in your own life toward living plastic-free. You're inspired and charged and you want to do more. There are lots of ways you can get involved in spreading your newfound plastic-free living awareness on a larger scale.

You can have a lasting impact by creating ripples of awareness with every action you take. Buckminster Fuller described the principle of precession as "the effect of bodies in motion on other bodies in motion."[3] So each moving body is creating its own ripples of influence; those ripples interact with the ripples of others, and together the impact grows and grows. Below we run through a few examples of ways to start creating your own unique ripples, alone or with the communities that surround you, ranging from the local to the global.

Start with a Pledge

Why not start by making it personal with a pledge to yourself. The Plastic Pollution Coalition offers up the following "4Rs Pledge" as a way to make yourself accountable:

- REFUSE disposable plastic whenever and wherever possible. Choose items that are not packaged in plastic, and carry your own bags, containers and utensils.

- REDUCE your plastic footprint. Cut down on your consumption of goods that contain excessive plastic packaging and parts. If it will leave behind plastic trash, don't buy it.

- REUSE durable, non-toxic straws, utensils, to-go containers, bottles, bags and other everyday items. Choose glass, paper, stainless steel, wood, ceramic and bamboo over plastic.

- RECYCLE what you can't refuse, reduce or reuse. Pay attention to the entire life cycle of items you bring into your life, from source to manufacturing to distribution to disposal.

You can take the pledge here: www.plasticpollutioncoalition.org/take-action-1

Participate in Plastic-Free Events or Start Your Own Movement

There is power and inspiration in doing something with many others at the same time for a shared purpose that will make the world a better place for all.

COMMUNITY AND COASTAL CLEAN-UPS

One way to start tackling the plastic problem head-on is to simply start picking up plastic litter—and garbage in general—wherever and whenever you see it.

In our home community of Wakefield, Quebec, every spring there is a "Village Clean-Up" with a call put out to the whole community to spare a couple of hours one Saturday morning to help gather up all the garbage that has accumulated and is now visible after the snow has melted. Teams are organized to cover the full village, and gloves and bags are available to those who need them. Kids love it and get right into it and it becomes a fun challenge to find as much litter as possible—a bizarre kind of treasure hunt. Lots of fun, teachable moments are possible with an activity like this. Inevitably, most of the garbage collected is, you guessed it, plastic—in particular, single-use disposable plastic food packaging.

3   R. Buckminster Fuller, *Critical Path*, Sebastopol, CA: Estate of R. Buckminster Fuller, 1982, p. 344.

Coastal clean-ups are organized regularly all over the world and directly decrease plastic pollution.

How about taking part in what just might be the world's oldest and largest global garbage collection activity? Every September, the Ocean Conservancy organizes the International Coastal Cleanup, which engages people to gather up trash from the world's beaches and waterways, identify the types of trash and help change behavior. It has been going on for thirty years, and in 2015, more than 18 million pounds (8,165,000 kg) of litter was collected by almost 800,000 volunteers along over 25,000 miles (40,000 km) of coast around the world.[4] If you've made it this far through our book, you can probably guess what most of the top items collected were: yup, single-use plastic disposables, mostly food packaging. This data is used to create an Ocean Trash Index, which adds to what has become the world's largest database on marine debris. Through their Clean Swell app anyone can now add vital data to this database by logging trash found along coastlines quickly and easily on a mobile phone.

PLASTIC-FREE JULY
In 2011, Rebecca Prince-Ruiz got together with her colleagues at the Western Metropolitan Regional Council in Perth, Western Australia and they recruited 40 local households to go plastic-free for a month. The idea was to show that recycling is not the solution and that the emphasis should be put on refusing, reducing and reusing. It started small and local and grew each year until they opened it to the world in 2013.

The event builds awareness about the problems of single-use disposable plastics and challenges people to do something about them. People are encouraged to register to participate for however long they wish—a day, a week, a month or beyond—and to refuse all single-use plastic during that time. Or they can focus on the top 4 polluters: plastic bags, bottles, takeout coffee cups and straws. They are asked to keep a "dilemma bag," where they put any unavoidable single-use plastic they collect, and share the contents at the end.

4   More details available at: http://www.oceanconservancy.org/our-work/international-coastal-cleanup (accessed 3 March 2017).

It's now a global movement engaging over 60,000 people, schools and organizations from 130 countries annually, and hosts a website chock full of resources and tips for going plastic-free.

You can register and learn lots here: www.plasticfreejuly.org

PLASTIC-FREE TUESDAY

Instead of a plastic-free month each year, how about a plastic-free day each week?

Annemieke was so affected by all the articles about plastic pollution and its effects on wildlife that she started her blog, Plastic Minimalism, in 2013. Sharing her own steps toward a plastic-free life was not enough: she wanted to create more awareness about the adverse impacts of plastic consumption. In 2014, she launched the Plastic-Free Tuesday movement, which has a single foundational rule: One day a week with no plastic consumption and no plastic waste.

Participants are encouraged to share their experiences on social media and engage with the community. Annemieke now has a team of eight co-Plastic-Free Tuesdayers to help with running the movement, and they regularly invite guest bloggers to share plastic-free experiences or specialized knowledge. The website provides a wealth of plastic-free living tips and tools, and offers downloadable posters to spread the word about the plastic problem. They even provide a recipe for making your own homemade glue to put up the posters without plastic tape!

Check it out here: plasticfreetuesday.com (and this is Annemieke's original Dutch language blog: plasticminimalism.blogspot.nl)

START YOUR OWN MOVEMENT

Rebecca and Annemieke felt called for different reasons to take what personal development guru Tony Robbins would term "massive action" against the plastic in their lives. And that massive action has been massively successful in creating positively-charged precessional ripples all over the world.

Here's a beautiful, tangible example of the precession flowing from Rebecca's Plastic-Free July. In 2012, Melbourne, Australia resident Lindsay Miles saw a flyer in her local library for the Plastic-Free July challenge. She decided to give it a go. She was already eco-minded, and the full epiphany came when she watched the film "Bag It!" as part of the challenge activities. This opened her up to the issues and the plastic all around her. It also convinced her that she could not possibly go back to living her regular life after just one month. She began intensively researching and learning, and sharing her plastic-free knowledge and experience through her blog, aptly entitled Treading My Own Path (treadingmyownpath.com), and through a handy e-guide for plastic-free living called That's a Wrap. And now she is a movement of her own with a growing following.

So how about you? Do you feel inspired to tread your own path and start your own movement to help catalyze some massive change? What is it about plastic that most irks you? Is it the synthetic chemical toxicity? The strangling and choking of wildlife with plastic packaging? The secrecy of plastic manufacturers about all the chemicals in plastics? Whatever it may be, go for it. And if you're not interested in starting your own movement, then simply jump on board the many that are already up and running and changing the world.

Creating a Plastic-Free Community

Back in 2008, we organized a campaign in our home community of Wakefield, Quebec to reduce the use of single-use plastic bags. Wakefield is a certified Fair Trade Town, so as members of the Wakefield-La Pêche Fair Trade Committee, we created a Plastic Alternatives Subcommittee to deal with the issue. It was made up of talented and passionate local residents who volunteered to sit down and figure out how best to go about this.

We came up with a range of possibilities: push our municipality to ban the bags or to impose a fee on bags, or carry out an educational campaign to encourage people to bring their own reusable bags when shopping. We decided to start with the latter and see how it went. It was a huge success. After polling the local shop owners to get their take on the situation, we organized presentations in the local schools on the issue and had the students create powerful posters encouraging shoppers to bring their own bags. The shop owners were more than happy to display the students' charged artwork in their stores. We also provided an alternative reusable bag that the stores could sell to shoppers who did not have a reusable bag, but wanted to make the shift. The result was what one shop owner described as a 90 percent reduction in plastic bag use.

The Fair Trade Committee also created a highly popular local dish lending library. This allows anybody to sign out dishes, cups, glasses and utensils for events, which range from the annual Canada Day celebrations at the local community center to the winter solstice candlelight potluck walks organized at private homes. Our business also lends out large stainless steel water dispensers for community events and festivals and we organize screenings of films that address the plastics issue. Recently, we sponsored a screening of "A Plastic Ocean" at the Wakefield Docfest and organized a lively panel discussion following the film to discuss microplastics testing that had taken place in our local river. The screening included an art contest for students from the local schools. Including children is absolutely key to creating a plastic-free community.

As part of the microbead collection campaign organized by the 5 Gyres Institute in 2016 to remove plastic microbead-containing products from circulation, we recruited local families to make artfully decorated and informative collection boxes to put in local stores.

One of the most ingenious and effective plastic reduction efforts we have ever come across was implemented by our friends at Bodhi Surf & Yoga Camp and the non-profit organization Geoporters in Costa Rica. Over a year, community members of all ages participated in communal trash cleanups on the streets of the village of Bahia Ballena using GPS technology to map out the collected solid waste in every 24 cubic meter quadrant.

With Bodhi and Geoporter's assistance and training, community volunteers plotted this trash map on a satellite image of the area to pinpoint garbage "hot spots"—areas of dense trash accumulation such as near grocery stores and the community center—and strategically placed garbage bins throughout the village for proper disposal of trash. The garbage and recycling bins were made by community members as were hand painted signs with colorful positive messages in Spanish promoting eco-actions. Our favorite was the ubiquitous "*Yo no tiro basura*" (I don't throw garbage). The messages were deliberately personal and non-judgmental, rather than a judgmental order like "Don't litter." The result: A massive reduction in the trash throughout the community.

Those are a few ideas, but there's so much that can be done, and tons of room for creativity. There are some obvious possibilities: plastic bag bans, bottled water bans, styrofoam bans, microbead-containing product collection drives, film showings, expert speaker events and plastic-free living tips seminars. But don't be afraid to think outside the box.

And you can define community any way you like: your neighborhood, your local bar, your library, your school or university or workplace. Chances are, if you have a specific idea and you put out the word—by putting up a poster at your local library, for example—that you are interested in doing something to address the problem of plastic, you'll probably find that other like-minded folks will gravitate to you with ideas and energy to help out. In fact, doing so might help you discover the community around you that you never knew existed.

CITIZEN SCIENCE

High quality, verifiable scientific data is key for charting plastic toxicity and pollution problems and promoting regulatory and corporate changes. As a citizen, you can help gather that precious data by becoming a citizen scientist. No formal scientific training or education is required; just a desire to make a positive difference.

We recently had the opportunity to put on our citizen scientist lab coats and take to the water. A key step in dealing with the problem of microplastic pollution in waterways is understanding and measuring the extent of it. Over the summer of 2016, we took part in some microplastics sampling on our local Gatineau River, which is a huge part of our lives. We swim and play in it just about every day in the summer months. Ottawa Riverkeeper (ORK), through its Riverwatch Program coordinated by staff scientist Dr. Meaghan Murphy, got together with Dr. Jesse Vermaire of Carleton University to organize microplastics testing in surface waters throughout the Ottawa River watershed. Our local community-based volunteer organization, Friends of the Gatineau River, helped with this testing along the Gatineau River and we were invited to tag along.

The results? Microplastics in every sample. And it was the same for every single sample taken by ORK throughout the Ottawa River watershed. Most of the microplastics were microfibers, likely coming from synthetic fabrics that enter the river either from washing machine wastewater, or as airborne dust particles that settle on the surface of the water. This is important data.

How can you become a citizen scientist? Here are few suggestions:

- ORK is part of the Waterkeeper Alliance (waterkeeper.org), which has chapters all over the world. These dynamic non-profit organizations are taking action to protect waterways and ensure clean water. Contact a local Waterkeeper Alliance organization in your community and offer to help out with microplastics testing. If they are not doing microplastics testing, well, you have stumbled onto a magnificent opportunity to make a tangible difference. Offer to help them start up a citizen science microplastic sampling program and model it on the ORK Riverwatch program.

- Become a 5 Gyres Ambassador. In 2010, the nonprofit 5 Gyres Institute (www.5gyres.org) began a series of scientific firsts by researching plastic in all five subtropical gyres, as well as the Great Lakes and Antarctica, through expeditions. In 2014, the organization published the first Global Estimate of Plastic Pollution, finding nearly 270,00 tons (245,000 tonnes) and 5.25 trillion pieces of "plastic smog" worldwide. The 5 Gyres Ambassador program is designed to educate and empower 5 Gyres' global network of supporters to take action against plastic pollution. Jay's bucket list includes participating in a 5 Gyres expedition.

Citizen Scientist Trawling: A trawl can be towed alongside a boat or stationed in a river to capture floating plastic while filtering debris through a fine-mesh net.

There are some other excellent app-based citizen data collection tools out there—just like the Ocean Conservancy's Clean Swell app mentioned earlier (page 160)—which allow you to engage in the science on your own while walking on the beach:

- Litterati (www.litterati.org): A funky community focused on identifying, mapping and collecting the world's litter. Anyone with a smartphone can photograph, geotag and describe any litter they find anywhere in the world. The data is used to work with companies and organizations toward sustainable solutions to the global waste problem.

- Marine Debris Tracker (www.marinedebris.engr.uga.edu): Co-developed by environmental engineer and waste specialist Jenna Jambeck, the Marine Debris Tracker app allows anyone to log marine debris or litter anywhere in the world.

- Marine LitterWatch (www.eea.europa.eu/themes/coast_sea/marine-litterwatch): This app was developed by the European Environment Agency to collect and share data on marine litter on European beaches and coastal areas.

- Tangaroa Blue Australian Marine Debris Initiative (www.tangaroablue.org/amdi/amdi-program. html): Includes the Australian Marine Debris Database, which provides all citizens with a methodical way to document the marine debris they find around the Australian coastline. Uses an online form rather than an app.

YOUTHS TAKING ACTION

The future is bright and plastic-free. Youths all over the world are on the move and taking deep, impactful action against plastic toxicity and pollution. Here are a few of the most dynamic young individuals we have ever encountered—they are leading the charge:

- Olivia and Carter Reis of One More Generation (onemoregeneration.org): In 2009, when they were seven and eight years old, respectively, Olivia and Carter founded One More Generation (OMG) to help educate children and adults about the plight of endangered species. They put a special emphasis on plastic pollution. We've been honored to partner with them over the years in support of their dynamic initiatives, including most recently on their wildly successful global OneLessStraw Pledge Campaign, which masterfully targeted individuals, businesses and schools to engage people in saying "No" to plastic straws for the month of October 2016, and hopefully beyond.[5]

- Hannah Testa of Hannah4Change (www.hannah4change.org): Hannah is a force to be reckoned with. She single-handedly networked with a local senator to have February 15, 2017 declared Plastic Pollution Awareness Day in the state of Georgia.[6] She and the senator co-wrote the resolution for the declaration. This was the first event of its kind in the United States, and included exhibits and student artwork, as well as speeches by Hannah and other eco-dignitaries, politicians and business leaders. What's next for Hannah? Working with partner organizations to have a similar day declared in other states, with the goal of it becoming another Earth Day.

- Melati and Isabel Wijsen of Bye Bye Plastic Bags (www.byebyeplasticbags.org): Have you seen their TED talk? You must.[7] They founded the social initiative Bye Bye Plastic Bags to rid their home, the island of Bali, of plastic bags. They succeeded in convincing the Governor of Bali to ban plastic bags for all of Bali by 2018. They say, "Don't ever let anyone tell you that you're too young or you won't understand. We're not telling you it's going to be easy. We're telling you it's going to be worth it." They have partnered with reusable bag makers in Bali to create Welcome Alternative Bags, an open platform that offers a variety of eco-friendly alternative bags for retail and wholesale purchase.

- Milo Cress of the Be Straw Free Campaign (ecocycle.org/bestrawfree): In 2011, at the age of nine, Milo Cress started the Be Straw Free Campaign to encourage individuals and restaurants to pledge to go plastic straw free. He promotes an "Offer First" policy for restaurants to ask customers if they want a straw rather than providing one by default. After diligent lobbying, he had July 11, 2013 declared "Straw Free Day" by the Governor of Colorado.

Do you have a child or know of a child who is inspired and energized to get involved in tackling the plastics issue?

---

5   See the guest post Carter and Olivia did on our blog about the OneLessStraw Pledge Campaign: https://lifewithoutplastic.com/store/blog/onelessstraw-toward-one-more-generation (accessed 4 March 2017).

6   See the guest post Hannah did on our blog about how she created Plastic Pollution Awareness Day in Georgia: https://lifewithoutplastic.com/store/blog/how-i-got-february-15-2017-declared-plastic-pollution-awareness-day (accessed 4 March 2017).

7   You can see it here: https://www.ted.com/talks/melati_and_isabel_wijsen_our_campaign_to_ban_plastic_bags_in_bali (accessed 4 March 2017).

Here's a suggestion: Have them apply to attend the Plastic Ocean Pollution Solutions (POPS) International Youth Summit organized by Algalita Marine Research and Education (algalitayouthsummit.org). Algalita was founded by Captain Charles Moore, who was the first to discover the swirling soup of plastic debris in the Pacific Ocean that has come to be known as the Great Pacific Garbage Patch.

It's an amazing opportunity to supercharge that youthful inspiration and energy. The POPS Summit happens every February in Dana Point, California, bringing together about 100 youths from around the world for a weekend to share their original plastic pollution reduction ideas with their peers, to listen to inspiring speakers and to attend workshops covering topics including action planning, scientific research, film-making and public speaking, as well as pitching projects and ideas. One of the exercises at the 2017 Summit was for groups to create a 60-second long viral Internet sensation (song, dance, poem or skit) that highlights the problem with plastic pollution and includes a catchy hashtag and a call to action. And then each group performed it for everyone! We've been honored to be a sponsor of the Summit and love the reasons Algalita puts such concerted and beautifully-organized efforts into educating and mentoring youth in this way:

- They are powerful and effective leaders
- They are open-minded and full of energy
- They can make a lot with just a little
- They bring fresh ideas and look to the future
- They are excited to share
- When they talk, the world listens
- They are active social networkers

CONTACT YOUR ELECTED REPRESENTATIVE OR A CELEBRITY YOU ADMIRE

You may have noticed in the previous section that all of the featured youths went out of their way to contact their local politicians as a way of getting their message across and effecting concrete, publicly visible change. As Hannah has said, "you don't ask, you don't get." And frankly, youths have incredible asking power—much more so than adults in some ways. What politician wants to be known for denying a youth a reasonable request that will make the community a better place to live, and possibly garner favorable national and international attention?

We all know about star power. Well-known celebrities—actors, artists, athletes, authors, chefs, explorers, entrepreneurs, musicians, personal development gurus and talk show hosts—all have an automatic megaphone directly into the hearts and minds of their fans. There are good reasons why Leonardo DiCaprio was able to meet with Donald Trump to discuss climate change not long after his election as President—DiCaprio's eco-star status gets him in the door and the President looks good to DiCaprio fans for listening. Some celebrities who are already known for supporting causes that tackle plastic pollution include Ed Begley Jr., Jeff Bridges, Fran Drescher, Adrian Grenier, Jack Johnson, Bette Midler and Amy Smart. The Plastic Pollution Coalition includes on its membership page a long list of members who are "Notable Individuals."

If there is a politician or star out there you admire and respect, consider contacting them about a plastic toxicity or pollution issue—a plastic bag ban, a water bottle ban or concerns about endocrine disruptors in plastic products. If it's presented thoughtfully and clearly and backed up with credible sources, it may strike a chord that could lead them to look deeper into the issue and take action toward legislative change or to engage their following toward positive plastic-free change. Just remember that they are busy people who are constantly being asked for things, so do your homework first and be prepared to explain your request.

PRESSURE YOUR FAVORITE BRANDS TO GO PLASTIC-FREE
Do you have a favorite food or drink, but it irks you to no end that it is only available packaged in plastic?

In this age of light-speed social media messaging, some large corporations are increasingly receptive to requests for change in the direction of health and environmental sustainability, and may even take action on their own. We've talked about how individual actions can lead to powerful precessional ripples of awareness. Well, the same can happen at the corporate level. One wonderful example is when the large Danish supermarket chain Coop found out the microwave popcorn it was selling in its 1,200 stores included potentially carcinogenic, endocrine-disrupting fluorinated chemicals in the lining of the popcorn bags.[8] It removed the popcorn from all the stores and challenged the suppliers to find an option. After about six months, Liven, a Spanish supplier, came up with a stronger natural cellulose bag that did not need a coating.

So if there are particular products that have plastic parts or packaging or chemicals you disapprove of, try contacting the company to express your disapproval. You can take it a step further and send them back the product or packaging with a letter explaining why. If you have an alternative solution, be sure to explain that. It can be easy to criticize, but when you propose a realistic solution (even if it's one that may be costly to the company) you'll likely be taken more seriously and seen as more credible.

UNLEASH YOUR INNER PLASTIC-FREE ARTIST
Plastic has become a popular and powerful medium for multimedia artists all over the world—and with good reason. It is versatile, colorful and easily manipulated. Part of the power lies in the messages this plastic art conveys: chilling reminders of how single-use disposable plastics such as bags and bottles have invaded our lives and world. We are often bowled over by the frequently uncanny etheric beauty of such plastic art, and how it stimulates in the viewer worlds of contrasting and conflicting thoughts and emotions. You might find the colors, textures and imagery stunningly beautiful, but you feel like you shouldn't. The material is toxic and globally polluting, after all. And that's the power of plastic art: it makes you think, feel and reflect . . . deeply, personally and globally.

8   Brian Bienkowski (2015) "What's Poppin' in Denmark? Popcorn with Safer Packaging" Environmental Health News (accessed 4 March 2017: http://www.environmentalhealthnews.org/ehs/news/2015/oct/denmark-chemicals-fluorinated-popcorn-solution-endocrine-disruptor).

Here are a just few artists whose stunning artwork serves as a poignant form of aesthetic activism (and there are many more out there):

- Dianna Cohen (www.diannacohen.com): As mentioned in the introduction, Dianna Cohen is co-founder and current CEO of the Plastic Pollution Coalition, and it is through her art that anti-plastic activism found her. She was using plastic to create three-dimensional wall pieces and larger installations for years when she noticed the plastic was cracking and breaking down. She initially thought this meant the plastic was organic and ephemeral, but did some research and discovered the toxic-polluting reality.

- Chris Jordan (www.chrisjordan.com): The photographs in Chris Jordan's artwork "Midway: Message from the Gyre" have had a profound impact on people all over the world and raised massive awareness about the plastic pollution issue. You've probably seen them (just Google "bird with plastic in stomach"). They show "the detritus of our mass consumption"—plastic—in partially decomposed open carcasses of dead baby albatrosses who were fed lethal quantities of colorful plastic their parents mistook for food while foraging in the polluted Pacific Ocean.

- Pam Longobardi (driftersproject.net): In her words, "Plastic objects are the cultural archeology of our time." In 2006, she discovered mountains of ocean plastic debris on the remote shores of Hawaii, and began the Drifters Project, which involved cleaning beaches, making art and working with communities. Her touring, ever-evolving installations are made from beach-collected plastic which is re-situated "within the cultural context for examination."

- Max Liboiron (maxliboiron.com): Academic, activist and artist Max Liboiron directs a marine science and technology laboratory specializing in citizen science and grassroots environmental monitoring of plastic pollution. Her scholarly work feeds her artwork, and, seemingly, vice versa. Her art spans various media ranging from elaborate interactive trash installations to small sea globe souvenirs containing rock from a closed landfill that is underwater at high tide and contains plastics from the Hudson River in Brooklyn. She challenges the viewer, mixing plastic with non-plastic and asking, "Is it plastic, or not?"

- Sheila Rogers (www.sheilarogersfineart.com): A collector of shells along shorelines, Sheila Rogers found the shells were being overtaken by plastic so she began collecting the plastic and making art with it. This is how she describes her artwork: ". . . the plastic is sorted by color, secured in large acrylic boxes, and displayed in an arrangement of complementary colors. From a distance, the beauty of the color-coded organization lures viewers into a fanciful encounter with interesting art pieces. Yet upon closer view, the shocking revelation of single-use plastic trash manifests."

- Vilde Rolfsen (vilderolfsen.com): The Plastic Bag Landscapes by Norwegian photographer Vilde Rolfson are just that; airy images that could be depicting Narniaesque caves or castles of illuminated aquamarine or ruby red ice. But no, they are crinkled plastic bags that were found in the streets of Oslo.

- Jeremy Carroll (www.facebook.com/jeremycarrollstudio): [9] Here's some really disturbing artwork that puts things in perspective. Artist and photographer Jeremy Carroll's exhibit is called Entanglement, and shows real live humans tangled up in typical marine plastic waste that is normally shown strangling and suffocating aquatic wildlife. He also highlights some typical "human" food and drink such as a plate of spaghetti or a mug of root beer crafted from plastic.

---

9 See also: "Jeremy Carroll, Marine Pollution," L'Oeil de la Pohotographie, 25 February 2017 (accessed 4 March 2017: http://www.loeildelaphotographie.com/en/2017/02/25/article/159939624/jeremy-carroll-marine-pollution).

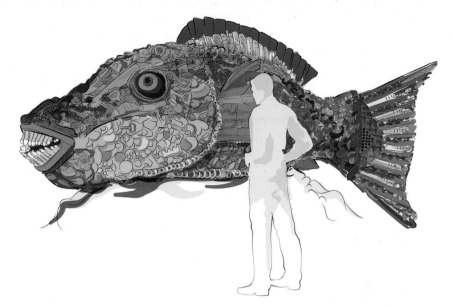

Priscilla the Parrotfish, from the Washed Ashore traveling exhibit of sculpture, crafted from ocean plastic debris.

- Washed Ashore (washedashore.org): Washed Ashore is a non-profit community art project founded by artist and educator Angela Haseltine Pozzi in 2010, after she was motivated to do something about the enormous amounts of plastic pollution washing up on pristine Oregon beaches. She recruited hundreds of volunteers to clean up the beaches and they used the debris to create massive arresting sculptures of the sea wildlife most affected by plastic pollution. The larger than life sea sculptures make up traveling exhibits that visit venues ranging from SeaWorld to the Smithsonian.

What about you? Do you have a plastic art project in you? Why not let out your inner artist? Release your innate creativity and send a beautifully disturbing message to the world about the pain plastic is causing. There is no shortage of material for you to work with, that's for sure. Just head on down to the edge of a waterway or stroll through an urban landscape and, unfortunately, the chances are that you will find ample supplies for your plastic art projects. But better they become meaningful art than end up in the gut of a Northern Fulmar. Through the ages, across societies, it is so often the artists who are the true visionaries of the times.

CHAPTER 7

FINAL WORDS:
EMBRACING A CIRCULAR LIFE WITHOUT PLASTIC

In 1962, biologist and conservationist Rachel Carson published her classic book and call to action, *Silent Spring*, which documented in chilling detail the toxic effects on wildlife of a widely used and apparently harmless pesticide commonly known as DDT (dichlorodiphenyltrichloroethane). She explained how the chemical was clearly harmful as it weakened the eggshells of raptors and other birds, leading to the death of their young. In scientist-speak this is called "reproductive failure."

With *Silent Spring*, she put a powerful public spotlight on the dangerous effects of synthetic chemicals in the environment. She explained in a manner accessible to all how such human-made toxins directly harm wildlife and have the potential to harm humans. When it was published, she was dying of advanced breast cancer. Practically single-handedly, she ignited a global environmental movement and influenced the eventual banning of DDT.[1]

In 2015, a stunningly disturbing research paper entitled "Threat of Plastic Pollution to Seabirds is Global, Pervasive and Increasing" was published in the U.S. scientific journal *Proceedings of the National Academy of Sciences* (PNAS) by respected researchers from the Commonwealth Scientific and Industrial Research Organisation and Imperial College London.[2] Here are few of their key findings based on an extensive global risk analysis of plastic exposure and ingestion by 186 seabird species:

- Nearly 60 percent of all sea bird species have plastic in their gut.

- It is estimated that 90 percent of all seabirds alive today have eaten plastic of some kind.

- Based on current rates of plastic ingestion by birds and exponentially increasing global plastic production, plastic will be found in the guts of 99 percent of all seabird species by 2050.

There is now a voluminous amount of research and information available about plastic pollution and the toxic effects of various plastics—much of it presenting similarly jarring findings and projections. Why should this study stand out from the increasing stream of revealing studies emerging on the health and environmental effects of plastic pollution? Because it highlights what might be the canary in the coal mine pointing to plastics being a new silent spring.

1   E. Griswold (2012) "How 'Silent Spring' Ignited the Environmental Movement," *The New York Times Magazine*, online edition: 21 September 2012 (accessed 4 March 2017: http://www.nytimes.com/2012/09/23/magazine/how-silent-spring-ignited-the-environmental-movement.html).

2   C. Wilcox, E. Van Sebille and B.D. Hardesty (2015) "Threat of Plastic Pollution to Seabirds is Global, Pervasive and Increasing," *Proceedings of the National Academy of Sciences* 112(38):11899–11904. See also S. Torok (2015) "Almost All Seabirds to Have Plastic in Gut by 2050" Commonwealth Scientific and Industrial Research Organisation (accessed 4 March 2017: http://www.csiro.au/en/News/News-releases/2015/Marine-debris).

The carcass of a baby laysan albatross fed a lethal amount of plastic by parents who mistook plastic trash in the ocean for food. (Adapted from a photo by Chris Jordan, www.chrisjordan.com)

One leading marine biologist thinks this is the case, and we would agree, especially when considered alongside the steadily increasing body of scientific research highlighting the endocrine-disrupting effects of plastic chemicals ranging from bisphenol A (BPA) to phthalates.

Boris Worm, a professor at Dalhousie University and a specialist in global marine biodiversity and conservation, penned a comment to the above research paper where he suggested exactly that:

> Carson specifically highlighted how DDT was a persistent pollutant that accumulated in the environment and threatened the survival of many bird species by interfering with their breeding cycle. In PNAS, an analogous argument is made for plastic pollution, only this time a "silent spring" may be looming in the oceans.[3]

In a radio interview,[4] he explained that his rationale for this conclusion flows from the following ominous parallels with the DDT silent spring documented by Rachel Carson 55 years ago:

- Plastic, like DDT, is a global phenomenon and can be found everywhere, as the above research is one indication. DDT is still used in some countries and is widely found throughout the global environment, including in the Arctic where it is consumed by fish and seals, and then humans further up the food chain. It is still found in the Great Lakes despite being banned in North America well over 40 years ago.

3   B. Worm (2015) "Silent Spring in the Ocean," *Proceedings of the National Academy of Sciences* 112(38):11752–11753.

4   CBC Radio (2015) "Plastics—A New Silent Spring?" *Quirks and Quarks*, 12 September 2015 (accessed 4 March 2017: http://www.cbc.ca/radio/quirks/quirks-quarks-for-sep-12-2015-1.3224539/plastics-a-new-silent-spring-1.3224613).

- The problem is not going away on its own. Both plastics and DDT are persistent pollutants that remain for centuries. The plastic really never disappears. It just gets broken down into smaller and smaller pieces.

- Global production is massive. Approximately 1.8 million tons (1.6 million tonnes) of DDT have been produced—a huge amount by any measure. That same amount of plastic is produced every two days now. This leads to an enormous amount of badly managed waste plastic ending up in the environment and being ingested by wildlife.

- Both plastic and DDT affect reproductive development. DDT has been shown to adversely affect reproduction in wildlife, especially birds and aquatic wildlife. Plastic-derived endocrine-disrupting chemicals ranging from BPA to phthalates have been shown to promote reproductive disease.[5]

- Both plastic and DDT may not appear directly poisonous on their own, but their toxic effects can manifest through impacts on hormonal systems. DDT was sprayed directly on skin and added to paint for children's rooms to control mosquitoes—it is still used in some parts of the world as a pesticide. Plastics are ubiquitous in children's toys—including, unbelievably, toys that are still made with the highly toxic polyvinyl chloride (PVC) plastic resin.

- Plastic toxins and DDT both bioaccumulate and become increasingly concentrated as they move up the food chain. Miniscule amounts of DDT in water can increase in concentration up to ten million times as they are continually ingested by plankton, then small fish, larger fish, fish-eating birds and humans. Apart from the toxins inherent to plastics, plastic in aquatic environments act like little sponges, adsorbing and absorbing other chemicals in the surrounding water, and can concentrate them up to a million times more than the surrounding water.

As Dr. Worm notes, seabirds are fitting canaries in this global marine coal mine. They live on the ocean and feed there, but come back to land regularly to nest, where they can be closely monitored and studied in ways that other ocean wildlife cannot. Thus, they are sentinels for monitoring the state of the oceans and, by extension, the state of the global environment.

Attempting to clean up global plastic pollution is a step in the right direction, but the extent of the pollution is far beyond a level where even the most effective cleanup methods can have a tangible long-term effect, given the constant flow of plastic into the environment and the fact that we are dealing with a dispersed smog of microplastic particles all over the world. The only realistic solution is to stop the introduction of new plastic into the global environment at the source.

The "O" in our Life Without Plastic logo is a turtle. There are levels of significant meaning behind this. Turtles are among the aquatic wildlife most tragically affected by oceanic plastic pollution. They eat it regularly—floating plastic bags look a lot like tasty jellyfish—and die painful, slow deaths as it clogs their digestive systems. In various North American Aboriginal cultures—including Chantal's Huron–Wendat heritage—the turtle symbolizes Mother Earth stoically carrying the world on her back, including the burdens of humanity. With plastic, humanity has created a burden for which we must all take responsibility. Yes, we are all turtles, responsible for the well-being of our families and the world as a whole.

---

5   M. Manikkam, R. Tracey, C. Guerrero-Bosagna and M.K. Skinner (2013) "Plastics Derived Endocrine Disruptors (BPA, DEHP and DBP) Induce Epigenetic Transgenerational Inheritance of Obesity, Reproductive Disease and Sperm Epimutations," *PLoS ONE* 8(1):e55387.

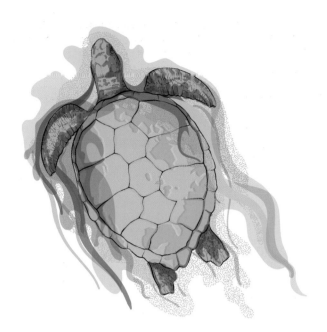

Jay grew up with a research scientist father—an insect-studying entomologist—who was a firm advocate of a holistic ecosystem approach to science, and life in general, for that matter. The term "ecosystem" was coined by British botanist Sir Arthur Tansley in 1935 to describe "the idea of progress towards equilibrium, which is never, perhaps, completely attained, but to which approximation is made whenever the factors at work are constant and stable for a long enough period of time."[6] The problem now is that the "factor" of plastic has tilted us dangerously away from an equilibrium that can sustainably support life on Earth for the long-term. With toxic microplastic pollution permeating every corner of the planet, our global ecosystem is in a process of deadly intoxication. The load of Mother Earth turtle has become significantly heavier and synthetically lopsided.

If we combine this with another fundamental issue of our times—climate change—we begin to see just how interrelated our global ecosystem actually is. Both plastics and climate change are fed by the "factor" of toxic, polluting fossil fuels: oil, coal and natural gas. Understanding this interconnectedness helps us see that all our actions—collective and individual—are necessary and can make a real tangible difference toward preserving life on Mother Earth.

So we need to reduce plastics at the source, and we do see this happening through large-scale collective actions that are catalyzing a new industrial revolution in the way things are made—including plastics. The movement toward a circular economy where waste does not exist is growing around the world, as witnessed by the groundbreaking work of the Ellen MacArthur Foundation. Currently, its New Plastics Economy project is bringing together key stakeholders to re-think and re-design the future of plastics, starting with the fundamental problem of plastic packaging.[7] This goes hand-in-hand with the cradle-to-cradle life cycle approach to product development that is being implemented through the work of the visionary Cradle

---

6   As cited in: Eugene P. Odum, *Ecology and Our Endangered Life-Support Systems*, Sunderland, Massachusetts: Sinauer Associates, Inc. Publishers, 1989, p. 38.

7   More information available here: https://www.ellenmacarthurfoundation.org/programmes/business/new-plastics-economy (accessed 4 March 2017).

to Cradle Products Innovation Institute.[8] These complementary approaches view plastic as a valuable resource to be captured and reused as safely and completely as possible rather than simply discarded as waste. And new plastic development should not be driven by fossil fuels; rather, it should be focused on the safest and most sustainable bioplastics, ideally 100 percent plant-based, free of chemical additives and compostable.

But really, it all boils down to individual action, whether it is toward personal or collective change. That means *you*. Even the big collective actions start with one person. Ellen MacArthur had an idea and grew it into a global movement. And frankly, it's the billions of individual actions that, when combined, are most impactful and lay the groundwork for larger collective action and change. They also inspire other individuals to act. We are seeing this all over the world as the zero waste movement takes on an electric momentum. Zero waste bloggers and stores are popping up everywhere.

At the beginning of Chapter 3 (page 17), we talked about the fact that we all have "plastic" brains. That is, our brains are capable of transforming and changing due to the innate neuroplasticity of the human brain. Our plea is simple: Please use your personal cerebral plasticity to create some new plastic-free habits that will help reduce your consumption of plastic. Even just one simple habit shift—such as saying no to plastic straws—is utterly stupendous and will have a concrete effect by decreasing the demand for new plastics.

The essence of this book is to provide you and your family with some easy-to-implement tools for staying healthy and helping rid our world of toxic, polluting and synthetic plastics. The task may appear daunting, but it doesn't have to be if you take it one small step at a time. And take heart, you are far from alone on your plastic-free journey. The plastic-free wave is rising fast, and if you have this book in your hands, you are most definitely riding it with the rest of us all over the world. We are a fun, engaged movement and a community growing at light speed. There is no end to the creative ways one can live without plastic

Thank you for being the circular plastic-free change our world so needs. Together we can stop this pernicious plastic silent spring in its tracks, and lighten the load on dear Mother Earth turtle so a healthy equilibrium is restored.

Onward!

---

8   More information available here: http://www.c2ccertified.org/ (accessed 4 March 2017). See also Michael Braungart and William McDonough, *Cradle to Cradle: Re-Making the Way We Make Things*, London: Vintage Books, 2008.

RESOURCES

GENERAL RESOURCES FOR ALL KINDS OF TIPS ON PLASTIC-FREE LIVING

(also check out the Zero Waste sites listed at the end of the Resources section)

- Being-PALL: Plastic A Lot Less (being-pall.com)
- My Plastic Free Life (myplasticfreelife.com)
- Plastic Free July (plasticfreejuly.org/living-plastic-free.html)
- Plastic-Free Tuesday (plasticfreetuesday.com)
- Treading My Own Path (treadingmyownpath.com)

SHOPPING FOR PLASTIC-FREE ITEMS

In all cases when shopping for anything, be sure to take into account the packaging. Remember that single-use disposable plastic packaging is at the root of the global plastic pollution problem. If something is packaged in plastic, ask if you can get it without the packaging and encourage the seller to use plastic-free packaging. Ask that your online orders be shipped without plastic packaging. This is completely possible. We have been doing it for the past ten years.

In suggesting products below, the focus is on things that are made with natural and organic ingredients and are packaged with minimal or no plastic. Note that we have provided what is currently on our radar, but there are likely many more plastic-free options out there beyond what we have listed below.

ONLINE STORES FOCUSED ON PLASTIC-FREE PRODUCTS

- Less Plastic (lessplastic.co.uk)
- Life Without Plastic (lifewithoutplastic.com)
- Monomeer (www.monomeer.de)
- Noplastic.ca (noplastic.ca)
- Sans BPA (www.sans-bpa.com)
- Sin Plastico (www.sinplastico.com/en)

PLASTIC-FREE ITEMS
Personal Care Products
DIY BLOGS AND WEBSITES

- Beth Terry of the My Plastic Free Life blog (myplasticfreelife.com/plasticfreeguide)
- Crunchy Betty blog (crunchybetty.com/start)
- Etsy, the unparalleled online marketplace for vintage, handmade and craft goods (www.etsy.com)
- #NoToPlastic (notoplasticblog.wordpress.com)
- Rebecca Prince-Ruiz and her colleagues at Plastic Free July (www.plasticfreejuly.org/personal-care.html)
- Wellness Mama (wellnessmama.com)

SOAP

- Aquarian Bath (www.aquarianbath.com/soap.html)
- Chagrin Valley Soap & Salve Company (www.chagrinvalleysoapandsalve.com/products/for-the-body/soap-bars)
- Dulse & Rugosa (www.dulseandrugosa.com)
- Lush (www.lush.com)
- Serenity Acres Farms (www.serenitygoats.com)
- Tierra Mia (www.tierramiaorganics.com/collections/body)
- Unearth Malee (www.unearthmalee.com/product-category/organic-soap)
- Urban Forest (urbanforestsoap.com/soap)

SHAMPOO BARS

- Aquarian Bath (www.aquarianbath.com/shampoo-bars-solid-shampoo-hair-soap.html)
- Chagrin Valley Soap & Salve Company (www.chagrinvalleysoapandsalve.com/products/natural-shampoo-bars)
- Dulse & Rugosa (www.dulseandrugosa.com)
- Emerson (www.emersonsoaps.com)
- Lush (www.lush.com)
- Nature Skin Shop (www.natureskinshop.com/hair/shampoo-bars)
- Pachamamai (www.pachamamai.com/savon/30-shampoings-naturels)
- Unearth Malee (www.unearthmalee.com)
- Urban Forest (www.urbanforestsoap.com/shampoo-bars)

SKINCARE LOTION
- Aquarian Bath (www.aquarianbath.com/skin-care-herbal-organic.html)
- Chagrin Valley Soap & Salve Company (www.chagrinvalleysoapandsalve.com/products/for-the-body/moisturizers)
- Dulse & Rugosa (www.dulseandrugosa.com)
- Farm to Girl (farmtogirl.com/collections/all)
- Organic Essence (orgess.com/shop)
- Unearth Malee (www.unearthmalee.com/product-category/body-care)

DEODORANT
- Aquarian Bath (www.aquarianbath.com/skin-care-herbal-organic/deodorant-natural-organic.html)
- Chagrin Valley Soap & Salve Company (www.chagrinvalleysoapandsalve.com/products/for-the-body/organic-deodorant)
- Hoda's Herbals (www.hodasherbals.com/collections/frontpage/products/healing-deodorant)
- Lush (www.lush.com)
- Organic Essence (orgess.com/product-category/deodorant)
- Mountainess Handmade (www.etsy.com/shop/mountainess)
- Primal Pit Paste (primalpitpaste.com)
- Routine (www.routinecream.com)
- Whiffcraft (www.whiffcraft.ca/product-category/coconut-oil-deodorant)

LIP BALM
- Aquarian Bath (www.aquarianbath.com/skin-care-herbal-organic/lip-balms.html)
- Burt's Bees (www.burtsbees.ca/natural-products/lips-lip-care-beeswax-lip-balm/beeswax-lip-balm-tin.html)
- Chagrin Valley Soap & Salve Company (www.chagrinvalleysoapandsalve.com/products/for-the-face/lip-butter-balms)
- Lush (www.lush.com)
- Mountainess Handmade (www.etsy.com/shop/mountainess)
- Organic Essence (orgess.com/product-category/lip-balm)
- Unearth Malee (www.unearthmalee.com/product-category/body-care)

COSMETICS
- Keeping It Natural (www.etsy.com/shop/KeepingItNatural)
- Kjaer Weis (kjaerweis.com)
- RMS Beauty (www.rmsbeauty.com)

Feminine Hygiene
DISPOSABLE NON-TOXIC PADS AND TAMPONS
- Azalea (www.wholefoodsmarket.com/products/tampons-applicator-regular-absorbency)
- Natracare (www.natracare.com)
- Organyc (www.organyc-online.com/home)
- Seventh Generation (www.seventhgeneration.com/feminine-hygiene)
- Tampon Tribe (tampontribe.com)

REUSABLE PADS AND TAMPONS
- Femallay (www.femallay.com)
- Gladrags (gladrags.com)
- Lunapads (lunapads.com)
- Sckoon (www.sckoon.com)

MENSTRUAL CUPS
- DivaCup (divacup.com)
- Femallay (www.femallay.com)
- The Keeper (keeper.com)
- Menstrual Cup Co.—Numerous brands (menstrualcup.co/menstrual-cup-brands)
- Mooncup (www.mooncup.co.uk)
- Sckoon (www.sckoon.com)

SEA SPONGE TAMPONS
- Femallay—Sea Clouds (www.femallay.com)
- Jade & Pearl (jadeandpearl.com/sea-pearls)

Shaving Equipment
- Fendrihan (www.fendrihan.com)
- Life Without Plastic (www.lifewithoutplastic.com/store/home-and-living/bath-and-body/shaving.html)
- Men Essentials (www.menessentials.ca)
- Rockwell Razors (rockwellrazors.com)

Waxing
- Gentle Bees (gentlebees.co/product/body-hair-remover-pro-sugar-wax)
- Nurture From Nature (www.etsy.com/shop/NurturefromNature)
- Parissa (parissa.com)
- Samasweet (www.etsy.com/ca/shop/Samasweet)
- Sundos & Silk (www.etsy.com/shop/SundosandSilk)

Dental Care

NON-PLASTIC COMPOSTABLE TOOTHBRUSH

- Life Without Plastic (www.lifewithout plastic.com/store/home-and-living/bath-and-body/body-care.html)
- Neem Tree Farms (neemtreefarms.com/shop/neem-chew-sticks)

OTHER OPTIONS

- Brush With Bamboo (www.brushwith bamboo.com)
- The Environmental Toothbrush (www.environmentaltoothbrush.com.au)
- Green Panda (www.the-green-panda.com)
- Miswak Stick (www.miswakstick.com)
- WooBamboo (woobamboo.com)

TOOTHPASTE, TOOTH TABS AND TOOTH POWDERS

- Aquarian Bath Tooth Powder (www.aquarianbath.com/herbal-products/tooth-powders-natural-toothpaste-alternative-toothpowder.html)
- Georganics (www.etsy.com/uk/shop/Georganics)
- Hoda's Herbals Sparkle Toothpaste (www.hodasherbals.com/collections/frontpage/products/dazzling-toothpaste)
- Lush Toothy Tabs and Powders (www.lush.ca/en/face/teeth)
- Pachamamai Crystal (www.pachamamai.com/savon/home/52-crystal-dentifrice-solide-en-boite-rechargeable.html)

DENTAL FLOSS

- Dental Lace (www.dentallace.com)
- Eco-Dent GentleFloss (www.eco-dent.com/gentlefloss.html)
- Le Negri (www.lifewithoutplastic.com/store/plastic-free-dental-floss-from-natural-silk-in-metal-tin.html)
- Radius (madebyradius.com/products/natural-biodegradable-silk-floss)
- Vömel (www.sinplastico.com/en/75-dental-floss-20mts.html)

Insect Repellent

- Arcadia Natural & Handcrafted (arcadia-us.com/lip-balms-and-lotions/deet-free-bug-repellent)
- Chagrin Valley Soap & Salve Company (www.chagrinvalleysoapandsalve.com/products/for-the-outdoors)
- Hickory Ridge Soaps (www.hickory ridgesoaps.com/search?q=skeeter)
- Jade & Pearl, Beat It (www.jadeandpearl.com/beat-it-insect-repellent)

Cleaning

RECIPES

- Cleaning Essentials (cleaningessentials.com)
- Earth Easy (eartheasy.com/live_nontoxic_solutions.htm)
- Green Living Ideas (greenlivingideas.com/2008/04/27/natural-cleaning-recipes)
- Keeper of the Home (www.keeperof thehome.org/homemade-all-natural-cleaning-recipes)

CASTILE SOAP

- Dr. Bronners' Castile Soap (www.drbronner.com)

LAUNDRY DETERGENT

- Dizolve (www.dizolve.com)
- Pure Soap Works (puresoapworks.com/laundrypowder.htm)
- The Simply Co (thesimplyco.com)

SOAP NUTS

- Earth's Berries (www.Earthsberries.com)
- Eco Nuts (econutssoap.com)
- Eco Suds (ecosudssoapnuts.com)

Brushes

- Burstenhaus Redecker (www.Redecker.de)

HAIR BRUSHES

- Life Without Plastic (www.lifewithoutplastic.com)

STRAW BRUSHES

- Glass Dharma (www.glassdharma.com/accessories.php)
- The Last Straw Co (thelaststrawco.bigcartel.com/products)
- Life Without Plastic (www.lifewithoutplastic.com)
- Simply Straws (simplystraws.com/collections/accessories/products/brush)

SNOW BRUSH

- Life Without Plastic (www.lifewithoutplastic.com)

DISH WASHING, BOTTLE AND FOOD BRUSHES

- Ecochoices (www.ecochoices.com/ecohousekeeping/ecosponges.html)
- Life Without Plastic (www.lifewithoutplastic.com)

The Kitchen
GROCERY SHOPPING BAGS
- Credo Bags (www.credobags.com)
- EcoBags (www.ecobags.com)
- Envirothreads (www.envirothreads.com/organiccotton.html)
- Life Without Plastic (www.lifewithoutplastic.com)
- Stitchology (www.stitchology.com)

BAG & BOTTLE DRYER
- Wood Doing Good (wooddoinggood.com)

Other Bags
BULK, GREENS AND PRODUCE BAGS
- Credo Bags (www.credobags.com)
- EcoBags (www.ecobags.com)
- Envirothreads (www.envirothreads.com)
- Life Sew Sweet (www.etsy.com/shop/lifesewsweet)
- Life Without Plastic (lifewithoutplastic.com)
- Vejibag.com (vejibag.com)

BREAD BAGS
- Dans le Sac (danslesac.co)
- Life Without Plastic (lifewithoutplastic.com)
- Sax Bags (saxbags.com)

Food Containers
GLASS CONTAINERS
- Anchor Hocking (www.anchorhocking.com)
- Le Parfait (www.leparfait.com)
- Onyx Containers (www.onyxcontainers.com/17-airtight-glass-stainless-steel-containers)
- Pyrex (www.pyrexware.com/pyrex-storage)
- Weck (weckjars.com)

STAINLESS STEEL CONTAINERS
- Clean Planetware (cleanplanetware.com)
- EcoLunchbox (ecolunchboxes.com/collections/lunch-boxes)
- Klean Kanteen (www.kleankanteen.com/collections/food-canisters)
- Life Without Plastic (www.lifewithoutplastic.com/store/eating/bentos-and-boxes.html)
- Lunchbots (www.lunchbots.com/products)
- Onyx Containers (www.onyxcontainers.com/7-lunch-containers)
- Planetbox (www.planetbox.com)
- To-Go Ware (to-goware.mybigcommerce.com/food-carriers/?sort=pricedesc)
- UKonserve (www.ukonserve.com/shop-all-products-s/53.htm)

FOOD WRAPS AND COVERS
- Abeego (Abeego.com)
- Beeswrap (Beeswrap.com)
- The Edgy Moose (www.etsy.com/ca/shop/Edgymoosedesigns)

CUTTING BOARDS
- Bambu (www.bambuhome.com/collections/utensil-sets)

SCRAPERS/SPATULAS
- Bambu (www.bambuhome.com/collections/cutting-boards)
- Swedish Spatula: Flotsam and Fork (www.flotsamandfork.com/products/swedish-spatula)
- Maisy and Grace (www.maisyandgrace.co.nz/product/ryslinge-rubber-scraper)
- Uulki (uulki.com/shop/baking/uulki-rubber-spatula-set)

WATER FILTERS—BINCHOTAN CHARCOAL STICKS
- Black + Blum (black-blum.com)
- Kishu Charcoal (kishucharcoal.com)

WATER DISPENSERS (CERAMIC AND STAINLESS STEEL)
- Aqua Ovo (aquaovo.com/water-filters/ovopur-origin.html)
- Dinuba (dinubawater.com)
- Life Without Plastic (lifewithoutplastic.com)
- Water Crock Shop (watercrockshop.com)

SODA MAKER
- Soda Stream (sodastream.com)

INDOOR COMPOSTING
- Nature Mill (www.naturemill.net)
- No Food Waste (nofoodwaste.com)
- Worm Composting (worm-composting.ca/; unclejimswormfarm.com)
- Make your own: (apartmenttherapy.com/how-to-make-your-own-indoor-compost-bin-138645; www.ecowatch.com/how-to-compost-in-your-apartment-1881838055.html)

Coffee and Tea Tools
DRIP/POUR-OVER COFFEE MAKERS
- Chemex (www.chemexcoffeemaker.com)
- Hario (www.hario.jp)
- Melitta (www.melitta.com/en/1-Cup-Porcelain-Pour-Over-Coffee-Brew-Cone-1827.html)

FILTERS
- CoffeeSock (coffeesock.com)

FRENCH PRESS
- Bodum (www.bodum.com)
- Frieling (frieling.com/product/frenchpresses)
- Le Creuset (lecreuset.ca/product/french-press)

ELECTRIC DRIP COFFEEMAKER
- Ratio Eight (ratiocoffee.com/products/eight)

PERCOLATORS
- Farberware (www.farberwareproducts.com/products/coffee-makers)
- Presto (www.gopresto.com/products/products.php?stock=02811)

ELECTRIC KETTLES
The following are brands we have seen that offer models with all stainless steel interiors and no transparent plastic window indicating the water level—check them carefully!

- Black & Decker (www.blackanddecker.com/en-us/products/small-appliances/kitchen/coffee-and-tea)
- Hamilton Beach (www.hamiltonbeach.ca/kettles.html)
- Hario (www.hario.jp)

REUSABLE PODS
- Ekobrew (www.ekobrew.com)
- Mycoffeestar (www.mycoffeestar.com)
- Sealpod (sealpod.com)

COMPOSTABLE PODS
- Halo (halo.coffee/collections/all)
- PurPod100 (purpod100.com)

COFFEE AND TEA MUGS
- Klean Kanteen (www.kleankanteen.com/collections/insulated)
- Life Without Plastic (www.lifewithoutplastic.com/store/drinking/coffee-and-tea.html)
- Takeya (takeyausa.com/shop/coffee/coffee-tumbler)

Food Preservation: Canning, Freezing & Dehydrating
CANNING
- Le Parfait (www.leparfait.com)
- Weck (weckjars.com)

ICE CUBE TRAYS
- Life Without Plastic (www.lifewithoutplastic.com/store/stainless-steel-ice-cube-tray.html)
- Onyx Containers (www.onyxcontainers.com/15-ice-cube-tray)
- RSVP Internatonal (www.rsvp-intl.com/product/endurance-ice-cube-tray)

POPSICLE MOLDS
- Life Without Plastic (www.lifewithoutplastic.com/store/freezycup-in.html)
- Onyx Containers (www.onyxcontainers.com/8-ice-pop-molds)

FOOD DEHYDRATORS
- Excalibur (www.excaliburdehydrator.com/shop/dehydrators/dehydrators)
- Weston (www.westonsupply.com/Weston-Stainless-Steel-Food-Dehydrator-p/74-1001-w.htm)

PARCHMENT PAPER
- Beyond Gourmet Unbleached Parchment Paper (available on Amazon)
- If You Care Parchment Baking Paper (www.ifyoucare.com/baking-cooking/parchment-baking-paper)

The Bathroom
SHOWER CURTAINS
- Dream Designs (dreamdesigns.ca)
- Life Without Plastic (lifewithoutplastic.com)
- Rawganique (www.rawganique.co/Organic-Shower-Curtains-s/211.htm)

TOILET BRUSHES
- Life Without Plastic (lifewithoutplastic.com)

The Bedroom
MATTRESS
- Dormio (dormio.ca)
- Dream Designs (www.dreamdesigns.ca/collections/mattress)
- NaturaWorld (www.naturaworld.com/products/product_types/mattresses)
- Naturepedic (www.naturepedic.com/toronto)
- Obasan (obasan.ca)
- Shepherd's Dream (www.shepherdsdream.ca/product-info)
- Soma Organic Mattresses (www.somasleep.ca)

BEDDING
- Dream Designs (www.dreamdesigns.ca)
- NaturaWorld (www.naturaworld.com/products/product_types/pillows)
- Zen Abode (www.zenabode.com)

CRIB MATTRESS
- Natural Rubber: Obasan (obasan.ca), Green Buds Baby (greenbudsbaby.com)
- Spring: NaturePedic (naturepedic.com)
- Wool: Organic Lifestyle (organiclifestyle.com)

Clothing
CLOTHES
- Alternative Apparel (www.alternativeapparel.com)
- Ash & Rose (www.ashandrose.com)
- Bead & Reel (www.beadandreel.com)
- DL1961 (www.dl1961.com)
- Eileen Fisher (www.eileenfisher.com)
- Encircled (www.encircled.ca)
- Faeries Dance (www.faeriesdance.com)
- Fair Indigo (www.fairindigo.com)
- Gather & See (www.gatherandsee.com)
- Hempest (Hempest.com)
- HOPE Made in the World (hopemade.world)
- Ibex (shop.ibex.com)
- Indigenous (www.indigenous.com)
- Kasper Organics (www.kasperorganics.com)
- Kestan (kestan.co)
- Mayamiko (www.mayamiko.com)
- Mini Mioche (www.minimioche.com)
- Modernation (shopmodernation.com)
- PACT Apparel (wearpact.com)
- Patagonia (www.patagonia.com)
- People Tree (www.peopletree.co.uk)
- PrAna (www.prana.com)
- Purple Impression (www.purpleimpression.com)
- Raven & Lily (www.ravenandlily.com)
- SiiZU (siizu.com)
- Slum Love (www.slumlove.com)
- Shift To Nature (shifttonature.com.au)
- Thought Clothing (www.wearethought.com)
- Wallis Evera (wallisevera.com)
- YSTR (ystrclothing.com)
- Zero Waste Daniel (ZWD) (zerowastedaniel.com)

SHOES
- El Naturalista (www.elnaturalista.com/en)
- Indosole (indosole.com)
- Nisolo (nisolo.com)
- Rothy's (rothys.com/pages/about)
- Simple (simpleshoes.com)
- Toms (www.toms.com)

Babies and Kids
CLOTH DIAPERS
- Babee Greens (www.babeegreens.com)
- The Responsible Mother (www.responsiblemother.com)
- Sweet Papoose (www.etsy.com/ca/shop/SweetPapoose)

TOYS
- Ava's Apple Tree (www.avasappletree.ca/playtime)
- Camden Rose (www.camdenrose.com)
- Green Heart Shop (greenheartshop.org)
- Heartwood Natural Toys (heartwoodnaturaltoys.com)
- Little Sapling Toys (www.littlesaplingtoys.com)
- Natural Pod (naturalpod.com/shop)
- Nest (nest.ca)
- Nova Naturals (www.novanatural.com)

CHILDREN'S DISHES & BABY BOTTLES
- Born Free (www.summerinfant.com/bornfree)
- Klean Kanteen (www.kleankanteen.com)
- Life Factory (www.lifefactory.com)
- Life Without Plastic (lifewithoutplastic.com)
- Organic Kidz (www.organickidz.ca)
- Pura Stainless (www.purastainless.com/shop/infant)
- Timberchild (www.timberchild.com)

The Home Office
STATIONERY, FOUNTAIN PENS AND GLUE TINS
- Goulet Pens (www.gouletpens.com)
- Green Apple Supply (greenapplesupply.org)
- Life Without Plastic (www.lifewithoutplastic.com)

Pets
GROOMING BRUSHES
- Life Without Plastic (www.lifewithoutplastic.com)

PET WASTE COMPOSTING TOILET
- Doggie Dooley (www.doggiedooley.com)

COMPOSTABLE DOG FECES BAGS
- Biobag (www.biobagusa.com/products/retail-products/pet-waste-products-retail)
- Earth Rated (www.earthrated.com/en/home)

The Garden

TOOLS
- Bambu (www.bambuhome.com/collections/garden)

SOIL BLOCKERS
- Johnny's Selected Seeds (www.johnnyseeds.com/tools-supplies/seed-starting-supplies/soil-block-makers)
- Soilblockers (www.soilblockers.co.uk)

COMPOSTABLE PLANTERS
- Ecoforms (www.ecoforms.com)
- Western Pulp (www.westernpulp.com/nursery-greenhouse)

HOSES
- ClearFlow (clearflowwaterhose.com)
- Water Right (www.waterrightinc.com)

PLASTIC-FREE LIVING ON THE GO

The Lunch Box

SANDWICH BAGS
- Fluf (www.fluf.ca/collections/snack-packs)
- Life Without Plastic (www.lifewithoutplastic.com)
- Mother Earth Reusables (www.etsy.com/shop/MotherEarthReusables)
- Natural Linens Boutique (www.natural-linensboutique.com/shop-1/organic-reusable-sandwich-bags)

LUNCH CONTAINERS AND BENTOS
- Bento & Co (en.bentoandco.com)
- Eco Lunch Box (www.ecolunchbox.com)
- Fluf (fluf.ca/collections/classic-lunch)
- Joli Bento (jolibento.com)
- Life Without Plastic (www.lifewithoutplastic.com)
- Lunchbots (www.lunchbots.com)

THERMAL CONTAINERS
- Klean Kanteen (www.kleankanteen.com)
- Lunchbots (www.lunchbots.com)
- Thermos (www.thermos.com)

ICE PACKS
- Life Without Plastic (www.lifewithoutplastic.com/store/plastic-free-flask-ice-pack-6-oz.html)
- Onyx Containers (www.onyxcontainers.com/20-ice-cubes)

LUNCH BAGS AND BOXES
- L. May Manufacturing (www.lunchbox.ca)
- Life Without Plastic (www.lifewithoutplastic.com)
- LunchBox (www.lunchbox.com)
- Planetbox (www.planetbox.com)

TIFFINS
- Clean Planetware (cleanplanetware.com)
- Happy Tiffin (www.happytiffin.com/latch-tiffins.html)
- Life Without Plastic (www.lifewithoutplastic.com)
- Onyx Containers (www.onyxcontainers.com)
- To-Go Ware (to-goware.mybigcommerce.com/food-carriers)

RESTAURANTS AND TAKEOUT

Bottles and Mugs

CERAMIC
- Earth-In Canteen (www.earthinusa.com)

GLASS
- BottlesUp (www.bottlesupglass.com)
- Faucet Face (www.faucetface.com)
- First Glass Design (firstglassdesign.com)
- Love Bottle (lovebottle.com)
- Soul Bottles (www.soulbottles.de)

STAINLESS STEEL
- Camelback (www.camelbak.com/en/bottles/stainless-steel)
- Hydro Flask (www.hydroflask.com)
- Klean Kanteen (www.kleankanteen.com)
- S'well (www.swellbottle.com)

COFFEE AND TEA MUGS
- Contigo (www.gocontigo.com/mugs)
- Ecoffee Cup (ecoff.ee)
- Klean Kanteen (www.kleankanteen.com/collections/insulated)
- Life Without Plastic (www.lifewithoutplastic.com/store/drinking/coffee-and-tea.html)
- Takeya (takeyausa.com/shop/coffee/coffee-tumbler)

Utensils
- Bambu (www.bambuhome.com)
- Justenbois (www.justenbois.com/en)
- Life Without Plastic (www.lifewithoutplastic.com)
- To-Go Ware (to-goware.mybigcommerce.com/bamboo-utensils)

Straws
STAINLESS STEEL
- Ecojarz (ecojarz.com/search.php?search_query=straw)
- Life Without Plastic (www.lifewithoutplastic.com)

GLASS
- Glass Dharma (www.glassdharma.com)
- Simply Straws (simplystraws.com)
- Strawesome (www.strawesome.com)

PAPER
- Aardvark Straws (www.aardvarkstraws.com)
- Straw Straws (www.strawstraws.com)

BAMBOO
- Bambu (www.bambuhome.com/products/bamboo-straws)
- Brush With Bamboo (www.brushwithbamboo.com)
- Straw Free (strawfree.org)

REED
- Kids Think Big (kidsthinkbig.com/product/ktb-reed-straws)

STRAW
- Straw Straws (www.strawstraws.com)

Traveling
TRAVELING ESSENTIALS
- Bambu (www.bambuhome.com/collections/travel-accessories)
- Life Without Plastic (www.lifewithoutplastic.com)
- Rawganique (www.rawganique.com)

PORTABLE WATER DISPENSERS
- Dinuba (dinubawater.com)
- Life Without Plastic (lifewithoutplastic.com)

Sports at the Gym and in the Great Outdoors
YOGA MAT
- Biovea (biovea.com)
- Dusky Leaf (duskyleaf.com)
- Jade (jadeyoga.com)
- Maduka (maduka.com)
- Rawganique (rawganique.com)

SLEEPING BAGS
- Holy Lamb Organics (www.holylamborganics.com)
- Wool Sleeping Bag (www.woolsleepingbag.com)

TENTS & TIPIS
- Arctic Canada Trading (arcticcanadatrading.com)
- Canvas Camp (www.canvascamp.us)
- Canvas Tent Shop (www.canvastentshop.ca)
- Fort McPherson (fortmcpherson.com)
- Salcedo Custom Tipi (www.salcedocustomtipi.com/custom.html)

RADIATING THE PLASTIC-FREE LIFESTYLE
Compostable Tableware and Utensils
- Bakey's (www.bakeys.com)
- Bambu Veneerware (www.bambuhome.com)
- Do Eat (www.doeat.com/en)
- Ecowares (eco-ware.ca/products-4)
- Hampi Natural Tableware (www.naturaltableware.com)
- Leaf Republic (leaf-republic.com)
- Natural Value (naturalvalue.com)
- Repurpose Compostables (www.repurposecompostables.com)
- Verterra (www.verterra.com)

BOOKS
- Andrady, Anthony L., ed., *Plastics and the Environment*, Hoboken, NJ: John Wiley & Sons, 2003.
- Beavan, Colin, *No Impact Man: The Adventures of a Guilty Liberal Who Attempts to Save the Planet and the Discoveries He Makes About Himself and Our Way of Life in the Process*, Toronto: McClelland & Stewart, 2009.
- Braungart, Michael and William McDonough, *Cradle to Cradle: Re-Making the Way We Make Things*, London: Vintage, 2009.
- Colborn, Theo, Dianne Dumanoski and John Peterson Myers, *Our Stolen Future: Are We Threatening Our Fertility, Intelligence, and Survival? A Scientific Detective Story*, New York: Penguin, 1997.
- Dadd, Debra Lynn, *Toxic Free: How to Protect Your Health and Home from the Chemicals That Are Making You Sick*, New York: Penguin, 2011.
- Freinkel, Susan, *Plastic: A Toxic Love Story*, New York: Houghton Mifflin Harcourt, 2011.
- Gillespie, Manda Aufochs, *Green Mama: Giving Your Child a Healthy Start and a Greener Future*, Toronto: Dundurn, 2014.
- Humes, Edward, *Garbology: Our Dirty Love Affair with Trash*, New York: Penguin, 2012.
- Imhoff, Daniel, *Paper or Plastic: Searching for Solutions to an Overpackaged World*, San Francisco: Sierra Club Books, 2005.

- Johnson, Bea, *Zero Waste Home: The Ultimate Guide to Simplifying Your Life by Reducing Your Waste*, New York: Scribner, 2013.
- Leonard, Annie, *The Story of Stuff: How Our Obsession With Stuff is Trashing the Planet, Our Communities, and Our Health - and a Vision for Change*, New York: Free Press, 2010.
- Moore, Captain Charles, *Plastic Ocean: How a Sea Captain's Chance Discovery Launched a Determined Quest to Save the Oceans*, New York: Penguin, 2011.
- Smith, Rick and Lourie, Bruce, *Slow Death By Rubber Duck: How the Toxic Chemistry of Everyday Life Affects Our Health*, Toronto: Knopf Canada, 2009.
- Smith, Rick and Lourie, Bruce, *Toxin Toxout: Getting Harmful Chemicals Out of Our Bodies and Our World*, Toronto: Vintage Canada, 2013.
- Stevens, E.S., *Green Plastics: An Introduction to the New Science of Biodegradable Plastics*, Princeton, NJ: Princeton University Press, 2002.
- Taggart, Jennifer, *Smart Mama's Green Guide: Simple Steps to Reduce Your Child's Toxic Chemical Exposure*, New York: Hachette, 2009.
- Terry, Beth, *Plastic Free: How I Kicked the Plastic Habit and How You Can Too*, New York: Skyhorse Publishing, 2012 (updated in 2015).
- Tolinski, Michael, *Plastics and Sustainability: Towards a Peaceful Coexistence between Bio-Based and Fossil Fuel-Based Plastics*, Salem, MA: Scrivener, 2012.
- Vasil, Adria, *Ecoholic*, Toronto: Vintage Canada, 2007.
- Vasil, Adria, *Ecoholic Body*, Toronto: Vintage Canada, 2012.
- Vasil, Adria, *Ecoholic Home*, Toronto: Vintage Canada, 2009.

Children's Books

- Harper, Joel, *All the Way to the Ocean*, Claremont, CA: Freedom Three Publishing, 2006.
- Harper, Joel, *Sea Change*, Claremont CA: Freedom Three Publishing, 2015.
- McLaren, Goffinet, *Sullie Saves the Seas*, Pawleys Island, SC: ProsePress, 2011.
- McLaren, Goffinet, *Sullie Saves the Seas: A Story Coloring Book*, Pawleys Island, SC: St. Charles Place Publishing, 2011.
- Mech, Michelle, *Ocean Champions: A Journey into Seas of Plastic*, Salt Spring Island, BC: Michelle Mech, 2017.
- Moser, Elise, *What Milly Did: The Remarkable Pioneer of Plastics Recycling*, Toronto: Groundwood Books, 2016.

FILMS & VIDEOS

- Addicted to Plastic (www.crypticmoth.com/plastic.php)
- All the Way to The Ocean (vimeo.com/ondemand/allthewaytotheocean/160024055)
- A Plastic Ocean (www.plasticoceans.org)
- A Plastic Tide (news.sky.com/video/special-report-plastic-pollution-in-our-oceans-10742377)
- Bag It (www.bagitmovie.com)
- How Microbeads Are Causing Big Problems (youtu.be/Bic7QEVRNe4)
- Investigating Plastic Pollution: The Basics (www.algalita.org/video/plastic-pollution-a-serious-threat-to-the-environment-april-2013)
- Let's Ban the Bead (storyofstuff.org/movies/lets-ban-the-bead)
- Midway (www.midwayfilm.com)
- Open Your Eyes (youtu.be/9znvqlkIM-A)
- Plastic Paradise (plasticparadisemovie.com)
- Plastic Planet (www.plasticplanet-derfilm.at)
- Plastic Shores (plasticshoresmovie.com)
- Plastic State of Mind (youtu.be/koETnRONgLY)
- Straws (www.strawsfilm.com/media-horizon)
- Tapped (tappedmovie.com)
- The Story of Bottled Water (storyofstuff.org/movies/story-of-bottled-water)
- The Story of Microfibers (storyofstuff.org/movies/story-of-microfibers)

ORGANIZATIONS

Plastic Pollution

- Algalita Marine Research and Education (www.algalita.org)
- Be Straw Free (www.ecocycle.org/bestrawfree)
- Break Free From Plastic (www.breakfreefromplastic.org)
- City To Sea (www.citytosea.org.uk)
- Ellen MacArthur Foundation (newplasticseconomy.org)
- Mission Blue (www.mission-blue.org)
- Ocean Conservancy (www.oceanconservancy.org)
- One More Generation—OneLessStraw (onemoregeneration.org & onelessstraw.org)
- Plastic Change (plasticchange.org)
- Plastic Free Curriculum (www.plasticfreecurriculum.org)
- Plastic Free Island (www.plasticfreeisland.com)
- Plastic Oceans Foundation (www.plasticoceans.org)

- Plastic Ocean Project (www.plasticoceanproject.org)
- Plastic Free Philippines (plasticfreephilippines.com)
- Plastic Pollution Coalition (www.plasticpollutioncoalition.org)
- Plastic Soup Foundation (www.plasticsoupfoundation.org)
- Plastic Tides (plastictides.org)
- Riverkeeper (www.riverkeeper.org)
- Story of Stuff (www.storyofstuff.org)
- Straw Free (strawfree.org)
- Straw Wars (strawwars.org)
- Surfers Against Sewage (www.sas.org.uk/messageinabottle)
- Surfrider Foundation (www.surfrider.org)
- The 5 Gyres Institute (www.5gyres.org)
- The Last Plastic Straw (thelastplasticstraw.org)
- Think Beyond Plastic (www.thinkbeyondplastic.com)

Plastic Toxicity
- Breast Cancer Prevention Partners (formerly Breast Cancer Fund) (www.bcpp.org)
- Environmental Defense (environmentaldefense.ca)
- Environmental Working Group (www.ewg.org)
- Healthy Child, Healthy World (www.healthychild.org)

Zero Waste
- Be Waste Wise (wastewise.be)
- Cafeteria Culture (www.cafeteriaculture.org)
- Going Zero Waste (www.goingzerowaste.com)
- Litterless (www.litterless.co)
- Paris To Go (www.paris-to-go.com)
- PAREdown Home (www.paredownhome.com)
- The Zero Waste Girl (thezerowastegirl.com)
- Trash is for Tossers (www.trashisfortossers.com)
- Zero Waste Chef (zerowastechef.com)
- Zero Waste Guy (zerowasteguy.com/blog)
- Zero Waste Home (www.zerowastehome.com) (And check out the BULK food app to find bulk food stores near you, or to add in a new one you've found in your neck of the woods: zerowastehome.com/app)

ACKNOWLEDGMENTS

Writing a book is an act of birth. And while it's the parents that make the baby, they generally benefit from the support of many. This is certainly true in our case.

Thank you to our families who have encouraged us from the start on this plastic-free living journey. Special thanks to Luella Sinha and Malamarie Sinha for their diligent assistance in doing research for the book.

Thank you to our fabulous Life Without Plastic team of Sarah Wylie, Alise Marlane, Carmencita Checa, Aura Macabugao, Charitha Eathalapaka and Morgan Nordstrom for keeping things rolling during the writing process. Particular thanks to dear, committed Sarah for her hours spent helping to pull together the handy Resources section.

Thank you to our home community of Wakefield, Quebec, which is filled with all kinds of artists, musicians, builders, farmers and activists who embrace plastic-free living. You have supported us from the start and continue to do so in so many ways.

Thank you to our loyal and passionate customers who never cease to inspire and surprise us with innovative ideas for new products and probing questions about all things plastic and plastic-free.

Thank you to plastic-free living guru Beth Terry, creator of the blog My Plastic Free Life and author of *Plastic Free: How I Kicked the Plastic Habit and How You Can Too*, whose creative lifestyle and writings constantly amaze and inspire us, and whose friendship we cherish.

Thank you to the dynamic growing global community of activist individuals, organizations and progressive companies seeking to make the world a better place by tackling the problem of plastic pollution. Special thanks to the following for inspiration and support over the years: Dianna Cohen and the Plastic Pollution Coalition, Captain Charles Moore and the Algalita Marine Research Foundation, Anna Cummins and Marcus Eriksen and the 5 Gyres Institute, and Lauren Singer of Trash Is for Tossers. We are making a difference!

It has been a joy and privilege to work with the wonderful team at Page Street. That first email from our editor Elizabeth Seise filled us with excitement, opening the door to the realization of a long-held goal. She and publisher Will Kiester have made the writing and publishing process rather dreamy. Thank you for taking a chance on us and helping us realize the dream of this book, our baby.

Our deepest waves of gratitude go to our son Jyoti: the ray of luminous light who started us on this incredible plastic-free journey and brightens the way every day.

ABOUT THE AUTHORS

Credit: Franziska Heinze

Chantal Plamondon and Jay Sinha are the co-founders of Life Without Plastic, an online shop and information resource for safe, high quality, ethically sourced and Earth-friendly alternatives to plastic products for everyday life. They live in the rolling Gatineau Hills of Wakefield, Quebec, Canada (in a twist of ironic black humor—though it's really not funny at all—their beloved hometown recently became the location for an expanded polystyrene factory!).

Chantal Plamondon is an ecopreneur and lawyer born and raised in Ste-Thérèse, Quebec, Canada. She attended McGill Law School and went on to obtain a masters degree in law with a specialization in business ethics from the University of Ottawa. She also graduated from HEC Montréal with a degree in Management. Starting a multiple bottom line, conscious business has always been at the top of her life goals. Since co-founding Life Without Plastic with Jay, she's been dealing primarily with strategic development, product sourcing and accounting. This passion to protect the environment was passed on to her from her Huron-Wendat mother who told her about the importance of being grateful for what the Big Turtle, our planet Earth, offers us every day. She hopes that some day everything produced on our planet will go back to feed the Earth and its creatures in a healthy nutritious way, without any bits of plastic being caught between the teeth of the Big Turtle.

Jay Sinha is an ecopreneur, scientist and lawyer who hails proudly from the windy prairies of Winnipeg, Manitoba, Canada where the sun shines bright and the sky is huge. He has always been captivated by nature, and his environmental protection instincts really kicked into gear when doing a grade six project on acid rain. Now he sees chilling parallels between yesterday's acid rain and today's borderless smog of toxic microplastics. An honors degree in biochemistry from the University of Western Ontario taught him about the microscopic world within and around us all. He spent a year living and traveling in Europe, and in India exploring his Bengali roots—all the while absorbing firsthand how we are one people, regardless of whether we're from Grenoble or Kolkata . . . or Winnipeg. Continuing his international and eco-oriented life focus, he completed civil and common law degrees at McGill University in Montreal, followed by a dip back into science with a graduate diploma in ecotoxicology from Concordia University—all the better to understand the toxic effects of plastics. He is a writer at heart who hopes his words will help people, and contribute to making the world a better place.

INDEX